Praise for *Supply Chains: A Manager's Guide*

"An excellent summary of the state of supply chain management going into the twenty-first century. Explains the essential concepts clearly and offers practical, down-to-earth advice for making supply chains more efficient and adaptive. Truly a survival guide for executives as they struggle to cope with the increasing competition between supply chains."

> —Christian Knoll, Vice President of Global Supply
> Chain Management, SAP AG

"Through real-world case studies and graphic illustrations, David Taylor clearly demonstrates the bottom-line benefits of managing the supply chain effectively. Although the book is written for managers, I recommend it for everyone from the executive suite to the shipping floor because they all have to work together to master the supply chain. But beware—you can expect many passionate employees demanding improvements in your company's supply chain after reading this book!"

> —David Myers, President, WinfoSoft Inc.,
> Former Board Member of Supply Chain Council

"A comprehensive, thoroughly researched, and well-designed book that gives managers the information they need in a highly readable form. I am already starting to use the techniques in this book to improve our international distribution system."

> —Jim Muller, Vice President of Produce Sales,
> SoFresh Produce

"Supply chain management is a deceptively deep subject. Simple business practices combine to form complex systems that seem to defy rational analysis: Companies that form trading partnerships continue to compete despite their best efforts to cooperate; small variations in consumer buying create devastating swings in upstream demand, and so on. In his trademark fashion, Taylor clearly reveals the hidden logic at work in your supply chain and gives you the practical tools you need to make better management decisions. A must-read for every manager who affects a supply chain, and in today's marketplace there are few managers who are exempt from this requirement."

—Adrian J. Bowles, Ph.D., President, CoSource.net

"David Taylor has done it again. With his new book, David makes supply chain management easy to grasp for the working manager, just as he did with his earlier guides to business technology. If you work for a company that is part of a supply chain, you need this book."

—Dirk Riehle, Ph.D.

"David Taylor has done a masterful job of defining the core issues in supply chain management without getting trapped in the quicksand of jargon. This concise book is well written, highly informative, and easy to read."

—Marcia Robinson, President, E-Business Strategies,
author of *Services Blueprint: Roadmap*

"Taylor has done a tremendous job of giving readers an intuitive grasp of a complicated subject. If you're new to supply chains, this book will give you an invaluable map of the territory. If you're already among the initiated, it will crystallize your insights and help you make better decisions. In either case, you can only come out ahead by reading this book."

—Kevin Dick, Founder of Kevin Dick Associates,
author of *XML: A Manager's Guide*

"My motto for compressing data is 'squeeze it til it gags.' In the current business climate, that's what you have to do to costs, and Taylor shows you many ways to squeeze costs out of your supply chain. He also writes with the same economy: This book contains exactly what you need to manage your supply chain effectively. Nothing is missing, and nothing is extra."

—Charles Ashbacher, President, Charles Ashbacher
Technologies

Supply Chains

Supply Chains

A Manager's Guide

David A. Taylor, Ph.D.

✦ Addison-Wesley

Upper Saddle River, NJ • Boston • Indianapolis • San Francisco
New York • Toronto • Montreal • London • Munich • Paris • Madrid
Capetown • Sydney • Tokyo • Singapore • Mexico City

The publisher offers excellent discounts on this book when ordered in quantity for bulk purchases or special sales, which may include electronic versions and/or custom covers and content particular to your business, training goals, marketing focus, and branding interests. For more information, please contact:

> U.S. Corporate and Government Sales
> (800) 382-3419
> corpsales@pearsontechgroup.com

For sales outside of the U.S., please contact:

> International Sales
> international@pearsoned.com

Visit us on the Web: www.awprofessional.com

Library of Congress Cataloging-in-Publication Data

Taylor, David. A., 1943–
    Supply chains : a manager's guide / David A. Taylor.
        p. cm.
    Includes bibliographical references and index.
    ISBN 0-201-84463-X (alk. paper)
    1. Business logistics. I. Title.
    HD38.5.T39 2004
    658.7—dc21   2003056020

Copyright © 2004 by David A. Taylor

Text printed in the United States on recycled paper at Courier in Westford, Massachusetts.

ISBN 0-201-84463-X

3 4 5 6 7   CRW   07 06

Third printing, October 2006

Contents

PART I
Challenges

1.
The New Competition

2.
The Rules of the Game

3.
Winning as a Team

8.
Maintaining Supply

9.
Measuring Performance

PART IV
Planning

10.
Forecasting Demand

11.
Scheduling Supply

Contents

12.
Improving Performance

PART V
Design

13.
Mastering Demand

14.
Designing the Chain

15.
Maximizing Performance

Acknowledgments

I'd like to thank Kevin Dick, Jill Dyché, Dirk Riehle, and Jill Mizano for their thoughtful and constructive reviews of this book. I am especially grateful to Kevin, whose exceptional grasp of economics and information technology was of great help to me in bridging the gap between these two disciplines. I am also grateful to John Fuller, Mary O'Brien, Tyrrell Albaugh, and the rest of the team at Addison-Wesley, together with freelance copy editor Carol Noble, for taking such good care of the book at each stage of its development. But my deepest appreciation, as always, goes to my wife, Nina. She not only supported and encouraged me throughout the two-year writing effort, she drew on her own outstanding skills as a writer and business strategist to greatly improve the finished product.

Introduction

In May 2001, Nike announced that it had lost sales in the preceding quarter because of problems in its supply chain. The amount of income lost was impressive: a cool $100 million. Three months later, Cisco Systems announced that it was writing down unusable inventory due to some confusion in *its* supply chain. The amount of its write-down was even more impressive: $2.2 billion. Isolated incidents? Only in terms of magnitude—supply chain failures are becoming increasingly common, and they are costing companies dearly. In addition to their impact on profits, problems in the supply chain have a devastating effect on stock prices, causing an average loss of $350 million in shareholder value with each reported incident. That's a steep price to pay for a single mistake.

Supply chain failures can be devastating

The flip side of this coin is that, as Dell and Wal-Mart demonstrate every day, getting the supply chain right can yield a tremendous competitive advantage, allowing new players to overthrow entrenched industry leaders. Why is the supply chain so important to success? Because it's the new frontier of business. Modern manufacturing has driven most of the excess time and cost out of the production process, so there is little advantage to be gained on the shop floor. But supply chains are still notoriously wasteful and error-prone, and they offer huge opportunities for gaining competitive advantage. The result is a fundamental shift in the nature of competition. The fight for market dominance is no longer a battle between rival companies. The new competition is supply chain vs. supply chain.

Competition is shifting to supply chains

What makes this new competition so challenging is the level of cooperation it requires. To forge winning teams, companies have to tear down the barriers between the functional silos within their organizations, and they have to replace adversarial supplier

Cooperation is the key to success

relationships with a win-win collaboration across the chain. Bringing about this level of cooperation isn't easy, but the best companies are already doing it, and they're starting to distance themselves from the rest of the pack.

Supply chains are every manager's business

As a by-product of this new competition, supply chain management has escalated from a support function to a core competence that cuts across the entire company. Managing the chain can no longer be left to specialists; in the new competition, the supply chain is every manager's business. If your company touches a physical product as it moves toward the market, it's part of a supply chain, and it will succeed in the new competition only if you and your fellow managers understand how to make the chain as efficient and effective as it can be.

This is your guide to the new competition

This understanding can be hard to come by because supply chain management is a deep and technical subject. Most books on supply chains offer either simplistic formulas for success, in which a single solution fits every problem, or the kind of detailed analysis that only a practitioner could love. This book is my attempt to provide the balanced overview you need, giving you enough information to make intelligent decisions without dragging you into a morass of detail. Think of it as your playbook for the new competition.

The book is organized around your needs

The book is organized into five parts of three chapters each, as shown in Figure I. Part I lays out the business challenge, Part II describes the tools you need to meet this challenge, and the remaining parts explain supply chain management at three levels: operations, planning, and design. These last three parts all have the same structure, with one chapter each on demand, supply, and performance. This common structure provides a unique nine-chapter matrix for understanding and solving supply chain problems. At the back of the book, you'll find sources for the facts cited in the text, some suggested readings, and a glossary of common terms.

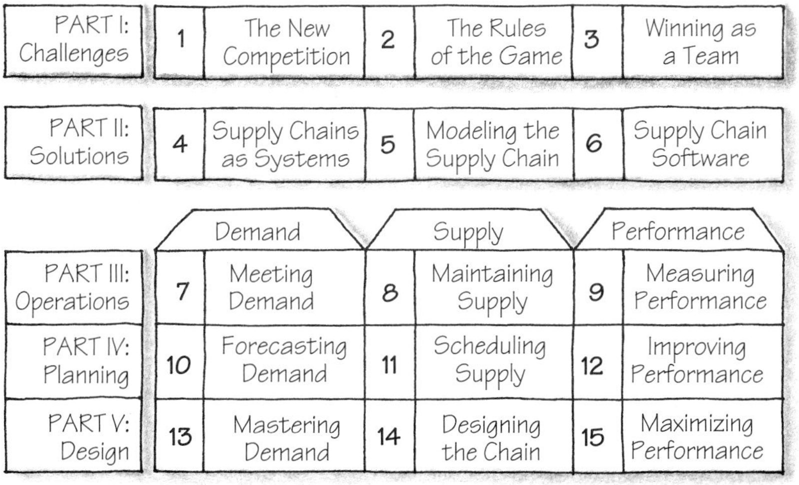

PART I: Challenges	1	The New Competition	2	The Rules of the Game	3	Winning as a Team
PART II: Solutions	4	Supply Chains as Systems	5	Modeling the Supply Chain	6	Supply Chain Software
		Demand		Supply		Performance
PART III: Operations	7	Meeting Demand	8	Maintaining Supply	9	Measuring Performance
PART IV: Planning	10	Forecasting Demand	11	Scheduling Supply	12	Improving Performance
PART V: Design	13	Mastering Demand	14	Designing the Chain	15	Maximizing Performance

Figure I
Organization of the Book

The fast track makes your job easier

I assume you're busy and don't have a lot of time for reading, so I use something I call the *fast track* to help you absorb the material quickly. As you can see from this page, the fast track summarizes the key point of every paragraph. This is the fifth book I've written using this technique since I developed it 15 years ago, and I continue to use it because loyal readers all over the world have threatened to shoot me if I don't. In fact, many managers have told me that the best thing about my books is they don't actually have to read them—they get everything they need by skimming the fast track and looking at the drawings. I'm never sure whether to be flattered or offended by this observation, but there it is.

You can read the book selectively

Feel free to jump around in the book. Part I is an executive briefing on chain-based competition; if all you need is the big picture, here it is. Part II is an introduction to supply chain tools; depending on your needs, you can study it, skim it, or skip it. The matrix organization of the remaining parts allows you to tackle the material in slices, reading Part IV to learn about planning, say, or Chapters 7, 10, and 13 for a tour of demand management.

There's a glossary to help with the jargon

Like all technical disciplines, supply chain management has developed jargon to help practitioners communicate with each other and keep outsiders at bay. To ease your way into the subject, I use specialized terms only as necessary and keep abbreviations to a minimum. But I also want to give you a working vocabulary in the subject, so I do introduce the appropriate terms as they come up, setting them in bold type and defining them in the glossary.

The Web site offers graphic simulations

An excellent way to further your understanding of supply chains is to experience them directly using simulation models of the sort described in this book. If you'd like to see supply chains in action, direct your browser to *www.supplychainguide.com.* The site also offers in-depth discussions of advanced topics, reviews of books about supply chains, and links to software vendors, service providers, and other online resources. You can also find my current e-mail address there if you would like to drop me a note about the book or ask me a question about supply chains.

David A. Taylor, Ph.D.
San Mateo, California
May 2003

About the Cover

The image on the cover of this book is *Kroeber Series #39* by
photographer Jay Dunitz. In 1980 Dunitz discovered a jumble
of discarded metal scraps left to the elements by sculpture students
at the University of California at Berkeley. By rearranging these
pieces and photographing them in bright sunlight, Dunitz created
transient sculptures of his own that are now preserved in his book
Pacific Light, published by Beyond Words in 1989. This is the third
book by David Taylor to be graced by an image from the Kroeber
Series, the first being his internationally acclaimed *Object Technology:
A Manager's Guide*. When asked about his love of these images,
Dr. Taylor explains: "My goal in writing is to identify the most
powerful ideas, arrange them in the way that best reveals their
underlying structure, and convey them with as much clarity as
possible. I can't imagine a better graphic realization of that goal
than the images of Jay Dunitz."

PART

I

Challenges

PART I: Challenges	1	The New Competition	2	The Rules of the Game	3	Winning as a Team
PART II: Solutions	4	Supply Chains as Systems	5	Modeling the Supply Chain	6	Supply Chain Software

		Demand		Supply		Performance
PART III: Operations	7	Meeting Demand	8	Maintaining Supply	9	Measuring Performance
PART IV: Planning	10	Forecasting Demand	11	Scheduling Supply	12	Improving Performance
PART V: Design	13	Mastering Demand	14	Designing the Chain	15	Maximizing Performance

1

The New Competition

The way you manage the supply chain can make or break your company. Some of the most spectacular business successes over the past 20 years have come from finding more effective ways to deliver products to consumers, but there have been some major wrecks along this same road. It's a high-stakes game, and you don't have a lot of choice about playing; if your company touches a physical product, it's part of a supply chain and your success hangs on the weakest link of that chain. Why? Because the nature of competition is shifting away from the classic struggle between companies. The new competition is supply chain vs. supply chain.

The Thrill of Victory

Siemens CT of Forchheim, Germany, makes computed tomography X-ray machines for hospitals and diagnostic labs all over the world. The machines cost about half a million dollars apiece and they are custom-built for each customer. Four years ago, Siemens CT found itself faced with rising costs and price erosion that threatened its position in this lucrative market. The group's response was to completely reinvent the way they provision, assemble, and deliver their products. They cut out two layers of middle management, switched the entire company to team structures, aligned incentives with supply chain success, and let creativity run rampant. Among other changes, the teams tightened the links with suppliers, eliminated all interim warehousing, adopted just-in-time production techniques, and switched to airfreight deliveries for customers outside of Europe.

Siemens CT reinvented its supply chain

Today, Siemens CT has an award-winning supply chain that sets a new standard for best practices in its industry. Lead time for their custom-built machines is down from 22 weeks to just 2 weeks. The

Lead time went from six months to two weeks

rate of on-time deliveries has gone from 60% to 99.3%, and *on time* now means that deliveries occur within a two-hour window—an impressive feat for a delivery that requires closing off a street and hauling in a crane. The cost of achieving these stellar results? Zero: These gains in performance were accompanied by a 40% reduction in inventory, a 50% reduction in factory workspace, a 76% reduction in assembly time, and a 30% reduction in total costs. The company also managed to double its output to 1,250 machines a year without increasing its head count.

Gillette slashed $400 million of inventory

Siemens' stunning success would be hard to match, but the company is not alone it its willingness to reinvent the supply chain. At the end of the 1990s, the Gillette Company, a $9 billion supplier of consumer goods, found itself losing market share because of escalating costs. In January 2000 it created a new kind of operating group, combining purchasing, packaging, logistics, and materials management in a single organization with the authority to completely rework its supply chain. Over the course of the next 18 months, the group reduced the total inventory in the chain by 30%, eliminating 40 days' worth of materials costing $400 million. The supply chain organization believes that it is just now getting up to speed, but it has already saved the company $90 million.

Chrysler reinvented its chain in 1990

Supply chain victories like these make for exciting news, but there is nothing new in the techniques these companies applied. At the end of the 1980s, Chrysler Corporation was on the ropes, ending the decade with a fourth-quarter loss of $664 million. Desperate for a way out of its financial morass, the company decided to experiment with some of the techniques being used by Japanese carmakers. Just as Siemens CT and Gillette would do a decade later, Chrysler formed cross-functional teams bringing together design, engineering, manufacturing, procurement, marketing, and finance, and it gave those teams the authority they needed to reinvent the supply chain. The teams cut the supplier base in half, brought the remaining suppliers in on the design of a new generation of cars, and developed long-term relationships based on trust rather than coercion. Instead of hammering suppliers on price as it had in the past, Chrysler asked for suppliers' help in finding ways to save the carmaker money. More surprisingly, the company offered to split the savings with the suppliers rather than asking them to pass all the savings on to Chrysler.

Chrysler called its sharing program the supplier cost reduction effort, or SCORE. The company announced SCORE in 1990 to a highly skeptical supply base. But once suppliers realized that this wasn't a trick—that Chrysler was serious about partnering with its suppliers and sharing the winnings—the ideas came flooding in. By 1995, the company had implemented 5,300 ideas suggested by suppliers, for a net annual savings of $1.7 billion. The cost of developing a new vehicle dropped by as much as 40%, and the time required for the development process fell from 234 weeks to 160 weeks. At the same time, Chrysler's profit per vehicle leapt from an average of $250 in the mid-1980s to $2,110 in the mid-1990s, an increase of 844%.

SCORE saved Chrysler $1.7B a year

Chrysler isn't the only company that staved off disaster by revamping its supply chain. In 1997 Apple Computer was losing $1 billion a year and was on the verge of bankruptcy. The most visible change the company made was to bring back Steve Jobs, but it was radical surgery on its supply chain that actually saved the company. Among other changes, Apple killed off 15 of its 19 products, adopted just-in-time production techniques for those that remained, overhauled its sales forecasting system, and began a relentless effort to minimize inventory. Within two years, the company went from holding a month's worth of inventory, with a value of $437 million, to a few days' worth, valued at just $25 million. Inventory went down by 94%, gross margins went up by 40%, and Apple is still in business today.

Apple reduced inventory by 94%

The supply chain made Amazon profitable

Speaking of still being in business, Amazon.com Inc., one of the few surviving dot-coms, announced its first-ever profit as of the fourth quarter of 2001. This profit was not so much a vindication of the e-commerce model as it was the result of an intensive, year-long effort to fix the company's sloppy supply chain. The problems had been so bad that 12% of incoming inventory was routed to the wrong storage location, resulting in a great deal of wasted time and energy as the company scrambled to track down its own goods. A year later, after installing better inventory controls, the company had that figure down to 4%—far from perfect, but no longer crippling. Amazon also started combining its shipments to gain economies of scale, sending 40% of those shipments out in full truckloads and driving them directly to destination cities. The results: an 18% reduction in inventory, removing $31 million worth of idle merchandise from Amazon's books, and a 17% reduction in fulfillment expenses, for a further savings of $22 million. These savings may be small compared to the preceding examples, but Amazon's $5 million net profit clearly wouldn't have been possible without them.

Cost reductions are only part of the story

The victories achieved by Siemens, Gillette, Chrysler, Apple, and Amazon illustrate the tremendous impact of supply chain performance on the cost of doing business. These savings are vitally important, and managers know this well: Cost reduction is the number-one reason that companies initiate supply chain improvements. But there's an even bigger opportunity here: Supply chain improvements are good for the bottom line, but they can be even better for the top line. Getting the supply chain right can give a company a tremendous competitive advantage, and sometimes that advantage is enough to overturn an entire industry structure.

Dell transformed the computer industry

The shining example of this kind of victory is the way Dell Computer systematically dismantled the rest of the personal computer industry. Prior to Dell, personal computers were manufactured in volume, shipped to retail stores, and sold individually to customers—pretty much like washing machines, televisions, and other appliances. It worked, but it required massive amounts of inventory, and customers were limited to a relatively small set of configurations. Dell changed all that by adopting a direct sales strategy, building every PC to order, and shipping it directly to the customer (Figure 1.1). Initially a mail-order house, Dell was one of the first to recognize the potential of the Internet, selling its first computers on line in 1996. Four years later it was doing $50 million a day from its Web site alone. In 2001, Dell became the largest producer of personal computers in the world, a position it surrendered only briefly after the merger of the former market leaders, HP and Compaq.

It's common knowledge that Dell's success was built on a combination of direct sales with build-to-order production, but Dell wasn't the first PC company to try this strategy. What really makes the company so successful is the way it executes the strategy. Dell is absolutely relentless about pulling time and cost out of its supply chain. Suppliers are located right next to Dell's assembly plants, and they deliver a constant stream of components on a just-in-time basis. Monitors are shipped directly from the companies that make them and merged in transit with Dell's own shipments, arriving in matching Dell boxes in

Dell's success rests on its supply chain

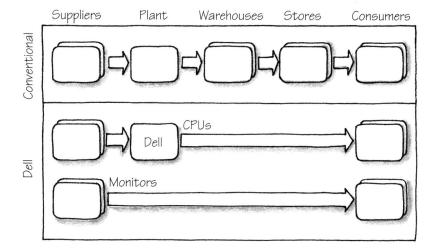

Figure 1.1
Dell's Supply
Chain Strategy

a single customer delivery (as shown in Figure 1.1). The company has forecasting and planning down to a science, and it enjoys the financial advantage of a negative cash-to-cash time—it actually gets paid for its products before it buys the components. The perfection of techniques such as these gives the company a full five percentage points of profit advantage over its competitors, a virtually unassailable advantage in what is now almost a commodity market.

Supply chains are the last untapped vein

Supply chains are as old as commerce, but the opportunities they now present are without precedent. Modern manufacturing has driven so much time and cost out of the production process that there is only one place left to turn for competitive advantage. As business-engineering guru Michael Hammer recently put it in his new book *The Agenda*, the supply chain is the last untapped vein of business gold. The examples in this section make it clear that this vein runs deep, but no one knows just how much gold is in there because the real potential of supply chains is just now being discovered. Today, supply chain management is far more important than manufacturing as a core competence; so much so that it's possible, as Nike and Cisco Systems have amply demonstrated, to dominate the market for a product without owning so much as a single factory. The future of supply chains looks bright indeed.

The Agony of Defeat

Supply chains are double-edged swords

Cutting-edge supply chains are double-edged swords. Wielded with skill, they can slice open new markets. Improperly handled, they lead to deep, self-inflicted wounds. For all the advantages that can come from getting the supply chain right, getting it wrong can be catastrophic.

Kmart launched a $1.4 billion overhaul

By the end of the 1990s, Kmart Corporation's supply chain was crippling its ability to match the prices offered by Wal-Mart and Target, and in the discount retail business price is everything. Worse, when the company did manage to lure back customers with its Blue Light specials, the products weren't in the stores when people came in to buy them; the supply chain couldn't deliver them in time for the sale, even with plenty of advance warning. Kmart was floundering, and it decided that it needed new technology to solve its problems. In May of 2000, the company announced an unprecedented $1.4 billion investment in software and services to overhaul its supply chain, including warehouse management software from EXE Technologies and planning systems from i2 Technologies.

A year and a half later, before the systems ever went live, Kmart announced that it was abandoning most of the software it had purchased and taking a $130 million write-off. What went wrong? Nearly everything, it seems, but the company did admit to a lack of clarity about its strategy, saying it needed to rethink its supply chain strategy first before implementing its systems. This was the right idea, but it seems to have arrived late and left early. Not long after the write-off, Kmart announced that it was buying $600 million worth of warehouse management software from Manhattan Associates, and that this purchase would solve its problems. Perhaps in a further effort to take some pressure off its supply chain, Kmart also announced that it was closing 250 stores. The company is now in bankruptcy.

The company is now in bankruptcy

Even companies that once got it right can still to get it wrong. After years of success with its SCORE program, Chrysler completed the famous "merger of equals" that led to DaimlerChrysler. Like the merger itself, the SCORE program quickly degenerated, and relationships with suppliers soured. The company has now resorted to demanding unilateral price reductions from suppliers in order to stave off mounting losses. Chrysler's moment in the sun has passed.

Chrysler failed to keep SCORE

Nike, the virtual enterprise that became the world's largest shoe company, has also managed to get itself into trouble with its supply chain. In February of 2001, the company announced that it had lost

Nike threw the switch and lost $100 million

$100 million in sales the previous quarter because of snafus in its supply chain. The debacle came right after the company went live with i2 Technologies' planning system. After a year of installation work, Nike decided it was time to throw the switch, and the new system immediately created havoc across the chain. Nike blamed i2, with the chairman complaining to analysts, "This is what we get for our $400 million?" (quoted in *Computerworld*; see the Notes on Sources). The vendor, in turn, complained that Nike had pushed the system into service too quickly and had required too many customizations. Whoever is to blame, both companies lost big. Nike's stock dropped 20% the day it made the announcement, and i2's fell 22% that same day.

Cisco blew $2 billion on excess inventory

Even Cisco Systems, the paragon of supply chain management, is capable of the occasional misstep. In May of 2001, the company reported that it had to write off some inventory as unusable—to the tune of $2.2 billion, the largest inventory write-down in the history of business. The problem stemmed from a breakdown in communication up the supply chain (Figure 1.2). Cisco was competing for large contracts in a booming market for Internet hardware. Having no production capacity of its own, Cisco passed all its anticipated demand directly on to its contract manufacturers. Those contractors added this to the demand they saw coming from Cisco's competitors, some of which were bidding on the same business, and each contractor looked at the demand independently, leading to double and triple counting of the same demand. The result: Component suppliers worked overtime to fill orders that were never placed, and Cisco wound up holding the bag.

Broken chains beat down stock prices

As these examples illustrate, supply chain failures can be devastatingly expensive. But there is an even bigger price to be paid than the immediate impact on cash flow. Nike and i2 both lost a fifth of their market value the day Nike went public with its problems. The size of these drops is exceptional, but their occurrence is not. A

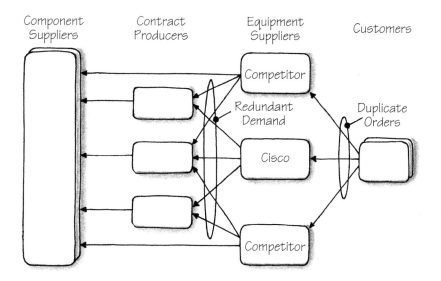

Figure 1.2
Cisco's $2 Billion
Blunder

recent study conducted at Georgia Tech examined more than a thousand news reports of supply chain problems between 1989 and 1999, looking to see whether these reports had an impact on stock prices. The answer they got was a resounding yes: Companies reporting problems suffered an average drop in their stock price of 7.5% the day of the announcement. When the researchers examined the prices six months before and after the announcement, they discovered that the prices actually began to fall well before the announcement, suggesting that the bad news had a tendency to leak, and the prices showed no signs of recovering after the fact (Figure 1.3). The total drop over 12 months was 18.5%.

These percentage drops are obviously large, but the full impact is better conveyed by actual valuations. On the day of the announcement, the average drop in shareholder value for the company making the announcement was $143 million. Over the course of a year, the average loss was more than $350 million. But even this figure underestimates the total loss because prices were rising at 15% per year during that period, so the real impact may be nearly twice the

**The average
loss of value is
$350 million**

Figure 1.3
The Market
Reaction to
Supply Problems

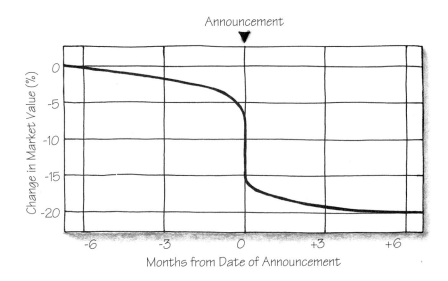

calculated amount. But even at the most conservative calculations and considering only the one-day loss, the researchers conclude that the 1,131 supply chain problems they examined in their study caused a loss of more than $160 billion in shareholder value. Clearly, the market doesn't react well to supply chain failures.

Investors punish all kinds of failures

The study also revealed that investors don't really care who caused the problem. When the reporting company accepted the blame for the incident, its stock dropped 7.1%. When it blamed its suppliers, its stock dropped 8.3%. And when it blamed its customers—usually for changing their requirements during the lead time—the company's stock dropped 10.9%. The message is clear: If a company reports a problem with its supply chain, it's going to get hammered in the stock market, regardless of who's at fault. If anything, pointing the finger at a trading partner only increases the punishment.

A High Stakes Game

Why does getting the supply chain right have such a big impact on success? Because the stakes are so high: Holding and moving merchandise is a very expensive proposition. Collectively, U.S. companies spend a trillion dollars a year on their supply chains, just under 10% of the nation's GDP. About a third of this cost is for holding inventory and the rest is for moving it around, with a bit of change left over for administration. As large as these figures may seem, they used to be substantially higher, totaling about 15% of GDP at the beginning of the 1980s. Deregulation of the transportation industry coupled with inventory reductions brought the total down to 10% by the early 1990s, and it has remained stable at that level ever since.

U.S. supply chains cost 10% of GDP

The same percentage holds good for individual companies, which spend an average of just under 10% of their gross income on supply chain functions. What is striking about the figures for individual companies is the tremendous advantage that some companies have over others in this regard. A recent survey of supply chain costs across a variety of industries yielded an average of 9.8% of revenue devoted to supply chains, a perfect match to the overall value. But the survey also revealed that the top quartile—the 25% best performers—had an average cost of just 4.2% of revenue. These companies spend less than half as much on their supply chains as the competition, giving them a full five-point advantage in profits. Continuing surveys reveal that the gap is not closing, but widening. The message is clear: If your company is on the wrong side of the supply chain gap, the sooner it makes the leap the better.

Some companies enjoy a huge advantage

Actually, the advantage is more dramatic than these figures might suggest, because in business a penny saved isn't really a penny earned. Depending on profit margins, it is usually closer to a nickel or a dime. Suppose you're running a company with $100 million in

A penny saved is a nickel earned

sales, 10% supply chain costs, and a 10% gross profit, as shown in the first panel of Figure 1.4. How could you increase your overall profit by 50%? One way is to increase sales by 50%, as shown in middle panel of the figure. The other way is to imitate the best-in-class companies and bring your supply chain costs down to 5%, as shown in the last panel. At the level of gross margins, this $5 million savings is the equivalent of $50 million in additional sales. This is not to suggest that you wouldn't prefer to get the profit from growth rather than cost reductions. But the fact that a 5% reduction in costs can produce the same increase in profits as a 50% increase in sales is certainly a valuable insight.

Small savings can lead to big profits

Here is a real-world, albeit anonymous, illustration of how supply chain savings translate into profits. A major electronics company found that it had $500 million in excess inventory. Its carrying costs were 50% of the purchase price, so it was paying $250 million a year to hold the extra material. Given the company's profit margin of 10%, it would need $2.5 billion in additional earnings to equal the bottom-line benefit of eliminating that excess inventory. In the retail sector, where profit margins of 2% are common, the impact

Figure 1.4
Supply Chain
Costs and Profit

	Current		Increase Sales by 50%		Reduce Costs by 5%	
Revenue	100%	$100	100%	$150	100%	$100
Supply Chain Expense	10%	$10	10%	$15	5%	$5
Other Expense	80%	$80	80%	$120	80%	$80
Gross Profit	10%	$10	10%	$15	15%	$15

of savings in the supply chain can be even more dramatic. With margins that thin, reducing supply chain costs from 10% to 8%—still nowhere near best-in-class performance—can increase profits as much as doubling sales.

Given the enormous stakes involved, the pressure to pull time and cost out of the supply chain is becoming relentless, and the demands are only going to increase as everyone gets better at the game. In addition to the financial drivers, several other factors are combining to put pressure on supply chains, including shorter product life spans, faster product development, rising globalization of sourcing, increasing demand for customization, and intensive quality initiatives such as the Six Sigma program. Given the challenges involved in getting the supply chain right, this may not be a game you are eager to play, but nobody gets to pass on this one. Every company that touches a product is part of a supply chain, and every company that is part of a supply chain has to deal with these problems sooner or later. The only choice you have is whether to tackle the problem now or wait until it tackles you.

You can't avoid the game

The New Competition

Very few companies are prepared to handle the new pressures being placed on their supply chains. A recent survey of executives in manufacturing companies found that 91% of them ranked supply chain management as either "very important" or "critical" to the success of their companies. Yet most acknowledged that they had problems with their chains, and only 2% regarded their chains as excellent. When asked about their strategies to improve their chains, 59% reported that their company had no strategy at all. Think about this for a moment: By their own reports, these managers realize that getting the supply chain right is essential, and they know they haven't done it yet, but most haven't even formulated a strategy for attacking the problem.

Few companies know how to fix their chains

No one group is responsible for success

It would be nice to say that these results are unusual, but the same pattern shows up in survey after survey: Companies realize that they are in trouble with their supply chains, but they don't really understand the problems, much less know how to fix them. Why so helpless? There are lots of reasons, but the root cause seems to be this: No one in the company is responsible for running the supply chain. Engineering designs the product, marketing sets prices and runs promotions, sales cuts deals with customers, purchasing negotiates with suppliers, manufacturing controls the inventories, logistics arranges transportation, accounting handles the cash flow, and so on. All the key activities take place in different groups with different agendas and conflicting goals. Worse yet, most of these groups go all the way up to the CEO before they come under common management. And the CEO is not the right person to be planning and operating the supply chain.

Teamwork is required to gain control

Given this level of disorganization, it's hardly surprising that supply chains are out of control. The amazing thing is that these chains function at all. Clearly, the first step toward regaining control is to assemble the key decision makers from each group and get them working together to find solutions. Did you notice that all the supply chain successes described in the first section of the chapter started out by forming a team to take responsibility for the chain? That's no coincidence: Cross-functional teams are a recurring theme in companies that run good supply chains. The most successful companies usually go further by designating a single top-level executive who has full responsibility for the chain.

The problem is bigger than any one company

Even if a company gets its act together and forms a crack supply chain team, it's still not ahead of the game. Today, the very nature of competition is changing, and it's not an easy change to absorb. Ever since the Industrial Revolution, the battles have been company against company, and the weapons have been the techniques of production. Today, that game is largely played out. Good design, efficient production, and quality construction, while not yet universal, have become the basic qualifications for making it into the top ranks. Among the serious players, it's now the supply chain that makes the difference between winning and losing.

Think about it this way. From the consumer's point of view, supply chains are irrelevant. All the hardball negotiations about price and terms, all the careful synchronization of deliveries, all the delays and the scrambling to keep products moving down the chain— none of these things matter to consumers. Most of them don't even know what a supply chain is, much less appreciate the problems of running one. In the ordinary course of events, the only member of the chain consumers ever see is the retailer, and their only sense of what lies upstream is summarized in the notion of a brand. For them, it all boils down to who can sell them the best product at the best price.

Consumers only care about results

From an individual company's point of view, this is hardly fair. Should a manufacturer be punished because a distributor runs out of stock? Should a retailer lose sales because a producer has a quality problem? But this isn't about fairness; it's about winning a new kind of competition. Like it or not, the fates of all the members of a supply chain are becoming increasingly joined. The new competition is no longer company vs. company; it's supply chain vs. supply chain. If the members of a chain can work together to put the most quality in the consumer's hands at the lowest price, they win. If not, they lose. Figure 1.5 illustrates this point by showing how a supply chain that is consistently cost-effective across the chain can outperform chains that are superior to it in any one link.

The fates of companies are now joined

Cast in this light, the conflicting agendas and political infighting among functional departments seem like minor problems. The real challenge isn't getting your own people to work as a team; it's getting all the companies in your supply chain to form a larger team

A higher level of teamwork is required

Figure 1.5
Competing Supply
Chains

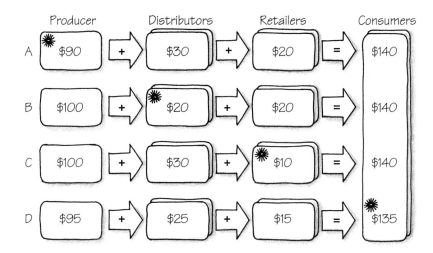

that can play and win the new competition. But how do you even approach a problem of this scale? Is vertical integration the answer? Will the techniques of supply chain collaboration do the trick? Is buying more software the solution? This book is here to answer these questions, but I'll give you a quick preview: Probably not, not likely, and no way.

This is a major shift in business

The new competition is a major upheaval that is affecting every aspect of how companies organize and operate. The required shift in thinking is so great—and the danger of not making the transition is so serious—that the National Research Council commissioned a study to articulate the problem and help prepare American manufacturers to meet the challenge. Their conclusion was that we are in the midst of a fundamental revolution in the nature of business, one that, in their words, "has the potential to alter the manufacturing landscape as dramatically as the Industrial Revolution." If you want to thrive in this new landscape, you have to understand how supply chains work—and how you can make them work better.

The challenge of mastering your supply chain may be daunting, but it's not insurmountable. Dell, Wal-Mart, and other supply chain leaders didn't succeed because they found a magic formula or were managed by business geniuses. They succeeded because they understood the core problems of supply chains, committed themselves to long-term solutions rather than quick fixes, and had the stamina to stick with those solutions until they worked. I can't help you with the stamina part, but I can explain the problems and show you how to find the best solutions. The next chapter kicks off that process by explaining how supply chains work and why they can be so difficult to manage.

2

The Rules of the Game

Supply chain management is a difficult game to master. It requires you to move a great many pieces in very specific ways, and you have to choreograph those moves to make each piece arrive in the right place at the right time. It's also a game that plays out on a grand scale, with a playing field that spans the entire planet. Fortunately, the rules of the game—the descriptions of the pieces and the ways they move—are simple enough to be summarized in a few pages. In a nutshell, supply chains consist of production and storage facilities connected by transportation lanes, and they exist to support the flow of demand, supply, and cash. The difficulty of managing supply chains comes primarily from the complexity that creeps into their structure and the variability that characterizes their flows. It's this complexity and variability that make an easy game hard to master.

Facilities and Links

A **supply chain** is basically a set of facilities connected by transportation lanes. Figure 2.1 illustrates one slice of the supply chain that brought you this book. **Facilities**, shown as rounded rectangles in the illustration, generally fall into one of two categories, depending on their primary function: **production facilities** and **storage facilities**. **Transportation lanes**, shown as arrows, are categorized by their **mode of transportation**; they include roadways, railways, waterways, sea lanes, air lanes, and pipelines. Viewed in the largest context, supply chains extend from the original **extractors** of raw materials, such as mines and farms, to the ultimate **consumers** of finished goods, the people who actually put those goods to their intended purpose.

A supply chain is a network of facilities

Figure 2.1
From Tree to Book

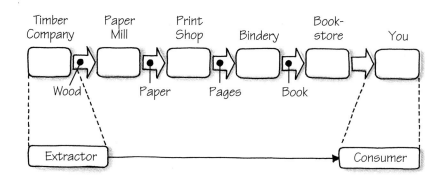

Facilities
contain
inventories

Facilities contain controlled quantities of materials called **invento-**
ries (Figure 2.2). Production facilities hold inventory in three different forms: **Raw materials inventory** consists of materials
ready for use in production; **work-in-process** (**WIP**) **inventory**
includes all the materials currently being worked on; and **finished**
goods inventory holds completed products ready for shipment.
Storage facilities vary: **Warehouses** usually contain only a single
kind of inventory, but **distribution centers** that do final assembly
contain all three kinds. **Cross docks**, which are used only to transfer goods between trucks, do not contain any separately managed

Figure 2.2
Three Kinds of
Inventory

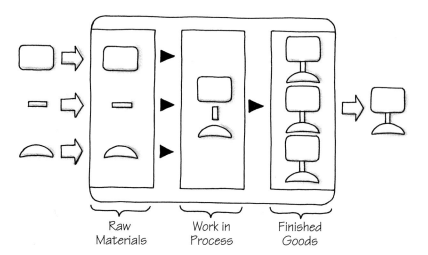

inventory. Retail stores also vary in this regard: Custom bicycle shops have all three types of inventory, warehouse-style stores contain only one, and some appliance stores carry none at all.

Lanes are used to move inventory between facilities along a particular mode of transportation, using a combination of vehicles and containers. Some vehicles, such as truck tractors and railway engines, can be decoupled from their containers, whereas other vehicles, such as delivery vans and tanker ships, have the container built in. Decoupling is an important consideration because it offers more flexibility in routing, dispatching, temporary storage, and other transportation activities. In the case of pipelines, the functions of the vehicle and the container are merged with the lane itself, with pumps providing the motive force and pipes containing the inventory in transit.

Each mode of transportation offers a unique mix of speed, cost, availability, and capability. For example, shipping by air is fast, expensive, available from all large cities, and limited to small and lightweight packages. By contrast, shipping by sea is slow, cheap, available only at cities with ports, and virtually unlimited with regard to size and weight. There are also different volume tradeoffs within each mode. In trucking, it is much cheaper to send **full truckload (FTL) shipments** than it is to use **less-than-truckload (LTL) shipments**, and the FTL option offers tighter control over the routing and timing of the shipment. However, using FTL shipments requires building up more finished goods inventory and may cause delays in shipments. Similar tradeoffs apply in the other modes.

Shipping within a limited geographical region normally uses a single mode from source to destination. For larger distances, including most international trade, shipments generally use two or more modes, a practice known as **inter-modal transportation**. For

Lanes are used by vehicles and containers

Transportation modes offer tradeoffs

Shipments can use multiple modes

example, a shipment might travel by rail to the nearest seaport, cross the ocean by ship, and travel the rest of the way by truck. Inter-modal shipments are usually enclosed in steel cargo containers that can be transferred between specially fitted rail cars, container ships, and tractor-trailers.

Lanes contain inventory in transit

Like facilities, transportation lanes contain inventory. This **in-transit inventory** bridges the gap between the shipping facility's finished goods inventory and the receiving facility's raw materials inventory (Figure 2.3). In-transit inventory is different from other forms in that it is unavailable for use, is at higher risk of loss from theft and accidents, and is subject to delays due to vehicle breakdown and lane congestion. Along with raw materials, work in process, and finished goods, in-transit inventory represents the fourth major type of inventory.

Containers are often used for storage

The distinction between in-transit inventory and the two inventories it connects is often blurred in practice. Trailers or railcars are frequently used to store finished goods at production facilities until full loads are produced, in which case the goods are still part of the plant's finished goods inventory. But if the storage is brief and the

Figure 2.3
Inventory in Transit

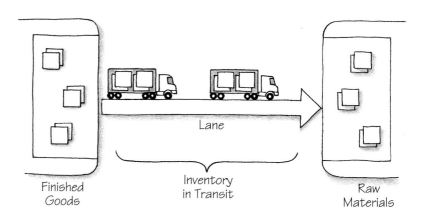

Finished
Goods

Lane

Inventory
in Transit

Raw
Materials

destination of the goods is determined by the choice of containers, the goods in the container may be treated as inventory in transit as soon as they are loaded. Similar issues come up at the destination, where full containers may sit for days or weeks in a yard before being unloaded. In one rather perverse practice, railway cars are actually kept on the move, circling in wide arcs around a facility, until there is space to park them in the yard. This is a very expensive way to hold inventory.

Although they don't make use of a separate transportation medium, **package carriers** such as UPS and FedEx are commonly viewed as a distinct mode when making transportation decisions. In reality, these **carriers** use a mix of air and highway transport to deliver their packages, using their own fleets of aircraft and trucks. As a practical matter, however, it doesn't matter how a package is conveyed because that decision is out of the shipper's hands, so using a package carrier is viewed as an alternative on a par with shipping by air, land, or water. The tradeoffs discussed for the other modes also apply to package carriers: They are fast, relatively expensive, available in most locations, and limited to relatively small, lightweight products.

Package carriers are viewed as a mode

Demand, Supply, and Cash

The essential goal in managing a supply chain is to achieve an orderly flow of goods from extractors to consumers. It should not be surprising, then, that the deepest roots of the discipline can be found in transportation management, which is responsible for moving finished goods to the next link in the chain. Over time, transportation management merged with a related function, materials management, to form the broader discipline of logistics, which handles the flow of materials all the way from suppliers through the three internal inventories and out to customers.

The basic goal is an orderly flow of goods

Demand and cash flow are equally important

What distinguishes the current discipline of **supply chain management (SCM)** from its predecessors is that it is equally concerned with two other flows: the flow of demand and the flow of cash up the chain, as shown in Figure 2.4. Without these other flows, the goods would never move: It's demand that provides the impetus for that movement, and it's cash that provides the motivation. The great insight of supply chain management is that the key to managing the flow of goods effectively lies in synchronizing all three flows. This synchronization becomes particularly difficult when, as shown in the "stack" notation in Figure 2.4, there can be any number of organizations at each link of the chain.

The basic dynamics of the flows are simple

The basic operation of a supply chain could hardly be simpler. Demand flows up the chain and triggers the movement of supply back down the chain. As supplies reach their destinations, cash flows up the chain and compensates suppliers for their goods. Naturally, the behavior of real-world supply chains is never quite this simple. But recognizing the fundamental elegance of supply chain dynamics provides the best foundation for understanding the complexities that inevitably arise.

Flows are discrete rather than continuous

With a few exceptions, such as oil moving through a pipeline, the three flows in a supply chain are discrete rather than continuous. That is, they move in distinct "packets" that convey particular

Figure 2.4
Three Basic Flows

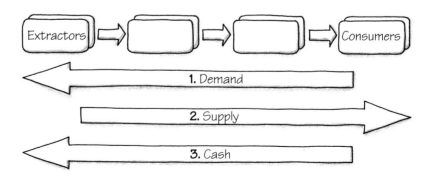

quantities at particular times. Demand is normally conveyed through orders, supply through shipments, and cash through payments (Figure 2.5). A great deal of supply chain management is concerned with balancing the tradeoffs between the size and the frequency of these packets. For example, economies of scale favor infrequent orders of large quantities of material, whereas reducing inventory carrying costs requires more frequent shipments of smaller quantities. For any given rate of flow, the smaller the packets become, the closer the chain comes to operating as a continuous flow rather than moving discrete lumps of demand, supply, and cash across the chain.

As Figure 2.5 illustrates, each exchange of demand, supply, or cash takes place between a **customer** and a **supplier**. In this book, these terms refer to the parties involved in a transaction across any link of the chain, regardless of their location within the chain. In other words, I use the terms in a relative rather than an absolute sense, the way the terms *buyer* and *seller* are used in discussing a purchase. This is a common usage for these terms but it's not universal; many writers use the term *customer* to refer to the ultimate consumer of the goods, and others use the term *supplier* only for

Each exchange has a customer and supplier

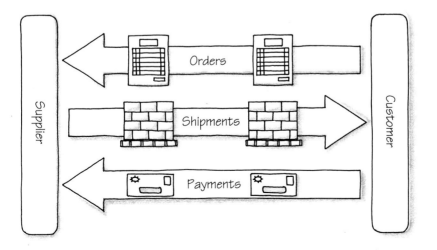

Figure 2.5
Packets of Demand, Supply, and Cash

upstream members of the chain who provide basic materials or assemblies. I avoid confusion in this book by always using the terms in the relative sense, but you should be aware of the inconsistent usage in other discussions. Be particularly alert to the differences in the way various authors use the terms *customer* and *consumer*; the muddling of these concepts often leads to pointless diatribes about who the "real" customer is.

Production may be to stock or to order

Orders trigger the flow of goods, but, depending on the production strategy, they may or may not trigger their immediate production by a supplier (Figure 2.6). In the **make-to-stock** strategy, a supplier makes products in advance of demand and holds them in finished goods inventory, satisfying demand from that inventory as orders come in. In the **make-to-order** strategy, the supplier doesn't build a product until it has an order in hand. There is also an intermediate strategy, **assemble-to-order**, in which a product is partially built in advance of demand, but final assembly is postponed until an order is received. Some companies use a mix of

Figure 2.6
Three Strategies for Production

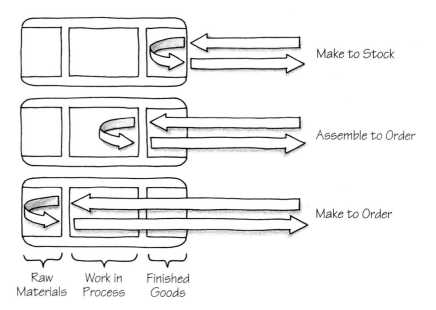

Make to Stock

Assemble to Order

Make to Order

Raw Materials   Work in Process   Finished Goods

these three techniques, but choose one as their primary strategy. For example, Sony uses make-to-stock, Boeing uses make-to-order, and Dell uses assemble-to-order.

The choice of production strategy has a major impact on the dynamics of a supply chain. With the classic make-to-stock strategy, inventory is produced in advance of and "pushed" down the chain toward consumers so that it will be on hand when they go to buy it. This strategy relies on demand forecasts to determine how much inventory to build and where to hold it. With make-to-order production, inventory is "pulled" down the chain by immediate orders. Forecasts are less important with make-to-order because there is no danger of making too much or too little inventory, though long-term forecasts are important to setting the correct levels of manufacturing capacity.

Production type determines push-pull strategy

These dynamics are often used to characterize supply chains as either **push chains** or **pull chains**, but in reality every chain is a mixture of push and pull. As long as consumers have a choice about what products they buy and when they buy them, the last link in the chain is always a pull link. At the other end of the chain, the extraction of raw materials from the earth almost always occurs in advance of demand for finished products. In effect, consumers pull and extractors push. Somewhere in between the two is the **push-pull boundary** (Figure 2.7), the point at which the flow of goods switches from being pulled by consumers to being pushed by extractors. In the case of the assemble-to-order strategy, for example, the push-pull boundary is located at the final assembly plant.

Every chain has push and pull segments

Actually, the push-pull distinction applies to every link in the chain, so it's possible for any link to operate in pull mode even though it is up in the push region of the chain. Ford's supply chain is a push chain right down to the dealer showroom, but it contains many links that are pure pull. For example, Johnson Controls

Any link can be push or pull

Figure 2.7
The Push-Pull
Boundary

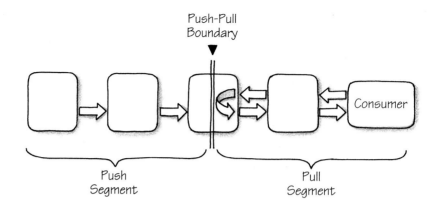

builds a seat from raw materials and delivers it to Ford within four hours of receiving an order, allowing the company to supply seats to Ford based on firm orders for specific configurations. In the context of a massive supply chain involving tens of thousands of companies building against anticipated demand, Johnson Controls is able to supply this particular component on a pull basis.

Cash flow receives the least attention

Of the three primary flows in supply chains, cash flow is the one that receives the least attention. This is understandable: Supply chains exist to move products to consumers, and orders are the mechanism for triggering that movement. But cash is the ultimate driver for the entire process; take it out of the equation and the whole business would come to a halt pretty quickly. Yet cash flow performance is the worst of the three, with producers routinely taking months to pay suppliers for goods that were shipped within days of being ordered. This situation is now changing, and accelerating the flow of cash is coming to be recognized as a key element of supply chain excellence.

Information also moves across the chain

In addition to the three key flows, there is something else that moves across the chain: information. Actually, information is already implicit in the three flows: Orders represent information about immediate demand, some products can be transmitted as information, and even cash can be exchanged in the form of information. But the more interesting kind of information isn't part of the actual transactions—it is exchanged in order to facilitate those transactions. This information includes demand forecasts, production plans, promotion announcements, and reports of all kinds. Unlike the three basic flows, information can move across the chain at any time, without being part of a particular transaction, and it isn't constrained to move sequentially up or down the chain. Instead, it can be broadcast simultaneously to any subset of the chain, ensuring that they are all operating with the same information at the same time (Figure 2.8).

One of the great insights into the behavior of supply chains is that information can often be substituted for inventory. Instead of requiring every member of the chain to maintain **safety stock** to buffer against uncertainty in demand, that uncertainty can be reduced by sharing information that helps members anticipate coming changes in the flows of demand, supply, and cash. Information is usually far cheaper than inventory, and it has the advantage that it can be in many places at the same time. The result: Substituting information for inventory is a key technique for improving supply chain performance and will be a continuing theme of this book.

Information can replace inventory

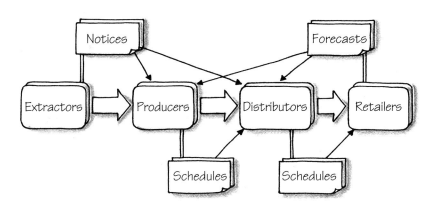

Figure 2.8
Information Broadcasting Across the Chain

Distribution and Procurement

Patterns make chains easier to understand

Although the basic elements of supply chains can be combined in an infinite variety of ways, there are two basic patterns that account for most of the structure. To see these patterns, consider how a supply chain looks from the perspective of a single plant. Every facility downstream of that plant is a destination for its finished goods and forms part of the plant's **distribution network**. Every facility upstream is a source of supplies, and forms part of its **procurement network**. These two networks of the supply chain are radically different from the plant's perspective.

Destinations are grouped into echelons

Some plants ship only to a single destination, but this is rare. The normal pattern is for each plant to serve as many destinations as necessary to satisfy demand within a particular geographical region. These destinations, in turn, may ship the goods onward to still more destinations, and so on, until the products eventually reach their ultimate consumers (Figure 2.9). The successive layers of this supply chain pattern are commonly referred to as **echelons**, and they are numbered outward from the plant as shown in Figure 2.9.

Figure 2.9
Echelons in Distribution

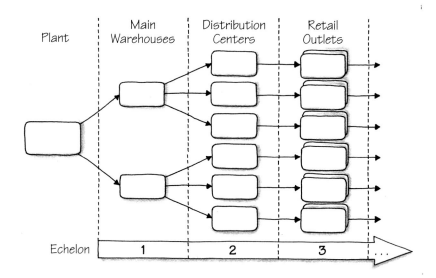

The business problem addressed by this portion of a supply chain is distribution, which is basically a matter of choreographing the flow of finished goods from the plant to consumers in a way that satisfies demand in a cost-effective manner. When multiple echelons are under the control of a single company, distribution managers often try to maintain an orderly distribution network by using only the links shown in Figure 2.9; that is, shipments are not normally allowed to skip echelons, and each destination receives shipments from only one facility in the echelon above it. Although these constraints simplify the management of a distribution network, they do not produce the most cost-effective solutions. Constraints on distribution patterns are now being relaxed as more sophisticated tools become available for designing and operating distribution systems.

This pattern is a distribution network

As you might expect, the difficulty of managing distribution goes up dramatically as the number of destinations increases. With more facilities to serve, the available inventory has to be divided more finely, increasing the risk of not having the right amount of product at any one facility. In addition, the time and expense of handling the goods increases with each echelon. On the other hand, transportation costs go down with more echelons because products can travel much of the distance in larger, more economical shipments. Finding the right balance between these opposing forces is one of the key tradeoffs in distribution design.

Distribution is harder with more destinations

Looking upstream, just the opposite pattern is observed. Although it is possible for a plant to obtain all of its supplies from a single source, this rarely happens. Ordinarily, the plant receives supplies from multiple sources, each of which receives its supplies from multiple sources, and so on, up to the point where the raw materials are obtained directly from extractors (Figure 2.10). The successive layers of this supply chain pattern are called **tiers**. Like echelons, tiers are numbered outward from the plant.

Source facilities are grouped into tiers

Figure 2.10
Tiers in
Procurement

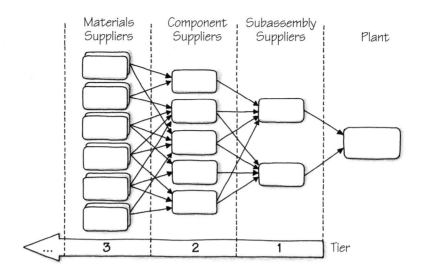

**This pattern is
a procurement
network**

The business function supported by this portion of a supply chain is procurement, which involves choreographing the flow of raw materials and subassemblies from their suppliers to the plant in a timely, cost-effective manner. As shown in the illustration, procurement networks tend to be less orderly than distribution networks, with overlapping sources being the rule rather than the exception.

**Procurement is
harder with
more sources**

Like distribution, procurement becomes more difficult to manage as the number of sources increases. The essence of successful procurement is having everything arrive as close to a production date as possible without paying more than is necessary to achieve that end. Simply by the laws of chance, the more suppliers involved, the more likely it is that at least one of them will miss its delivery date and delay a production run. In addition, the cost of placing orders and making payments goes up with the number of suppliers, as does the overhead of managing the additional relationships. As with echelons on the distribution side, adding tiers on the procurement side also increases the total time and expense required to bring production materials to the plant.

The basic distribution and procurement patterns described in this section can take on a wide variety of configurations. Most important, the sources and destinations may themselves be plants, each of which has its own distribution and procurement network. When there are multiple layers of plants, the distribution and procurement patterns overlap and the distinction between them blurs. For any one plant, the picture is reasonably clear, but for the supply chain as a whole, it can become quite complicated.

An important consideration in analyzing supply chains is identifying ownership boundaries. A sequence of facilities owned by the same company makes up its **internal supply chain**, and the links outside of the ownership boundary are its **external supply chain** (Figure 2.11). Internal supply chains often run more smoothly than external chains because they can be centrally controlled, and no buying and selling are required to move the goods. One of the big advantages of the classic strategy of **vertical integration**, in which a single company owns as much of the supply chain as it can acquire, is that it pits an internal supply chain against the competition's harder-to-manage external chains.

Ownership
boundaries
affect the flows

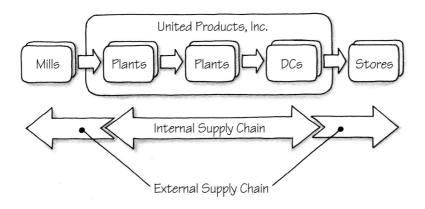

Figure 2.11
Internal and External Supply Chains

Complexity and Variability

Complexity and variability are key concerns

The basic elements of supply chains—the structures, dynamics, and patterns described in the preceding sections—are simple. Yet, as illustrated by the examples in Chapter 1, real-world supply chains are notoriously difficult to manage, and they are liable to catastrophic failure. This contrast between principle and practice invites a crucial question: Where does the difficulty come from? Underneath the many symptoms and their immediate causes, there appear to be two root causes to the difficulty of managing supply chains: complexity and variability. This last section of the chapter takes the measure of each.

Supply chain flows are linked in complex ways

The complexity begins with the way the three primary flows relate to one another. In principle, it's simple—orders trigger shipments, and shipments trigger payments. In practice, the relationship of orders to shipments and payments quickly becomes tortuous (Figure 2.12). A single production run generates orders to many different suppliers, and these orders are usually combined with orders for other production runs to achieve economies of scale in purchasing.

Figure 2.12
Orders, Shipments, and Payments

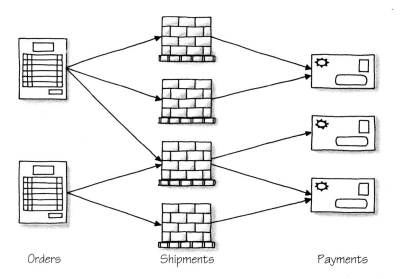

Orders   Shipments   Payments

The shipments fulfilling these orders may further combine orders to reduce the cost of transportation, but large orders may also be split across two or more shipments, and backordered items are often sent in still later shipments. Invoices usually cover multiple shipments, payments may cover multiple invoices, and so on. The simple linkages among the three basic flows are quickly obscured by these groupings and regroupings.

Another source of complexity is the way supply chains are managed, with different groups handling each of the three basic flows (Figure 2.13). On the customer side of a transaction, orders might be placed by a centralized purchasing department, shipments received by various local assembly plants, and payments made by a regional accounting department. On the supplier side, orders might be received by satellite sales offices, shipments made from regional distribution centers, and payments received by the accounting office of a parent firm. All of these groups operate according to different—and all too often, deeply incompatible—agendas, and no one group is responsible for the outcome of the entire transaction.

Different groups handle the three flows

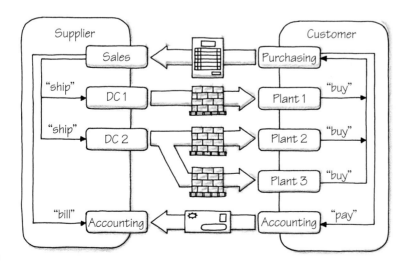

Figure 2.13
Different Groups Handling the Flows

Each flow requires extensive documentation

Complexity is also created by the proliferation of documents associated with orders. For each purchase order generated by a customer, a corresponding sales order is generated by the supplier—despite the fact that the majority of the information in the two documents is identical—and both must be matched against any governing contracts to make sure all of their terms are being honored. Each shipment resulting from the order requires its own documentation, including **packing slips, bills of lading, advance shipping notices,** and the like, and the billing and payment cycle generates yet another trail of paper. All of these documents must reference the controlling purchase and sales orders, and all the mappings among the documents must (or should) be carefully traced so that both companies are certain that what was ordered was shipped, and that what was shipped was paid for. And these are just the documents that flow between the companies; the number of documents required within each company can be much larger.

Supply chains usually have structural problems

Yet another source of complexity is the structure of the chain itself. The ideal supply chain is neatly organized into echelons and tiers, as described in the preceding section, and all transactions follow an orderly subset of links. In practice, these layered patterns are often obscured by a maze of ad hoc links and sequences that are crucial to the operation of the chain but make it very difficult to understand, much less manage. This is rarely by design; most chains are never actually designed. Rather, they evolve over time through a series of independent decisions—open a plant here, add four more suppliers for a component over there, shut down this warehouse instead of refurbishing it, and so on—few of which take the "big picture" into account.

Variability affects all business processes

The second core challenge of supply chains is coping with variability. No matter how well managed, all business activities exhibit natural variability in their duration, quality, and other attributes. Daily sales, delivery times, production yields, defect rates, maintenance times, and a thousand other aspects of supply chains all vary around some average value. For some purposes, it is sufficient to know this average and plan for it. But real-world supply chains don't ever "see" average values; what they deal with every day are the actual values that make up those averages. The more variability there is in those values, the more difficult and expensive it is to run the chain.

A great deal of supply chain management is devoted to coping with this variability. Inventories of finished goods act, in part, as a buffer against variability in demand, and raw material inventories offer comparable protection against variability in supply. Case in point: An audit of a major retailer found it needed $200 million in safety stock just to cover variability in its vendors' deliveries—a very expensive way to compensate for poor reliability. Redundant sources, such as alternate suppliers and transportation options, provide further protection against variation in the availability of materials and services. The list is long: Quality assurance programs attempt to reduce the variability in product quality, forecasting attempts to predict variation in demand, and so on. All of these efforts have some value in the attempt to cope with variability, but each extracts its own costs.

Inventory is used to buffer variability

Supply chains are particularly vulnerable to the effects of variability because they involve long sequences of interdependent activities. A relatively small delay in an upstream process, for example, can cascade down the entire supply chain, throwing off production schedules and disrupting any number of deliveries. Similarly, variation in the level of supply for upstream components relative to downstream demand can wreak havoc on a chain, as the electronics industry graphically illustrates with its sporadic chip shortages.

Variability in supply amplifies down the chain

Just as variability in supply can amplify down the chain, variability in demand can amplify back up the chain (Figure 2.14). The classic example of this **demand amplification** is a study conducted by Procter & Gamble in the early 1990s to investigate

Variability in demand amplifies up the chain

Figure 2.14
Demand
Amplification

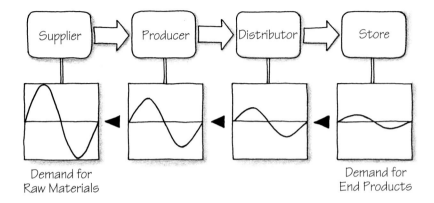

peculiar fluctuations in the demand for raw materials used in its
Pampers brand of diapers. These fluctuations puzzled the company
because babies generally go through diapers at a fairly constant
rate. Sure enough, a check of sales showed only minor, random
variations in the retail sales of Pampers. It turns out that these small
variations were being amplified up the supply chain, producing
large swings at the level of raw materials. The causes of this effect—
which P&G dubbed the **bullwhip effect**—are now well understood and easily countered (see Chapter 13), but demand
amplification continues to be a serious problem in many chains.

**Scale increases
the impact of
both problems**

The problems associated with complexity and variability are both
exacerbated by scale. In the early stages of industrialization, supply
chains consisted mostly of local companies working together to
bring goods to market, and complex mappings among the three
flows were not serious impediments to commerce. Today, with supply chains including thousands of companies spanning the entire
planet, complexity and variability have devastating effects on both
the efficiency and effectiveness of the supply process. The reasons
for this are not subtle; it's a simple matter of mechanics. As the number of contributors to a finished product goes up, the likelihood of
errors and delays inevitably escalates, and the ensuing disruptions
become increasingly severe with each additional link in the chain.

Supply chains aren't likely to get any smaller in the years to come, but both complexity and variability can be greatly reduced. The complexity of modern supply chains is ultimately a self-inflicted wound, the product of business practices that date back to the Industrial Revolution. Although variability itself is a fact of life, there is a ready arsenal of weapons to prevent it from attacking supply chains. The real business challenge doesn't lie in complexity and variability themselves, but in the failure to recognize the havoc they wreak on supply chains and make the necessary corrections. If you understand the importance of attacking these problems, and choose your weapons carefully, you can beat them.

That was a whirlwind tour of supply chains, but it gave you a quick look at the major landmarks and showed you the lay of the land, which should help you keep your bearings as you explore this region further. More important, you now understand the fundamental problems of supply chains and are ready to see how they can be solved, which is the subject of the third and final chapter of Part I.

Complexity and variability can be reduced

3

Winning as a Team

If complexity and variability are what make supply chain management a hard game to master, then the best tactics are those that lead to simplicity and stability. Indeed, most of the innovations in supply chain management over the past 20 years have attempted to both simplify and stabilize the flow of demand, supply, and cash. These innovations include the extension of just-in-time manufacturing techniques out to the supply chain, plus a variety of specialized programs for managing the replenishment of retail inventories. Unfortunately, the gains produced by these programs have often come at the expense of other links in the chain, and that doesn't improve the competitiveness of the chain as a whole. A brief look at game theory reveals why these programs are falling short and points the way to the winning strategy: integrating the members of the supply chain into a smoothly functioning team by making sure that every member's win contributes to the success of all the others.

JIT Supply Programs

Of the many efforts to improve the flow of raw materials into production facilities, most have involved extending the reach of the **just-in-time** (**JIT**) **manufacturing** method upstream toward suppliers. One of the key elements of the JIT approach is eliminating excess inventory throughout the production process by timing the movement of materials to each workstation to arrive just at the moment they are needed for the next operation. This practice minimizes inventories throughout the production process, helping manufacturing companies reduce holding costs, minimize obsolescence, and improve their return on assets. These benefits have led to the widespread adoption of JIT throughout industries that use repetitive production techniques.

JIT has transformed manufacturing

Frequent shipments reduce total inventory

Of the three inventories held in production facilities, the work-in-process (WIP) inventory is most easily reduced using JIT. But WIP is usually the smallest and least expensive of the inventories, and tackling the other two requires changing the way suppliers deliver raw materials and customers receive finished goods. In order to bring down the inventory of raw materials, JIT producers work with their suppliers to switch over from large shipments of materials that go to central receiving facilities to small, frequent shipments that go directly from trucks to the factory floor (Figure 3.1). The change is a dramatic one, often taking a company from monthly orders and shipments to multiple shipments a day with precisely timed arrivals. Most JIT producers have a similar program on the outbound side, using small, frequent deliveries to minimize their inventory of finished goods.

JIT requires close partnerships with suppliers

As soon as manufacturers begin to make these kinds of changes, JIT quickly expands from a production initiative to a much broader program that requires systematic changes in supply chain management. Toyota, the company that pioneered the JIT method in the 1970s, was keenly aware of this aspect of its program, and it worked closely with its suppliers to convert their operations to JIT as well, precisely coordinating the flow of goods from suppliers to production plants. In order to support the close relationship

Figure 3.1
Just-in-Time
Supply

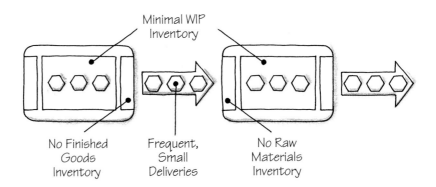

Minimal WIP Inventory

No Finished Goods Inventory

Frequent, Small Deliveries

No Raw Materials Inventory

required by this new kind of production, Toyota used a uniquely Japanese form of joint partnership, called a **keiretsu**, with its key suppliers. In Toyota's case, the keiretsu involved taking a 20% to 50% equity position in each supplier and replacing 20% of its key executives with Toyota personnel.

JIT practices offer important insights into how supply chains can be improved. Although the apparent focus of JIT is on reducing inventory, the true spirit of the method is a systematic pursuit of quality, one aspect of which is eliminating any unnecessary complexity. In the case of supply chain transactions, this philosophy has led to a much needed streamlining of the order-shipment-payment cycle. Instead of accumulating large orders mixing many different kinds of materials, producers place many orders for individual materials, often paying for these materials on delivery rather than accumulating lump sums. In addition, a great deal of documentation has been stripped away. For example, traditional orders are often eliminated in favor of continuously updated delivery schedules, and billing documents may be eliminated altogether. One of the great contributions of JIT to supply chain management is to provide a clear demonstration of just how simple the basic flows can become.

Simpler ordering reduces complexity

Along with reducing complexity, the JIT philosophy of quality also seeks to reduce variability in every stage of production. To this end, each operation is analyzed, refined, and rehearsed until it can be completed both quickly and consistently. In the case of supply chains, this level of rigor not only accelerates the movement of goods, it also adds an unprecedented level of precision to deliveries. This precision allows inventories of raw materials to be reduced to a fraction of their normal levels without causing shutdowns on the line.

Consistent performance reduces variability

Of course, not every form of variability can be eliminated, and herein lies the downside of JIT: It can make supply chains so fragile that any interruption in the flow of supplies brings the entire chain

JIT can make supply chains fragile

to a halt. Toyota learned this in 1997 when a fire at one of its suppliers shut down Toyota's production lines for an entire week. The following year, strikes in two GM parts plants led to the shutdown of almost all of the company's assembly plants within a matter of days. A year later, seven DaimlerChrysler plants and three GM plants were forced into half-shifts when flooding in one supplier's plant created a shortage of a single part. After the terrorist attacks of September 11, 2001, many plants in the United States had to be closed due to breakdowns in the transportation system. Ford, for example, shut down five North American plants due to parts shortages, many of them due to delays in bringing trucks across the Canadian border.

Manufacturers are now cautious about JIT

Shutdowns such as these can quickly wipe out the savings associated with reduced inventory levels. For a large manufacturer, having a plant shut down can cost as much as $10,000 a minute. Given this kind of financial impact, many firms that adopted JIT wholeheartedly are now rethinking their position and taking a more conservative approach. Honda, for one, now has a policy of maintaining dual suppliers for all its raw materials. Ford, while reaffirming its commitment to its JIT program in the wake of the terrorist attacks, immediately began developing plans to stockpile engines and other key parts at some U.S. plants.

Simplicity and consistency remain key goals

Even with appropriate risk management, JIT isn't the right approach for every supply chain. It doesn't work in job shops, which do not use production lines, and it's not relevant to process manufacturing. Even within its natural domain, repetitive production, it's not a good choice for low-volume products or for products with uncertain demand. But these are limitations, not defects; for the right kind of production environment, JIT can lead to dramatic improvements. More important, however, is the way the JIT effort illustrates how much can be done to reduce complexity and variability in supply chains. JIT's emphasis on simplicity and consistency can be used to advantage at every link of the chain, regardless of whether other aspects of the technique are employed.

Retail Replenishment Programs

The second major class of supply chain programs deals with the distribution side, and is concerned with replenishing retail inventories. Historically, the link between retail stores and their immediate suppliers has been a difficult juncture in the supply chain. In the past, retail inventories were managed by independent storeowners, who often lacked sophisticated tools for forecasting demand and planning replenishment. Yet this is precisely the point in the chain that can be the hardest to manage because it is the first point to feel the impact of changing consumer preferences. It is also the point where the chain becomes visible to the consumer, so it's critical to manage it well. If the desired product isn't on the shelf when a consumer walks in to buy it, even the most perfect sequence of supply operations is a failure.

Retail replenishment is a tough problem

The first generation of retail replenishment programs was based on shifting the control of inventories (Figure 3.2). In the traditional arrangement, retailers manage their own inventories and replenish them as they see fit. The problem with this arrangement is that producers are often in a better position than retailers to track emerging patterns in demand. In addition, producers can remove cost and uncertainty from this link in the chain by centralizing control of the replenishment process. One way to leverage these advantages is **consignment**, in which producers retain both ownership and control over inventories of their products at a retailer's site. Consignment has proved to be an effective tool for selling products that retailers might not be willing to carry on conventional terms, but it's not the first choice for producers because they have to wait longer before they get paid for their products.

Early efforts shifted control of inventory

Figure 3.2
Inventory
Management
Relationships

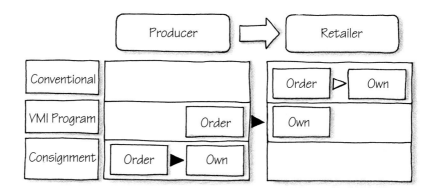

**VMI transfers
ownership but
not control**

A more recent development, **vendor-managed inventory (VMI)**, is shown in the middle row of Figure 3.2. The innovative aspect of VMI is the way it separates control from ownership, both of which usually transfer at the same time. In VMI, a producer receives continuous updates on a retailer's inventory level and replenishes it as needed, with the retailer taking ownership of the goods on delivery. This gives producers better visibility of sales of their products, helping them anticipate demand and better plan supply. The retailers benefit because they no longer have to track inventory levels or place orders for products under a VMI program. They also save money because they usually need less inventory, sometimes as little as half of what they would otherwise keep in stock.

**Quick response
applies JIT to
the retail link**

In addition to VMI, several other programs have been developed to smooth the flow of goods through retail stores. One of the earliest was the **quick response (QR)** program, an effort on the part of the apparel industry in the 1980s to combine some of the techniques of JIT with technologies for monitoring inventory levels in real time. As shown in Figure 3.3, electronic **point of sale (POS)** systems automatically captured data about clothing sales as they occurred, then transmitted this data to producers using **electronic data interchange (EDI)** connections. Producers responded with daily shipments of pre-tagged items that could go directly from their trucks to the selling floor.

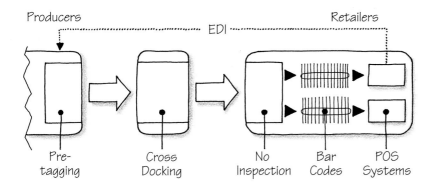

Figure 3.3
The Quick
Response Program

In the late 1980s, the apparel industry rolled out an extension of the QR program known as **continuous replenishment (CR)**. As shown in Figure 3.4, this program incorporated VMI for better inventory control, and it introduced joint forecasting so that producers and retailers could pool their understanding of consumer demand to better predict future sales. Another important aspect of this program was that a replenishment agreement acted as a standing purchase commitment. This allowed members of the program to eliminate individual purchase orders altogether, further streamlining the replenishment process.

Continuous replenishment added VMI

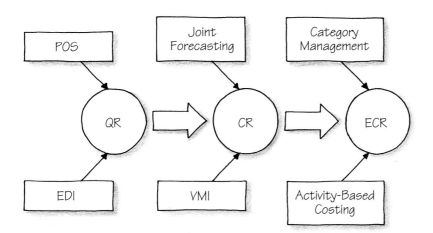

Figure 3.4
Retail
Replenishment
Programs

ECR added category management

In 1993, the grocery industry launched its own version of continuous replenishment, calling it the **efficient consumer response (ECR)** program. ECR's major contribution was the addition of **category management**, which organizes promotion and replenishment activities around groups of products that consumers view as roughly equivalent in satisfying their needs. This addition helps grocery stores determine the best mix of products to put on their shelves to make sure their customers' needs are met even if there are occasional shortages. This program also encourages the use of activity-based costing (described in Chapter 9) to determine the profitability of each product category.

The programs attack complexity and variability

Like the JIT programs described earlier, retail replenishment programs reflect a continuing effort to simplify and stabilize supply chain flows. For example, the elimination of orders in continuous replenishment removed a major source of time and cost that added no value to the end consumer. These programs also pioneered important techniques for coping with variability, including some that aren't employed in the JIT effort. Most notably, the use of real-time data on sales allows retailers to respond quickly to variations in consumer buying patterns, and the addition of joint forecasting allows retailers to prepare for some of these shifts before they hit the stores.

CPFR is the most ambitious program yet

The most ambitious replenishment program to date is **collaborative planning, forecasting, and replenishment (CPFR)**, a multi-industry effort that was formalized in 1998 (Figure 3.5). Although CPFR is not a direct extension of any of the preceding programs, it draws on the experience gained with all three. Being the first clean-sheet design since the commercialization of the Internet, CPFR abandons EDI and private networks in favor of Internet communication. In addition to the direct communication of real-time data, trading partners use centralized information servers to view and update shared plans and forecasts.

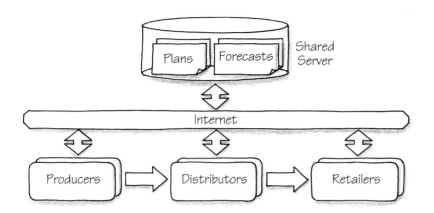

Figure 3.5
The CPFR Program

In short, the CPFR program relies on advanced, Internet-based tools to pool information about demand and supply, allowing trading partners to coordinate their inventory decisions and smooth the flow of goods across the chain. The use of such tools offers important advantages, but it also requires companies to make substantial investments in new technologies. Another obstacle is cultural: CPFR requires companies to share highly detailed information about their operations, and many are reluctant to do that. CPFR is beginning to win converts, but it's too soon to tell how widely the program will be embraced.

Adoption of CPFR has just begun

The Problem with Programs

All of the programs described in this chapter were introduced with great fanfare, and there are solid statistics to demonstrate that each of them has succeeded in reducing inventories and accelerating the flow of goods across the chain. These glowing reviews are bolstered by continuing reports in the business press about the remarkable economies produced over the past two decades through the relentless reduction of inventory. There's just one problem with these impressive results: They may not be real. Last year, a team of researchers at Ohio State University conducted a comprehensive analysis of the inventory levels reported by U.S.

All the programs have declared victory

corporations over the past 20 years, and they reached a startling conclusion: The Great Inventory Reduction of the late twentieth century never happened.

The programs aren't reducing inventory

The study did reveal a modest overall decline in total inventory since 1980, but most of that was due to a small number of industries that made structural changes in their supply chains. For example, the elimination of distributors and retailers in the direct sales model perfected by Dell, together with other advanced supply chain techniques, allowed the computer industry to cut its total inventories in half over the 20-year period. These are truly impressive gains, and they have contributed to the dramatic reductions in prices within this industry. But for other industries, including the two that have most ardently pursued retail replenishment programs—apparel and grocery—inventory levels have remained absolutely flat over the life of those programs.

They're just moving inventory elsewhere

What's going on here? Are these programs just a sham? No; the problem is subtler than that. The inventory levels of the companies participating in these programs have, in fact, dropped, but it now appears that most of those reductions were achieved by displacing inventory within the chain rather than actually eliminating it. This may be good for the companies reporting success, but it's hard on other members of their chains, and it does nothing to make those chains more efficient or competitive overall. These programs may be intended to create a new level of cooperation in the supply chain, bringing companies together as true trading partners, but, as often happens in business, the benefits of that cooperation appear to accrue mostly to the dominant party.

Retailers have slashed their inventories

The renowned success of Wal-Mart in mastering its supply chain provides a good case in point. Through a variant of the classic vertical integration strategy, Wal-Mart has largely eliminated the distributors, carriers, and other middlemen that used to intervene between producers and retail outlets (Figure 3.6). The scale of this effort is staggering: Wal-Mart's trucks carry 50 million pallets of goods each week to 500 million square feet of retail space to serve 15 million customers a day. With economies of scale such as these, Wal-Mart has been able to eliminate a great deal of excess cost in its supply chain. These efficiencies are reflected in the national data: Retail is one of the few sectors that has made dramatic progress in reducing its total inventory, neatly paralleling the rise of mega-retailers such as Wal-Mart.

Wal-Mart's massive scale also allows it to dictate terms to manufacturers, reversing the historical dominance of producers in the supply chains for consumer goods. For example, companies that want access to Wal-Mart's vast retail channel have to ship large volumes of goods to many different locations, meet precise delivery schedules with high reliability, and react instantly to changing levels of demand throughout the Wal-Mart empire. These requirements translate directly into increased inventories of finished goods, and that's exactly what the data show. In the industries that serve mega-retailers such as Wal-Mart, inventories of finished goods have not just remained flat, they have actually gone up over the last 20 years.

Manufacturers now hold more finished goods

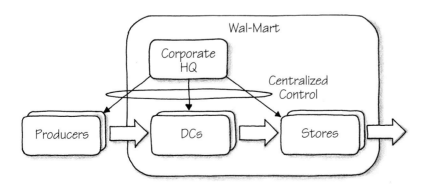

Figure 3.6
The Wal-Mart Model

Producers push the problem upstream

Of course, producers can compensate for this pressure to some extent by streamlining their internal operations and putting pressure on their own suppliers for more prompt performance, reducing their inventories of raw materials and work in process. And that's just what the data indicate; it is reductions in raw materials and WIP inventories that have kept total inventories from rising. Of course, increasing the pressure on suppliers to hold inventory to the last minute and respond rapidly to demand signals requires them to keep more finished goods on hand, and so on, up the chain. In short, the dramatic reductions in inventory achieved at the retail level have come, in large part, from pushing inventory up the chain, not from taking it out of the chain.

JIT also pushes inventory up the chain

This pattern of pushing inventory up the chain is also found in JIT programs. Here again, requiring suppliers to make precisely timed deliveries and respond rapidly to changing consumption reduces a producer's inventory of raw materials at the cost of forcing suppliers to hold more finished goods to buffer variability in demand. The standard response to this problem is for the suppliers to adopt JIT as well, but that only works if customers and suppliers precisely synchronize their operations. When U.S. companies first adopted JIT in the 1980s, they sometimes found that total inventory costs went up rather than down. The problem wasn't within the four walls: Both customers and suppliers ran exemplary JIT shops, each keeping on-site inventory to a minimum. The problem lay in the link between them. In order to handle coordination problems, companies often kept inventory in third-party warehouses to provide a buffer stock (Figure 3.7). The inventory hadn't been eliminated after all; it had just been moved to more expensive facilities.

JIT pushes inventory down the chain as well

One important difference between programs at the production level and those at the retail level is that producers are in the middle of the chain rather than at the end, so they have the option of

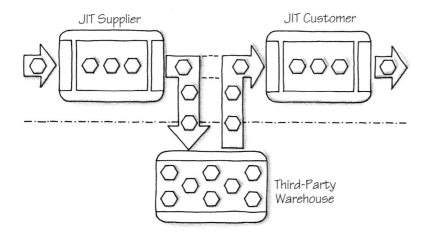

Figure 3.7
Hidden Inventory
in JIT

pushing inventory downstream as well as upstream (Figure 3.8). Not surprisingly, this is exactly what happens. The best example comes from the automobile industry; having sorted out most of the supplier aspects of JIT, U.S. auto plants now operate with as little as three hours of inventory on hand. But the inventory of cars and trucks sitting at dealerships now runs as high as three months' worth of supply. JIT may be a success for the automakers, but it isn't making their supply chains more efficient. Of all the ways in which the industry could hold inventory, finished goods is by far the most expensive form.

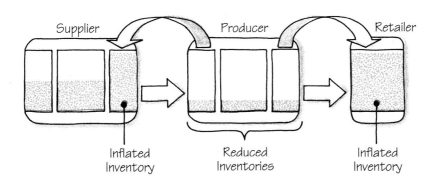

Figure 3.8
Producer
Displacing
Inventory

Trading partners still act like competitors

Viewed in the larger context of trade relationships, this pattern of pushing the burden up and down the chain rather than eliminating it altogether is not surprising. Although adjacent members of a supply chain are often called trading partners, more often than not this is a euphemism to draw attention away from a relationship that remains economically adversarial. No matter how much they may wish to cooperate, the bottom line is that the members of a supply chain are in competition with each other to increase their share of the consumer's dollar. When competition *between* chains drives down prices, the competition *within* chains heats up as each member of the chain tries to maintain its profit margins. If there is any imbalance of power within the chain—and there almost always is—the profits eventually gravitate to the power players, and the smaller players have to take what they can get.

True partnership is a real possibility

Supply chain relationships don't have to be like this. When companies act as true trading partners, working together to pull time and cost out of the chain, they can create a situation in which everyone makes more money. Chrysler's SCORE program—at least in its early years—was an excellent example of how much can be achieved this way. The company's $1.7 billion in savings didn't come out of its suppliers' hides; suppliers saved money right along with Chrysler. The savings came from finding better ways to build a car. What made this program different is that SCORE fostered true innovation rather than just escalating the competition for a fixed amount of money. The Ohio State researchers mentioned at the beginning of this section reached the same conclusion, based on their study of national data. In their words, "efforts to increase efficiency through the exercise of power simply change the location of the inefficiency." The only way to get genuine improvements is to redesign the supply chain to increase its efficiency as a whole.

The idea of replacing competition between trading partners with cooperation, creating win-win relationships, is so obvious and so often repeated that it no longer has much currency. Attempts to build such relationships can and do succeed, but failure is the more common result, and today's managers are right to be suspicious of trading partners that talk about building win-win relationships without showing where the additional winnings will come from. They know that no matter how friendly things get, there will always be a dollar-for-dollar tradeoff between their profits and those of their "partners," so cooperation will never truly replace the natural competition between them.

Win-win relationships are hard to build

The dilemma, then, is this: Adjacent members of a supply chain may have very real opportunities to increase their shared profits, but the underlying tension over how the profits are divided can prevent them from realizing those opportunities. And even if they do find a way to increase their total profit, they may do so by push-ing inventory or other costs onto other members of the chain. This situation makes any attempt to improve the performance of the chain as a whole a difficult proposition at best. The only way out of the dilemma is somehow to separate the effects of cooperation from those of competition, recognizing that both exist and devising a way to distribute the profits from cooperation in a manner that is fair to all parties. That's hard to do under the best of circumstances, but the techniques of game theory can make it a little bit easier.

Game theory offers some vital insights

Insights from Game Theory

When trading partners compete with each other over a fixed sum of money, they are playing what game theorists call a **zero-sum game**. In zero-sum games, there's a fixed amount of money at stake, and players compete to see who can win the largest share. In Figure 3.9, two players, A and B, are competing for stakes of $100. The range of possible outcomes, from A taking everything to B get-ting it all, forms the diagonal line labeled the *win-lose line* in the dia-gram. The outcome of the game is a single point on this line. For

Transactions are played as zero-sum games

Figure 3.9
A Zero-Sum Game

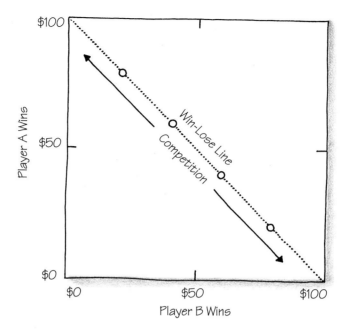

clarity—these aren't standard terms—I'll call the line describing the possible outcomes the *tradeoff curve,* and I'll refer to the point describing the outcome as the *tradeoff point.* In the case of a zero-sum game, the tradeoff curve is the same as the win-lose line, and movement of the tradeoff point along this line represents competition in its purest form. Most supply chain transactions play out as zero-sum games, with the two parties vying with each other to push the outcome in their direction along the win-lose line.

Few transactions are really zero-sum

If there are ways in which the parties involved in a transaction can influence the total winnings in addition to determining how they divide up those winnings, the transaction turns into a non-zero-sum game. A non-zero-sum game can go either way, depending on the relationship between the two parties. If that relationship is cooperative, the parties can push the tradeoff curve up into the win-win region, as shown in the left panel of Figure 3.10. If the relationship is antagonistic, they can do each other more harm than good, moving the tradeoff curve down into the lose-lose region.

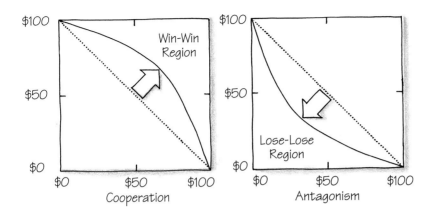

Figure 3.10
Non-Zero-Sum
Games

The core contribution of game theory to economics is the insight that few business transactions are restricted to pure competition. Much of what we think of as win-lose transactions are actually much richer than this.

The focus of the following discussion is on moving trading relationships up into the win-win range, but that shouldn't obscure the fact that relationships often degenerate into lose-lose propositions. It is all too easy for the adversarial aspects of competition to dominate a relationship, even to the point where harming the other party becomes more important than winning the game. This is often seen in the competition between supply chains, where price wars and other forms of "cutthroat" competition can plunge companies into the lose-lose region. But it is also found *within* supply chains, as evidenced by the hidden JIT inventory shown in Figure 3.7 and in the higher carrying costs of inventory at auto dealers rather than plants. One of the dangers of thinking of trading relationships as zero-sum games is that it is all too easy for struggles along the win-lose line to slide off the line into the lose-lose region.

On a more positive note, trading partners that want to improve their combined profits rather than just fight over a fixed amount of money can look for ways to change their relationship into a positive-sum

Lose-lose relationships are common

Cooperation can increase the total winnings

game. This is not to say that they can eliminate the element of competition altogether; no matter how far they push the tradeoff curve into the win-win region, there can still be a struggle over who gets the lion's share of the winnings. The difference is a matter of emphasis rather than kind. In a cooperative game, the players focus on how to increase their total winnings and relegate the allocation of those winnings to a secondary concern. In a competitive game, the winnings are considered fixed and the allocation is everything.

SCORE put cooperation ahead of competition

This is why Chrysler's SCORE program was so successful. It completely recast the relationship to focus on cooperation and provided a simple set of mechanics to resolve the competitive element. Current prices were taken as a given, and reductions in those prices were limited to actual savings resulting from improved techniques. That limited the competitive element to the amount of the savings, and the program was very flexible within that range. In the early days, Chrysler often accepted whatever savings a supplier chose to pass on, without questioning the actual amount. Some suppliers no doubt kept more than half of the savings, but others passed along most or even all of the savings in an effort to win more business. Since everyone was winning at this point, no one worried too much about keeping score.

Cooperation requires changing the relationship

The first lesson to be drawn from game theory, then, is that trading partners should place most of the emphasis on maximizing the total winnings. The more successful they are in this effort, the less important the allocation of those winnings becomes. This often requires a major shift in the way customers and suppliers view their relationship, and making that shift is often harder than finding opportunities for savings. In fact, studies of why supply chain partnerships so often fail reveal that the failure is usually due more to attitudes than economics. It takes a sustained effort to build a positive-sum relationship, but, at least for key links in the chain, the return on that investment of time and energy can be among the best in business.

Of course, the question of just where to place the tradeoff point in any given exchange doesn't ever go away, and even the best of relationships can become tense when there is freshly minted money lying on the table. There are many ways to resolve this question, but the preferred choice should always be to pick the point that maximizes the total winnings, compensating for any inequities through some other exchange. This is not only the best "average" outcome across the two companies, it is also the way to maximize the competitiveness of their supply chain.

Competition is never completely eliminated

This is best seen through an example. Suppose a customer and sup-plier are each spending $5 a unit to verify the quality of a certain component. Figure 3.11 shows how this situation can be repre-

Tradeoffs aren't always symmetrical

Figure 3.11
Allocating Cost Savings

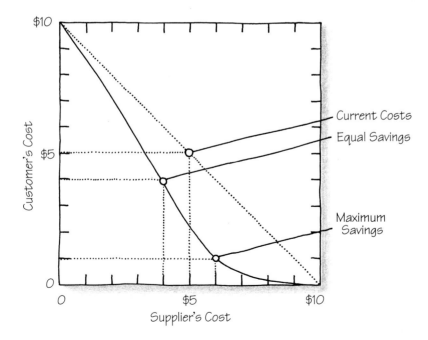

61

sented as a zero-sum game. In this case the cooperative region is in the lower left rather than the upper right because the companies benefit by reducing costs, whereas in the earlier example they benefited by increasing profits. The tradeoff curve in the diagram represents the results of a joint study showing that a cooperative inspection program could eliminate several redundant operations, reducing the total expenditure on quality control. According to the study, the tradeoff curve is asymmetrical; the largest savings will be realized if the supplier takes on more of the burden of quality assurance because this eliminates the additional expense of shipping and returning defective components. Assuming the companies can agree on this program, how should they split the savings?

The best policy is to maximize total winnings

In the real world, the most likely outcome is that the customer would express outrage at having to spend so much to compensate for poor quality and would insist that the supplier get its act together and eliminate the defects. But suppose that, in the spirit of cooperation, the two agree to share the savings equally, choosing the tradeoff point labeled *equal savings*. This isn't a bad choice; both companies spend less money on quality control, and the total costs for the component go down by $2, allowing the supply chain to improve its margins. But a better choice would be to pick the point that maximizes the total savings. In this example, the two companies can shave an additional $1 per component off their combined costs if the supplier actually increases its total cost. This may not be fair to the supplier, but this inequity is easily rectified by having the producer compensate the supplier in other ways. The simplest solution is for the producer to pay more for components shipped under the new quality program.

Relationships span many transactions

This last point—that the customer can compensate the supplier for its added expense through side payments or some other exchange—reveals another important contribution of game theory. Although it may make sense for companies to view spot purchases and other isolated transactions as zero-sum games, that kind of thinking breaks down when it comes to sustained relationships, which span multiple transactions and include multiple tradeoffs. Even if a company insists on applying zero-sum logic to an entire relationship, it is still better off choosing optimal points for individual transactions and making up the difference elsewhere. But the best relationship is achieved by setting the competitive component aside long enough to explore the full benefits that can be realized through cooperation. There is always a way to balance out the books later if one party doesn't realize its full share of the benefits in a particular transaction.

Another key insight from applying game theory is that decisions such as these can't be made intuitively; they are simply too complex for that. Even a trivial example of the sort shown in Figure 3.11 outstrips our ability to discover the best solution by thinking in terms of who "ought" to carry a cost or what a fair division of savings might be. The key to taking win-win relationships out of the realm of warm fuzzies and making them a working reality is to use formal models to find optimal values. For some decisions, a simple spreadsheet showing cost tradeoffs is enough; others may require modeling the entire supply chain. Chapter 5 provides an overview of the various kinds of models and their applications; the important point here is simply that modeling is an indispensable tool for making the complex decisions required in supply chain management.

Modeling reveals the real tradeoffs

Winning Through Collaboration

Although supply chain management has come a long way from its origins in transportation management, the discipline still tends to reflect the original focus on managing the flow of goods across a single link in the chain. As the examples in this chapter illustrate, it is all too easy for such point solutions to simply push problems up or down the chain rather than actually solving them. Even when two or more trading partners cooperate to improve their overall

Most efforts have been point solutions

position, they often do so at the expense of other members of the chain. In game theory terms, they are creating a local positive-sum game, but their cooperative relationship may actually drive their interactions with other members of the chain into the lose-lose region.

Competitiveness requires teamwork

This is not the way to build a winning chain. The new competition between supply chains isn't based on the effectiveness of individual links; it's based on the ability of the chain as a whole to bring better products to the market faster and cheaper than other chains. The key to doing this is to apply the logic of game theory across the entire chain, pushing the chain as a whole as far as possible into the win-win region. This can only happen if all the members of the chain are willing to play as a team, optimizing the tradeoffs at every link in order to pull time and cost out of the chain.

The goal is integrated planning and action

In effect, the members of this team need to plan and act with the integrity of a single organization, working together to simplify and stabilize the flow of demand, supply, and cash across the chain. This pooling of interests, this synergy of planning and acting, is the essence of supply chain integration. Succinctly put, supply chain integration means that the members of the chain come together to form a larger whole, one in which the parts are carefully aligned and synchronized so that the chain behaves as a single, coordinated system.

Vertical integration was the classic choice

Supply chain integration isn't an all-or-none proposition: It varies in both form and degree, as shown in Figure 3.12. The classic form, shown on the left side of the figure, is vertical integration, in which all the members of the chain are owned by the same company. Vertical integration is still practiced in some segments of the chain, as seen in Wal-Mart's ownership of the distribution channel, but it's hard to achieve across the entire chain today because so many companies are involved. Henry Ford was a great believer in vertical

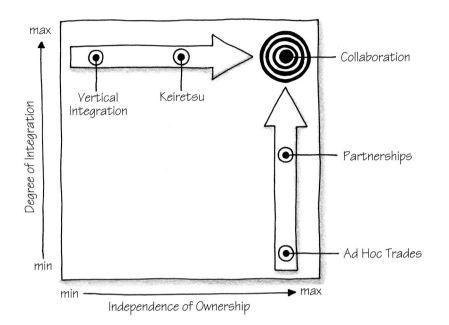

Figure 3.12
Strategies for
Integration

integration, and he made sure his company owned everything from rubber trees to sales lots. Today, Ford's supply chain includes more than 100,000 companies. Even if it were possible for Ford to own all those companies, the inevitable overhead and bureaucracy would negate most of the advantages of common ownership.

Today, it is far more common for companies to focus on their core competence and cooperate with other companies to assemble complete supply chains. But the form of that cooperation varies widely, as shown in Figure 3.12. The keiretsu is forged by establishing overlapping ownership and management among formerly independent trading partners, as described earlier in this chapter. It generally achieves levels of integration nearly as good as those of vertical integration, but this may be due as much to Japanese culture as to the business structure. The diametrical opposite of vertical integration is the ad hoc supply chain shown in the lower right of Figure 3.12, a group of independently owned companies bound only by need and market mechanisms. This kind of chain requires the least

Companies now focus on core competence

governance and is the most flexible, in that its membership can change with each transaction. But it would be hard to envision a less integrated solution to the problems of coordinating a chain.

Virtual integration is now the preferred path

Attempts to gain a high degree of integration without compromising independent ownership—an approach called **virtual integration**—are shown as movement up the right side of Figure 3.12. Partnership agreements between adjacent members of the chain are the usual first step toward vertical integration, but they are at best a partial solution because they only span a single link. True integration requires the members of a supply chain to coordinate the flow of demand, supply, and cash across the chain as a whole, not just across a single link.

Two trends point toward collaboration

As indicated in Figure 3.12, the current push for collaboration across the chain represents the natural convergence of two major trends in supply chain management. One trend is away from common ownership and toward independent companies. The other trend is away from ad hoc transactions and toward tighter integration. The place where those two trends meet—the spot marked with the bull's-eye—is the goal of supply chain collaboration: a team of companies achieving a high degree of integration across the supply chain while retaining independent ownership and control.

Collaboration isn't a new idea

Supply chain collaboration isn't a new idea; JIT, quick response, efficient consumer response, and the other programs described in this chapter are all early forms of collaboration, but they are limited to a small subset of the larger supply chain. In the future, collaboration has to span enough links in the chain to truly pull time and cost out of the chain, not just displace it within the chain.

Collaboration will be difficult to achieve

Achieving this level of collaboration will require managers to take a much wider perspective on the supply chain than they do today, thinking of their companies as part of a larger whole rather than the center of the business universe. This won't come easily; one recent survey revealed that more than 80% of all supply chain initiatives are completely contained within a single company, and most of the remainder deal only with immediate trading partners. Another survey, reported in *Supply Chain Management Review* (see Notes on Sources), reinforces the point with this rather bleak conclusion: "We did not find a single incidence of extensive analysis of the total supply chain to understand the inter-relationships or to set the goals," adding that ". . . no company has a model of the supply chain on which to test different modes of operation or the impact of different strategies."

This may be a bleak conclusion for the supply chain industry as a whole, but it represents a tremendous opportunity for companies that are ready to move to the next level. Integrating a supply chain through collaboration may not be easy, but you don't need to get your chain anywhere near the bull's-eye to score a big win. Given the current state of supply chains, just making progress in that direction can be enough to give you a solid competitive advantage. Imagine a perfectly integrated chain as a champion marathon runner, clicking off a steady stream of six-minute miles by maintaining perfect synchrony in every movement. The corresponding image for a conventional chain would be Dr. Frankenstein's monster lurching down the village lane, struggling to make an ad hoc assembly of muscles propel its body forward. If that's the competition, you don't have to be an Olympic runner to come in first. If you can walk, you can win.

You don't have to do it all at once

The essential message you should take away from Part I is this: Supply chains are the new arena of corporate competition, the core problem in managing supply chains is dealing with complexity and variability, and collaboration among trading partners is essential to coping with these problems. This is the mission; should you choose to accept it, you will need some specialized tools to help you succeed. Part II presents these tools by (1) explaining how to look at supply chains from a systems perspective, (2) showing you three different ways to model supply chains, and (3) giving you a quick tour of supply chain software. Once you have these tools in hand, you'll be ready to master your own supply chain.

PART

Solutions

PART I: Challenges	1	The New Competition	2	The Rules of the Game	3	Winning as a Team

PART II: Solutions	4	Supply Chains as Systems	5	Modeling the Supply Chain	6	Supply Chain Software

		Demand		Supply		Performance
PART III: Operations	7	Meeting Demand	8	Maintaining Supply	9	Measuring Performance
PART IV: Planning	10	Forecasting Demand	11	Scheduling Supply	12	Improving Performance
PART V: Design	13	Mastering Demand	14	Designing the Chain	15	Maximizing Performance

4

Supply Chains as Systems

Integrating a supply chain requires assembling an ad hoc collection of facilities into a coherent system that can function with a single purpose. In order to succeed in this effort, you need to know something about systems—how they are designed, how they work, and how they are controlled. In short, you need a little systems theory. This may sound like an abstract subject of limited relevance to your needs, but nothing could be further from the truth. As a manager, you deal with some of the most complex systems on earth every day, and your experience has already given you a basic understanding of how these systems work. The problem with this understanding is that it's largely intuitive, making it hard to use in solving new problems. This chapter will help you hone those intuitions into powerful business design tools.

Business Cybernetics

The formal study of systems dates back to the 1940s with the emergence of cybernetics, which took insights gained from the invention of computers and applied them to other domains. In cybernetics, a system is viewed as an assembly of components that interact to produce collective behavior. Computers are systems, of course, but so are plants, animals, ecologies, nations, companies, factories, and, yes, supply chains. The key insight of cybernetics is that there are common principles across all these different kinds of systems, principles that help explain the behavior of each. Knowing something about systems in general really does help you understand business systems in particular.

A system is an assembly of components

One of the key contributions of cybernetics was the insight that all systems can be seen as transforming inputs into outputs. When systems are constructed by people, as supply chains are, they are

A system transforms inputs into outputs

usually designed to produce outputs that have greater immediate value than the inputs. For example, computers take in large volumes of data and distill it into useful information; factories consume raw materials and produce finished goods; human beings take in food and transform it into . . . well, some improvements are less obvious than others. In this case, the output of interest is the energy extracted from the food, which in turn is transformed into physical movement and other forms of work.

Systems may have controls and monitors

Natural systems, such as ecologies, are usually self-regulating, and attempts to control them often do more harm than good. Systems made by people, on the other hand, are designed to be controlled and monitored so that their performance can be improved over time. Control is achieved by regulating the flow of inputs, and monitoring involves measuring the resulting outputs. In effect, these systems have the equivalent of knobs on their inputs and gauges on their outputs; changing the settings of the knobs changes the readings on the gauges (Figure 4.1). Inside the system, a number of components—which may be systems in their own right—interact to transform the inputs into the outputs. If the arrangement of the components in the illustration suggests the structure of a supply chain, that's probably not a coincidence.

Figure 4.1
A System

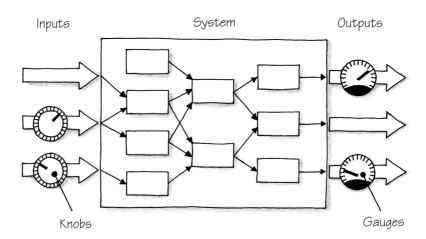

Notice in Figure 4.1 that not all the inputs have knobs, and not all the outputs have gauges. Even in the best-designed systems, there are usually some inputs that can't be controlled by the people operating the system. In the case of supply chains, economic cycles and natural disasters can have a profound impact on performance, but these are outside the span of control. Economists call these inputs **extrinsic factors** because, in contrast to **intrinsic factors** such as plant capacity and budget allocations, they originate from outside the boundaries of the system.

Similarly, it may not be possible to measure every output of a system. For example, measuring the contribution to consumer value added by each stage of a production process is highly desirable but notoriously difficult in most industries. Even if it *is* possible to measure every output, systems usually have so many outputs that it's not cost-effective to measure them all. The preferred approach, then, is to measure the set of outputs that are most helpful in monitoring and controlling the system. The problem of choosing the best set of outputs to measure is particularly difficult in the case of supply chains (see Chapter 9).

With just these few concepts in place, it's already possible to see why an understanding of systems is useful in managing supply chains. In essence, each manager in the chain is given responsibility for a set of knobs, and each one sees the readings on a set of gauges. The goal is for everyone to set their knobs just right in order to maximize the outputs of the chain. That isn't going to happen without some shared understanding of how the settings affect the operation of the chain, together with some coordination of the changes to get the best overall performance.

Figure 4.2 illustrates how this works by showing the relationships among three key processes in managing systems: understanding, prediction, and control. Understanding provides the insights necessary

Figure 4.2
Understanding,
Prediction,
and Control

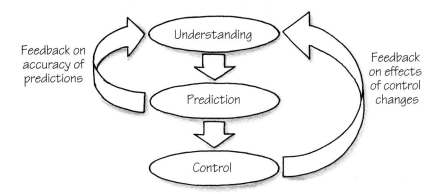

for you to predict how a system will behave in response to changes to its inputs. Prediction, in turn, allows you to control the system by making the best combination of adjustments. Comparing predicted with actual results deepens your understanding of the system, allowing you to make more accurate predictions and improving your control. Together, these core processes form the heart of any successful management process.

Understanding is usually neglected

Of the three processes, understanding is arguably the most important, yet it is also the most neglected. Instead, the emphasis proceeds in the other direction: Control is the primary concern, prediction is invoked only as needed to improve control, and understanding is viewed as an incidental by-product rather than the prime mover of the sequence. This reversal of priorities may be necessary in the short run, but it is self-defeating in the long haul. The image that comes to mind is driving a tandem truck down the freeway in reverse, making wild corrections to the steering in order to compensate for going about the matter backward. This book— not to mention my entire career—is devoted to getting understanding back out in front where it belongs.

Some systems don't require understanding

To be fair, some systems are so well designed that very little understanding is required to control them. Contemporary cars epitomize such systems, at least in regard to the basic controls. The harder you press on the gas pedal, the faster the car goes. The machinery and software that intervene between this input and the resulting output have become extremely complex over the years, but the mapping between the two is so straightforward that operators don't need to know a thing about the internals of the system. In computer terms such systems are referred to as being user-friendly, a state that remains an elusive goal for computers themselves.

Supply chains are anything *but* user-friendly. The basic mechanics, as described in Chapter 2, are pretty simple, but the behavior of the chain as a whole can be very difficult to understand, much less predict and control. One of the recurring themes of this book is that even the most benign attempts to control supply chains, such as offering quantity discounts to encourage volume purchases or running promotions to increase sales, can have wholly unintended and often disastrous effects on performance. When it comes to systems of this level of complexity, understanding is not a luxury; it's a necessity.

Understanding is essential for supply chains

A Rogues Gallery of Relations

One of the most basic characteristics of systems is the way in which they map values on the inputs to values on the outputs. This mapping, or **relation**, can take on a variety of different types, which range from the most straightforward to the truly bizarre. This section introduces you to the various kinds of relations you might encounter, using a device I call the Rogues Gallery of Relations.

Relations map inputs to outputs

To see why you need to understand relations, imagine controlling the system shown in Figure 4.3. It's about as simple as a system can get, with just a single component, a single input, and a single output. The values of the input and the output both range from 0 to 100. The input has a knob and the output has a gauge, so you have complete control of the system's input and full knowledge of its

The mapping can be viewed as a graph

Figure 4.3
The Simplest
System

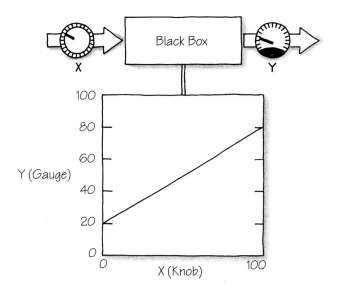

output. The component itself could have any degree of internal complexity, but we'll treat it as a "black box"—all that matters is the relationship between the input and the output. One possible relationship is shown graphically in the bottom of the figure. As you turn the knob from 0 to 100, the output goes from 20 to 80. With a bit of practice, you could quickly adapt to this control and produce any available output on demand. Over time, it would become as automatic as using the gas pedal in your car.

**Relations come
in many forms**

This system is easy to understand and operate because the relation between the input and output is so simple. Unfortunately, relations in real-world systems are rarely this simple. To see some other relations that might have been lurking in this system, take a look at the relations shown in Figure 4.4. Each panel illustrates a particular kind of relation, together with the name most commonly used for that type. All of these relations are found in supply chain systems, and knowing which one you are dealing with when you are changing an input is essential to achieving good control. As you proceed from left to right in the diagram, the relations become increasingly

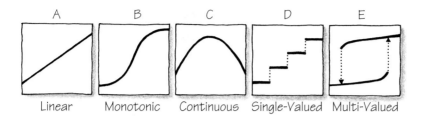

Figure 4.4
The Rogues Gallery
of Relations

difficult to understand and control, which is why I call them
rogues. A brief rundown on each rogue will help you recognize it
and deal with it successfully.

The relation shown in Panel A of the gallery is called a linear
relation because the mapping of inputs to outputs is described by
a straight line. This is the relation seen in Figure 4.3, and it isn't
really a rogue at all; it has every desirable quality, and it is the best-
behaved relation you could possibly hope for. Linear relations are
easy to understand, easy to predict, and—best of all—easy to control because increasing the input by a constant amount always produces the same, constant increase in the output. The world would
be a much more orderly place if all relations were of this clean, linear variety. Unfortunately, linear relations are just one special case.
All the other rogues in the gallery are decidedly nonlinear.

**Linear relations
are straight lines**

The monotonic relation in Panel B of the gallery is not as well
behaved. The only restriction on this relation is that increasing the
input never reduces the output. Beyond this, there are no guarantees regarding the shape of the curve. It could rise slowly, then
plateau for a while, then shoot up steeply, and so on. This makes it
much harder to use the knob to control the output because a small
adjustment in the knob could produce a big change in the output in
one part of the range and little or no change in another. The sample
curve shown in Panel B illustrates a system that is much more sen-
sitive in the middle of its range than it is near the ends. The effect of
repetition on brand recognition often exhibits this kind of relation,

**Monotonic
relations
always go up**

showing little or no increase until a certain threshold is reached, then rising quickly to a saturation point.

Continuous relations change smoothly

The continuous relation illustrated in Panel C is even less well behaved; the only guarantee with this relation is that the output will rise or fall smoothly with changes in the input, without any sudden jumps. But the actual mapping can take on any form whatever. Continuous relations make control harder still because increasing the input can drive the output higher, push it lower, or leave it unchanged. Unless you have some pretty good insights into how a system works, about the best you can do with this relation is sweep the knob back and forth and watch the gauge, trying to find the spot that gives you the best output. Many companies find themselves doing this in trying to manage the relation between price and profit, which usually follows a curve like the one shown in Panel C. Up to a certain point, raising prices increases revenue and profits go up. Beyond that point, further increases result in lost sales and profits start to go back down. Finding the price that produces the largest profits is rarely an easy process.

Single-valued relations change abruptly

The single-valued relation shown in Panel D is still harder to work with because even the smallest change in input can produce a huge leap in the output, with no smooth transition between successive levels. The only thing you can count on with this relation is that it will always produce the same output for any given input. Beyond that, anything goes. This rogue is quite common in supply chains, and it's almost always a monster of our own creation. For example, quantity discounts introduce discontinuities in the relation between price and quantity, so that increasing the quantity by a single item can cause an abrupt change in price for all the items in an order, possibly even reducing the total cost rather than increasing it as expected. This kind of behavior may not seem so bad simply because it's familiar, but quantity discounts are among the practices that make supply chains hard to predict and control.

The multi-valued relation illustrated in Panel E is the worst of rogues because it doesn't even promise to give you the same output for a given input. With this relation, a small change to the input can not only produce a sudden leap, it can shift the relation over to another curve altogether, so that reversing the change doesn't put things back the way they were. This relation may seem so perverse that it should never be permitted in supply chains, but it's there whether we like it or not. In fact, the example curve shown in Panel E is a naturally occurring pattern in the demand for fashion-based products, as explained in Chapter 10.

Multi-valued relations can do anything

Research on human thinking and decision making reveals that we have a great deal of trouble with the rogues described above. Simply put, we naturally assume that all systems are linear in nature, and we are very bad at detecting and understanding any other kind of relation. Nonlinear relationships are quite common in supply chains, so you will have to overcome your natural inclinations if you want to master supply chain management. I will help you with this throughout the book by pointing out nonlinear relationships whenever they appear, and by showing some of the ways in which the assumption of linearity is built into our thinking about supply chains.

We are biased toward linear relations

The Dynamics of Delay

The range of behavior that can be observed with just a single component barely hints at what can happen when two or more components are combined. Even the simplest combinations can produce behavior that is surprising and, for the purpose of understanding supply chains, quite revealing. Figure 4.5 shows three components hooked together to form a chain, with the output of each becoming the input of the next. The components don't actually do anything; as the relations below each component indicate, they just pass their inputs through to their outputs without changing them in any way.

Combinations produce new kinds of behavior

Figure 4.5
Combining
Components

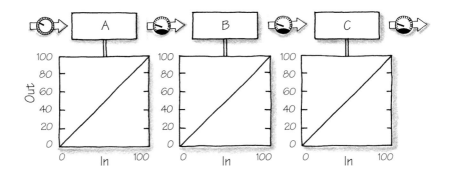

This system behaves identically to the single-component system explored in the preceding section (see Figure 4.3); the sequence of values generated by the knob—a sequence that is often called the signal—is immediately placed on the final output, just as it is in the simpler system.

Delays take components out of phase

It only takes a tiny alteration to make this system behave differently from the simpler one: a small delay from the time a component receives a change in its input to the time that change is reflected in its output. Figure 4.6 illustrates the impact of this delay by plotting the inputs to the three components over time. The original signal, labeled A in the figure, is faithfully replicated by the other two components,

Figure 4.6
The Effects
of Delay

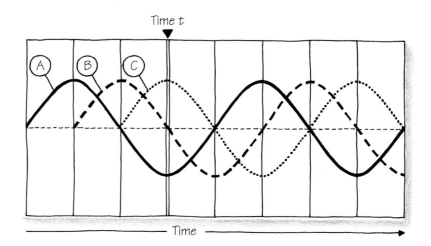

but the levels at the three components are no longer the same at any given time. In technical terms, the components are now said to be out of phase with each other. All systems involve some delays, so it is normal for their components to be out of phase. In supply chains, delays occur in all three flows—demand, supply, and cash—and they can range anywhere from minutes to months.

To see what kind of confusion these phase shifts can cause in a supply chain, imagine that Components A, B, and C are a retailer, producer, and supplier, respectively, and that the signal of interest is the level of demand being experienced by the chain. At the time labeled *t* in Figure 4.6, demand at the producer is right on the average value, but demand at the retailer is below average, and the supplier is experiencing unusually high demand. Based on the most current data, each company might reach totally different conclusions about how the chain ought to be responding to current demand. If any company tries to make a correction on its own, it is almost certain to throw the other two out of balance.

Phase shifts cause havoc in supply chains

If phase shifts were always as obvious as the ones shown in Figure 4.6, they could be detected and handled rather easily. But real-world supply chains are never this kind. Even if the original signal is transmitted faithfully all the way up the chain, the amount of the delay introduced by each component varies both within and across components. It takes very little variation of this sort to turn the neat curves of Figure 4.6 into wild, unpredictable swings. A further complication is that the original demand signal never varies in the smooth, cyclical manner shown in the figure; it usually carves out a jagged pattern that has little or no hint of regularity (see Chapter 10). The result: Phase shifts are rarely apparent even in the best of circumstances. All that the members of the chain know is that they are experiencing different levels of demand, and there may be no way to know whether those are simple delay effects or real disagreements that are cause for concern.

Phase shifts are usually invisible

Distortions introduce further complications

As puzzling as the effects of delay might be, much more confusion is introduced if there is any distortion of the signal from one component to the next. Real-world systems often show a pattern of increasing distortion as signals travel upstream, wreaking havoc among upstream components. Have you ever wondered why dense freeway traffic lurches along in waves of acceleration and braking rather than just flowing at a single, slow rate? Traffic studies have revealed that these waves can be triggered by just one or two drivers overreacting to the cars in front of them, triggering a ripple of exaggerated responses that spreads and amplifies for many miles behind them.

Economies of scale distort signals

Distortions of incoming signals can come from any number of sources, and they can be introduced accidentally or intentionally. In supply chains, the familiar economies of scale represent a common source of distortion: Customers order more than they need in order to get a quantity discount, producers run larger batches than necessary to reduce unit costs, and so on. Such decisions may save money in immediate operations, but the distortions they cause in the signals for demand, supply, and cash extract a much higher cost than most companies realize.

Demand amplification is one result

To see the problem in action, imagine that each component in the chain shown in Figure 4.5 increases the signal it receives by 50%. The result would be larger and larger swings of the signal as it moves up the chain, as shown in Figure 4.7. This is precisely what happens in the phenomenon of demand amplification described in Chapter 2. The bullwhip effect that caused the wild swings in the supply chain for Pampers wasn't a strange aberration of this particular chain, but a natural outcome of traditional practices found in all supply chains. Put another way, demand amplification is a problem of our own creation, one we have woven into the very fabric of supply chain practices. The only sure way to get rid of the problem is to eliminate the practices that cause it (see Chapter 13).

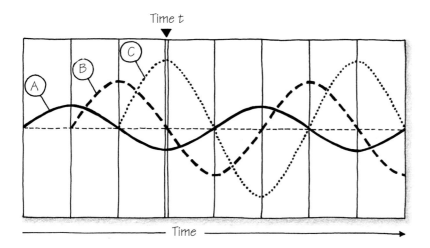

Figure 4.7
Combining Delay with Amplification

Feedback and Stability

In the systems discussed so far in this chapter, the signals all travel in the same direction, from the inputs toward the outputs. Although such systems exist, they are rare; most real-world systems have additional pathways that carry signals upstream as well, from outputs back to the inputs of earlier components (Figure 4.8). Such signals are called **feedback** because they feed information about the output back into the input, creating a loop in the system that wouldn't be there otherwise. Given that systems without feedback can be so hard to understand, adding a loop of this sort may seem like a perverse thing to do, but it turns out that the proper use of feedback is critical to producing useful, effective systems.

Outputs can be fed back into inputs

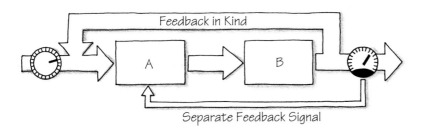

Figure 4.8
Introducing Feedback

Feedback comes in many forms

Feedback can take on many forms. The most basic kind of feedback simply takes a portion of the output and mixes it in with the incoming signal, as shown in the upper link of Figure 4.8. The more common kind of feedback in supply chains, shown in the lower link, uses a separate signal that communicates information about the current output to an upstream component rather than redirecting part of the original signal. Feedback can be entirely automatic, or it can require human intervention, as it does when an operator monitors a gauge and adjusts an input knob to achieve a desired output. In supply chains, using feedback effectively involves many people working together to analyze outputs and modify inputs.

Positive feedback amplifies incoming signals

The purpose of feedback is to provide information about current output to the upstream portions of a system, allowing them to tune their behavior to better regulate that output. To see how this works, imagine that the external signal going into Component A in Figure 4.8 is rising at a constant rate. Without feedback, the output will also rise at the same constant rate. However, if the output of Component B includes a feedback signal to A that causes it to amplify its response to the incoming signal, then the output of A will go up at an ever-increasing rate. This kind of feedback is called **positive feedback** because it amplifies the incoming signal strength. The result of positive feedback is an ever-accelerating increase in the output level, as shown in the left panel of Figure 4.9. If you have ever been at a presentation where someone turned the microphone amplifier up too high, you know exactly what happens with positive feedback—the signal just gets stronger and stronger until it overloads the system.

Negative feedback dampens signals

Now imagine altering the feedback mechanism so that the output of B is used to decrease A's response to the incoming signal rather than increase it. This arrangement is called **negative feedback** because it dampens incoming signals. With negative feedback, each increase in the original signal has a smaller effect on the output, as

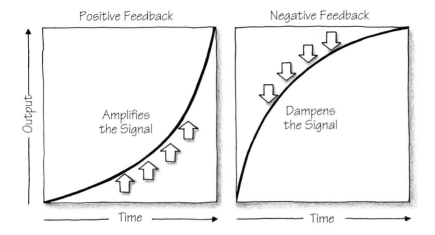

Figure 4.9
Two Kinds of
Feedback

shown in the right panel of Figure 4.9. This kind of feedback tends to keep a system within set bounds rather than pushing it toward extreme values.

As the examples suggest, the two kinds of feedback have radically different effects on a system. Positive feedback encourages movement in a particular direction and acts to promote unbounded growth. For example, compound interest on a bank account feeds the interest back into the principal, causing it to generate more interest during the next period, and so on. The same principle explains the exponential growth of start-up companies, markets, populations, and the like; it only takes a little positive feedback to translate a modest rate of growth into an exponential explosion.

Positive feedback fuels growth

By contrast, negative feedback limits movement in a particular direction, and it is most frequently used to promote stability in a system. A regressive tax system is an example of negative feedback because it reduces the increase in net income as gross income goes up. Negative feedback in economic systems is often expressed as the law of diminishing returns, in which each additional dollar invested in an activity produces a smaller return than the previous one. Of the two kinds of feedback, negative feedback is used much more

Negative feedback promotes stability

extensively in the design of systems because of its ability to keep a system within reasonable operating bounds.

Feedback is vital to supply chains

Feedback is the lifeblood of supply chains, and many of the supply chain initiatives described in Chapter 3 are designed to improve the flow of feedback up the chain. One of the advantages of vendor-managed inventory, for example, is that it lets suppliers directly monitor inventory levels in distribution centers and retail stores, giving them much earlier feedback on the flow of products and allowing them to tune their production accordingly. The use of point-of-sale systems in the quick response program improves this feedback by pushing the flow gauge all the way out to the cash register and detecting the movement of goods the moment it occurs.

All three flows benefit from feedback

In addition to facilitating the flow of goods down the chain, feedback facilitates the flow of demand and cash back up the chain. In fact, the signals that make up the feedback loops of supply chains can become so interwoven that it no longer makes sense to try to tease them apart. Are the sales data flowing upstream from retailers giving feedback on the flow of goods, or are they actually providing early information (sometimes called *feed forward*) about the demand that will soon flow up the chain? The difference isn't worth debating; the important point is that free exchange of information across supply chains provides the feedback necessary to regulate all three flows across the chain.

Information is replacing inventory

The great power of feedback in supply chains is that it reduces uncertainty by giving companies advance information about upcoming variations in demand and supply, allowing them to better cope with these variations. Without this advance notice, the only protection against variability in supply and demand is to hold enough inventory to handle the greatest demand and the lowest supply that are likely to occur, and inventory is a very expensive form of insurance. The insight that information can reduce the need for inventory has led to systematic efforts within many industries to replace inventory with information wherever possible. Indeed, substituting information for inventory is one of the most vital aspects of supply chain management, and techniques for achieving this goal are provided throughout this book.

This chapter provides only the briefest glimpse of a very deep subject, but it's enough to help you manage supply chains more effectively. The most important insight is the relationship among understanding, prediction, and control: You have to understand your chain in order to predict its behavior, and your ability to predict is what allows you to gain control. In each of these core processes—understanding, prediction, and control—you manipulate inputs and monitor outputs to see what happens, and your success depends in large part on how you select the inputs and outputs you want to work with. Another key to success is being prepared to cope with input-output relations other than the well-behaved linear relation we all naturally assume to be at work. You also need to bear in mind the importance of feedback in supply chains, making sure that you keep enough information flowing across your chain that it can respond to changing conditions quickly and effectively.

5

Modeling the Supply Chain

The examples in Chapter 4 show that even the simplest of systems can generate surprisingly complex behavior. How, then, are managers to understand such complex business systems as supply chains and manage them effectively? The answer, in a word, is modeling. The only way to understand complex systems is to construct simplified models of them, play with the models to see how they work, and then apply what you learn to the real-world system. You may not have thought about it this way, but you already do this with conceptual models all the time, even if the models are only in your mind. This chapter shows you how to use these mental models more effectively, and it introduces two more powerful kinds of models—mathematical and simulation models—that you can use as precision tools for prediction and control. You don't have to know how to build these more advanced models, but knowing what they are and when to use them is vital to managing a supply chain effectively.

The Case for Models

A model is nothing more than a simplified representation of a real-world system. This representation can take a wide variety of forms, including verbal explanations, whiteboard diagrams, mathematical equations, physical structures, and computer programs. All these models serve a common purpose: They take a system that may be hard to understand or dangerous to manipulate, and they render it in a form that is easier to understand and safer to play with.

Models are simplified representations

Models help with all three of the key business processes described in Chapter 4: understanding, prediction, and control (Figure 5.1). Building a model of a system requires that you analyze the system to identify its key components, figure out how those components

Modeling aids the three core processes

Figure 5.1
Modeling Supply
Chains

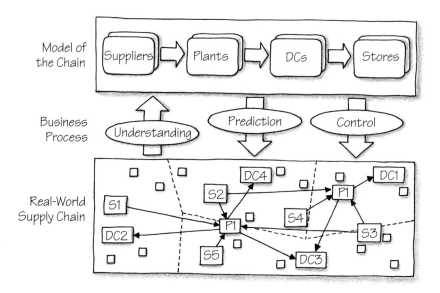

work, and then reassemble them in a way that replicates the essential behavior of the system. That basic sequence of analysis and synthesis is the surest way to understand complex systems. It's also the method underlying most scientific discoveries, engineering solutions, and business innovations.

**Models
generate
valuable
predictions**

Once you have assembled a model, you can use it as a test bed to generate predictions about how the system it represents would behave under a variety of conditions. Would building a new warehouse in Omaha reduce transportation costs as much as expected? Could the current supply chain support a 15% increase in demand? What would be the impact on cash flow of extending better credit terms to key customers? It's possible to answer "what if" questions such as these by changing the real-world system, but models provide answers faster, less expensively, and with a lot less risk to the company. Predictions generated by business models, in turn, increase your understanding of the real-world system, and you can use that increased understanding to further improve the quality of the model and its predictions.

To see how important predictions are to helping you improve your supply chain, think back to the example in Chapter 3, in which a customer and a supplier wanted to create a shared win by reducing their total inspection costs. The tradeoff curve shown in Figure 3.11 revealed that the best arrangement was for the supplier to spend a dollar more on inspection, allowing the customer to spend four dollars less. Where did this tradeoff curve come from? It could only be the result of a model that took into account the operations required for quality assurance, the cost of those operations, and their net effects on quality. In practice, a company wouldn't actually draw this tradeoff diagram once it had the model; it would simply use the model to find the lowest-cost solution. The only reason for drawing the diagram would be to help people understand why the new inspection program is a win for both companies.

Good models make for good decisions

Models are also used to control real-world systems, as shown on the right of Figure 5.1. This use of models is less obvious than the other two because the models used in control are usually implicit—that is, they are embedded in the design of business systems, but are never communicated to the people who own and operate those systems. This problem is particularly acute in the case of software. All the various kinds of supply chain software described in the next chapter are based on very specific models about how production, distribution, replenishment, sales, and other business processes are carried out. Unfortunately, most of the companies that buy this software have no idea what those models are until after they install the system and discover that the embedded models don't support the way they do business. The impact of this mismatch can range from a minor nuisance to a complete failure of the system, which is certainly a devastating way to learn about the importance of business models.

Models are also used for control

Business models come in a wide variety of forms, but most of them fall into one of the three broad categories shown in Figure 5.2. **Conceptual models** use diagrams and descriptions to represent a

There are three basic types of models

Figure 5.2
Three Kinds of
Models

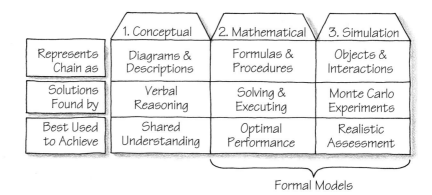

Represents Chain as	Diagrams & Descriptions	Formulas & Procedures	Objects & Interactions
Solutions Found by	Verbal Reasoning	Solving & Executing	Monte Carlo Experiments
Best Used to Achieve	Shared Understanding	Optimal Performance	Realistic Assessment

Headers: 1. Conceptual, 2. Mathematical, 3. Simulation

Formal Models

business system. They can be created on whiteboards, computer screens, or the backs of envelopes, and they provide simple, familiar structures for reasoning about the business. **Mathematical models** represent a business in terms of formulas and procedures, and they are solved by evaluating those formulas or procedures under a particular set of assumptions. **Simulation models** use software objects to represent the components of a business, and they are solved by "running" the model to see what happens when the objects interact with each other. Mathematical and simulation models are often referred to as **formal models** because they have strict forms and generate numerical predictions, in contrast to the informality of conceptual models.

Each type offers unique advantages

The distinctions among these three kinds of models are not hard and fast—hybrid forms are common. But the three types do represent three fundamentally different approaches to modeling, and each offers a unique set of capabilities and limitations. Because conceptual models are the easiest to build and understand, they are the best choice for achieving a shared understanding of the supply chain, particularly when managers are involved in the modeling process. Mathematical models are the most powerful, and they are best used to predict and optimize the performance of the chain. Simulation models are the most flexible, and they should be used to study the behavior of a model under the most realistic business conditions.

As a manager, you don't need to know how to use mathematical models and simulations; these formal models are usually implemented in software, and specialized skills are required to set them up and run them. But you do need to know how to use conceptual models because you are already applying them, whether well or badly, and you need to know what to expect of the other two types and when to trust their output. The next three sections provide a quick tour of the three kinds of models, and the final section offers some guidelines for using them to solve supply chain problems.

Choosing
the type is a
management
decision

Conceptual Models

The conceptual model is by far the simplest of the three types. This sort of model is basically a description of a business system and is usually expressed as some combination of diagrams and explanations. To a large extent, the format depends on the experience of the modelers—those with the most training in modeling usually rely on detailed diagrams with formal notation to reduce ambiguity. By contrast, those with little or no training tend to express their models as verbal descriptions mixed with stories about how the business works—stories that can often be formalized as scenarios. Although generally less precise than diagrams, descriptions and scenarios often capture the nature of the business in a way that formal diagrams cannot. The best conceptual models are usually a mix of diagrams, descriptions, and scenarios.

Conceptual
models are
the simplest

Regardless of how you express a conceptual model, the key is to find the right balance between precision and ease of communication. For systems analysts trained in the use of entity relationship (ER) diagramming, formal ER diagrams and detailed scenarios may be just the right tools. For managers who have never engaged in

The goal is
to facilitate
communication

business modeling before, the right balance may be a combination of simple diagrams and informal explanations. But even with managers, some conventions are necessary to make the diagrams and explanations make sense. Otherwise the output of the process may contain more myth than model.

This book uses convergent engineering

The diagrams in this book generally follow the conventions of convergent engineering, a modeling technique I developed specifically to help managers formulate useful business models. In this approach, a business system consists of three basic kinds of objects: organizations, processes, and resources. As shown in Figure 5.3, each of these objects plays a different role in the model, and the three relate to each other in ways that both constrain the model and make it more understandable at the business level. Briefly put, organizations own resources and execute processes; processes consume one set of resources and generate another set; and resources are the source of all cost and value in the system. There is much more to the approach than this, of course (see my earlier book, *Business Modeling with Object Technology*), but this one-sentence summary illustrates what I view as an appropriate level of formalism for

Figure 5.3
Organizations,
Processes, and
Resources

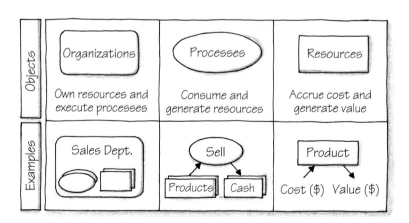

managers, and it should make the illustrations more meaningful to you as well.

Conceptual models can be developed by individuals, but for systems that cross organizational boundaries, as supply chains inevitably do, the best approach is to assemble a team of representatives from all the groups involved and hammer out the model together. Many software tools have been designed to support this group design process, but low-tech tools are often the most effective. Personally, I've always gotten the best results from a combination of white-board diagrams and 5×7 index cards. Each card represents one of the organizations, processes, or resources required for the model, and participants take turns role-playing these objects as they inter-act in the operation of the business. The resulting process is highly engaging, often contentious, and always educational as participants discover that each has a radically different understanding of how the business actually works. Once the group has assembled a con-sensus model out of its various conflicting perspectives, it has a solid foundation on which to build a better system.

Group modeling is the most effective

Although conceptual models form the basis for understanding sys-tems, they are of little value in prediction and control. It should be clear from the preceding chapter that even the simplest models can produce surprising interactions as soon as two or more components are hooked together, and our minds are simply not equipped to extrapolate the effects of these interactions. When we do try to puzzle out the behavior of a system, most of us tacitly assume that all the relations involved are linear. For reasons that psychologists are still teasing out, it is extremely difficult for us to extrapolate the behavior of nonlinear interactions, so we naturally tend to work within our limitations and oversimplify real-world relation-ships. Going beyond these limitations requires us to turn to more powerful kinds of models.

Conceptual models are poor at prediction

Mathematical Models

You already use mathematical models

Remember those word problems you hated as a kid? They went something like this: If a boat moving upstream in a river flowing at 2 miles an hour takes 4 hours to travel 3 miles, how many people were in the boat? These exercises were designed to teach you how to generate and apply mathematical models. And despite this early training, you do use mathematical models today. You just don't do it formally.

Production costing uses a linear model

For example, suppose your boss asks you how much it would cost to run batches of 1,000, 2,000, or 3,000 audio CDs. You know that it costs $1,000 to set up the run and a dollar to make each CD once the run begins, so your total cost would be $1,000 plus $1 times the number of CDs, giving you $2,000, $3,000, and $4,000 for the three quantities. In working up those numbers, you used one of the most common mathematical models in all of business—a linear model. In effect, your model predicts a linear relation between cost and the number of CDs produced, as shown in Figure 5.4.

Figure 5.4
Production Cost
by Volume

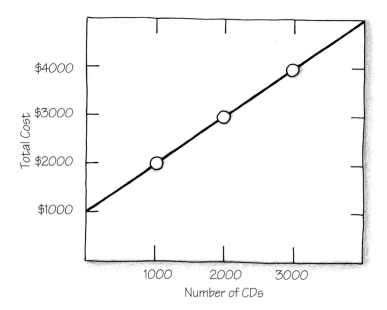

As this example suggests, a mathematical model is actually a special kind of system, one in which relations are specified using equations. The preceding example used the linear relation, the best-behaved rogue in the gallery of relations described in Chapter 4 (see Figure 4.4). But in this case the relation isn't just a graph of observed values—it's a mathematical equation that specifies a procedure for generating those values, as shown in Figure 5.5. The equation is actually a recipe for carrying out the calculation: First multiply two numbers together, then add a third number to the result.

Mathematical models are actually systems

Like all systems, mathematical models have inputs and outputs. In the linear model shown in Figure 5.5, the input is represented by the letter x and the output by y. As you twist the knob to vary the value of x, the reading for y moves up the graph in a straight line. The other two quantities, labeled a and b, are called **parameters**,

Models have inputs and outputs

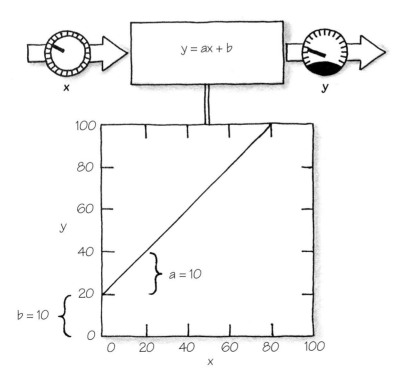

Figure 5.5
The Linear Model

and they are used to adjust the model to a particular set of circumstances. In the linear model, a changes the angle of the line and b changes its height. In Figure 5.5, a and b are both set to 1. In Figure 5.4, a is $1, the unit cost, and b is $1,000, the setup cost.

Parameters can be either inputs or outputs

Where do the values of parameters come from? Parameters are very interesting in this respect: They can act either as inputs or as outputs, depending on how you want to use the model. If you already know what these parameters are, as you did in the production costing example, you enter those values as setup inputs before you run the model, then feed in values of x to see what kind of graph they produce. If you don't know their values but already have some data plotted, you can do it the other way around—give the model the data and look for the parameter values that produce the best fit to the data. For example, if you didn't know the setup and unit costs but did know the total costs for 2,000, 3,000, and 4,000 CDs, you could plot the graph shown in Figure 5.4 and then read the values of the parameters right off the graph.

All mathematical models follow this pattern

The linear model is a particularly simple type, making it easy to understand and apply. The formulas used in mathematical models are often complex and hard to understand, particularly when the models use some of the more roguish relations such as nonmonotonic relations. But the basic pattern remains the same: All relations are expressed as equations, and any number of relations can be combined to create models of any size. There may be a long series of steps required to solve a large model, with specialized techniques for curve fitting when that process is applied, but the basic operation of the model remains the same.

Spreadsheets run mathematical models

Calculating numerical solutions for anything but the simplest of models can quickly become tedious, but this grunt work is almost always done by computers. The most common tool for mathematical modeling is a spreadsheet program such as Microsoft Excel.

Spreadsheets started as out tools for accountants, but their primary use today is in building business models. These models usually deal with financial flows, but the numbers can just as easily express the flow of supply or demand. For example, spreadsheets are often used to build demand forecasts, as described in Chapter 10. Of course, spreadsheets aren't the only tools for implementing mathematical models— many of the supply chain applications described in the next chapter use specialized mathematical models to perform their calculations.

Given the difficulty of building and using mathematical models, there has to be a good reason to use them, and there is. Unlike conceptual models, where the behavior of the model can be a subject of much debate, mathematical models are unambiguous; you plug in the numbers as inputs and you get clear, quantitative results. That's a powerful advantage in dealing with complex systems in which behavior can often be hard to understand, much less predict.

Mathematical models yield quantitative answers

There is, however, an even better reason for using mathematical models: In many situations, they can not only tell you what output you can expect from a given set of inputs, they can tell you what inputs to use in order to produce the *best possible* output. This remarkable ability, known as **optimization**, can be a tremendous tool for making decisions about how to run a supply chain. What optimization does is a lot like curve fitting, but instead of looking for parameter values that match a given set of outputs, optimization looks for values that produce the best outputs, and you get to tell it what constitutes "best." For example, you could model the way profit depends on both price and sales, including the interaction between the two, then solve the model mathematically to find the price that maximizes your profit.

Some models can find optimal solutions

In supply chain management, the most commonly used optimization technique is **linear programming** (**LP**). Linear programming is an extremely powerful management tool, one that comes about

Linear programming is a powerful optimizer

as close to magic as anything in business. Linear programming can be done in Excel, using its built-in **optimizer**, but the really powerful LP optimizers are found in the supply chain design and planning tools described in the next chapter. Skilled modelers use these systems to construct models that include thousands of parameters, representing such factors as historical demand levels, plant and warehouse capacities, material and labor costs, transportation rates, and required service levels. They then run the models to discover the best mix of products to build at each plant, the most cost-effective sources for each customer region, and other optimal values.

There are important restrictions on LP

There is a price to be paid for all this power: Linear programming makes some rather stringent simplifying assumptions about the real-world system. As the name *linear programming* suggests, one assumption is that all relations be of the well-behaved linear form, so all the true rogues in the gallery are banished. But in situations where the assumptions come reasonably close to the reality, the optimizations provided by linear programming can be immensely valuable. There are also variants of linear programming that relax some of these constraints. These alternatives usually take longer to compute solutions, but they are still guaranteed to produce optimal solutions.

Simulation Models

Mathematical models don't work for all systems

As the preceding paragraph suggests, much of the power of mathematical models comes from distilling complex relationships down into relatively simple mathematical forms. For systems with known relationships that can be captured in equations, mathematical models are usually the best way to go. But sometimes the relations among components don't conform to simple equations. Alternatively, they may fit an equation just fine, but there is no way of knowing what that equation might be. In such cases, simulation models are usually a better approach. Like a mathematical model, a simulation is a special kind of system, with inputs, outputs, and parameters. The difference is that simulations are a bit more literal than mathematical models: They just try to imitate the behavior of a system's components rather than distilling that behavior down to an equation.

In essence, building a simulation consists of programming a number of software objects to act out the roles of real-world objects, then running the system to see how those objects interact with each other under realistic business conditions. The objects represent customers and suppliers, orders and shipments, materials and products, vehicles and containers, and all the other elements of supply chains described in this book. In the program, these objects affect each other just as they do in the real world: Customer objects create order objects and send them to supplier objects, which ship product objects using vehicle and container objects, and so on. In a good simulation, these objects are modeled at a fine level of detail. The more detailed and accurate the simulation, the more precise and reliable the predictions about supply chain performance.

Simulations model real-world objects

As with mathematical models, simulations can be constructed using a variety of tools. A really simple simulation can be conducted with something as low-tech as index cards, with people holding the cards and acting out the roles of the various objects. Simulations can also be expressed in software using conventional programming languages. However, the most cost-effective approach is usually to use a commercial simulation system. These systems include graphical tools for building models, automated routines for testing them under different conditions, and reporting tools for analyzing the results. Although general-purpose simulators are available and can be used, the best choice is a specialized tool built just for simulating supply chains. These dedicated simulators include prebuilt objects for all the usual supply chain elements,

Dedicated supply chain simulators are best

allowing powerful simulations to be assembled and tested with a minimum of effort.

Testing consists of running the model

Once you have constructed a simulation model, you test it by running it as shown in Figure 5.6. First, you initialize the objects in the system by setting their parameters to reflect real-world production capacities, shipment times, material and labor costs, retail prices, and the like. You then start the simulator and feed it a sequence of inputs as they would occur in real time, including shifting levels of demand, seasonal variations in price, and so on. As the model runs, it generates outputs indicating the speed with which demand is satisfied, the amount of inventory held at each facility, the total cost to operate the system, and other measures of supply chain performance.

Simulations incorporate variability

Up to this point, running a simulation model is a lot like running a mathematical model: You set up the parameters, pass in the inputs, and see what you get in the way of outputs. But simulations go further than most mathematical models in that they allow the parameters and inputs to vary about some average value rather than being locked down to a fixed value. It is possible to incorporate this kind of variability into mathematical models, but in systems as large as supply chains, the computational power required is usually too great for these techniques to be of much value. Simulators, on the other hand, incorporate variability quite naturally—an important

Figure 5.6
Running a
Simulation

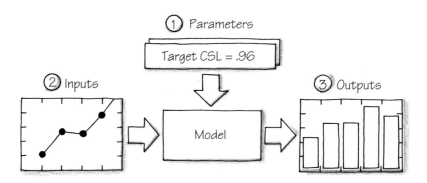

advantage because sales, shipments, prices, and countless other aspects of supply chains vary quite a bit in real-world supply chains, and this variability has a major impact on how the chains perform. It's not just a matter of causing variability in the outputs, although that certainly is one outcome. The more important concern about variability is how it affects the way you manage the chain.

As an example of this, consider a kind of variability that is especially problematical for supply chains: variability in demand. Imagine that you have a product—a particular kind of sofa, say—that is selling at a rate of 100 a week. You can simply use that value as a parameter of the model, but that simplification glosses over a very important reality: Some weeks you sell more than 100, and some weeks you sell less. In any given week you have to be ready to handle the actual sales for that week, not just the average sales, which means you need to maintain extra inventory to buffer variability in demand. How much inventory? It depends on how much variability you have. If your weekly sales vary quite a bit, like those shown in Case A of Figure 5.7, you need to be able to supply as many as

Variability in demand is especially important

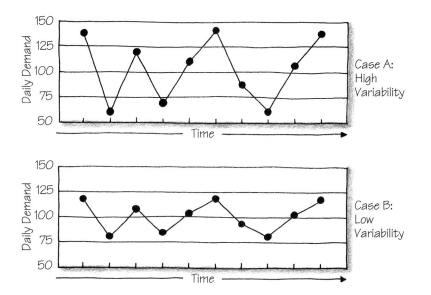

Figure 5.7
Variability in Weekly Demand

150 sofas a week to avoid running out. If you have only half this amount of variability, as shown in Case B, then 125 sofas will probably be enough. In either case, having just the average number of 100 sofas on hand pretty much guarantees that you will run out of stock at least half the time. A model based only on average demand would not produce a viable business result.

Distributions describe variability

The way models handle this sort of variability is by using distributions. If you take a large number of data points of the sort shown in Figure 5.7 and plot the total number of times you get sales of each number of sofas, the result will be distributions of values like the ones shown in Figure 5.8. The particular distribution shown follows a very common form, called the normal distribution, which has a mathematical formula with just two parameters: the mean, which is the formal name for the numerical average, and the standard deviation, which is a measure of the variability. In Figure 5.8, both distributions have a mean of 100, but the upper one has a standard deviation of 15, twice that of the lower figure. To capture

Figure 5.8
Distributions of
Weekly Demand

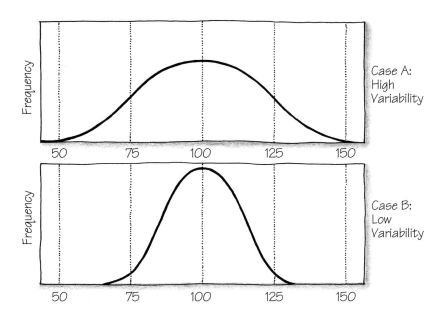

the variability in weekly demand, then, you tell the model to use the normal distribution and give it two parameters—the mean and the standard deviation—rather than just the mean. Given this richer input, the model can randomly vary the level of demand to reflect the way it varies in reality, producing a much more accurate simulation.

Adding variability to a simulation makes it more accurate, but it also complicates matters because the results of running the model now have a random element to them. If the output can vary each time you run a model, you can't just run it once and take the results as definitive. Instead, you have to run it many times and average the results to see how the model is most likely to behave under a realistic range of circumstances. This technique of running a model many times with random values is called the **Monte Carlo method**, in recognition of the role that chance plays in the outcomes. It may sound tedious to do many runs and pool the results, but simulation tools handle all that automatically. The only real cost to the multiple runs is the time spent waiting for the results.

The Monte Carlo method uses multiple runs

A Monte Carlo series provides a detailed look at how a supply chain design will perform under a single set of realistic business conditions. This may be sufficient to validate the results of mathematical modeling, but it doesn't do anything to improve those results. The way to do that is to vary the design in some systematic manner, running a Monte Carlo series on each variation and comparing the results. For example, you could seek the optimal level of safety stock under a variety of demand situations by simulating each level and comparing the results. Alternatively, you might want to compare the cost and benefits of varying the number of warehouses over a specified range.

Improvements come from comparing models

Although simulations are better than mathematical models at exploring the effects of variability, they aren't as good at finding optimal solutions. The best you can do with a simulator is to vary

Simulations don't support optimization

the value of one or more parameters in a systematic way and look for the one that gives you the best fit. That can be tedious, but most simulators support a technique called **hill-climbing** to accelerate the process. Rather than try out every possible value of a parameter, the simulator starts with a value provided as input, runs the model to determine how well it performs using that value, and then explores nearby values to see if it can improve on that performance. For example, if the parameter illustrated in Figure 5.9 was initialized at a value of 30, the simulator would try out values just above and below 30, quickly discovering that only an increase in the value improved performance. Through a series of such tests, it would gradually home in on 50 as the best value.

Hill-climbing is efficient but not guaranteed

Hill-climbing is a great time-saver in simulation work, but there is no guarantee that it will find the best possible value. The most common problem, as shown in Figure 5.9, is that it can converge on a solution that is the best within a region, but fail to find a better solution that lies farther out. In the example, initial values below 80 will tend to move toward 50 as the best choice, even though a better result can be obtained with a value of 110. There

Figure 5.9
Hill-Climbing to
Find the Best Value

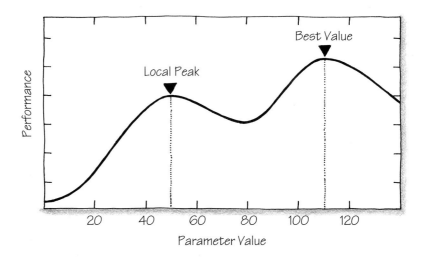

are variations of hill-climbing that increase the likelihood of finding the best value, but the fact remains that, unlike optimizers, simulators are not guaranteed to find the best possible solution.

Combining Models

The fact that three very different kinds of business models are available begs the question of which one is best. The answer to that question depends on two things: The nature of the problem you're trying to solve, and the kind of answers you are looking for. This final section of the chapter offers a few suggestions about when and how to use each of the three kinds of model.

There is no "best" type of model

The most important consideration is to apply each kind of model to the problems it is best at solving. If your goal is to understand how the current supply chain works and explore ways to improve it, the best choice may be a well-stated conceptual model. In fact, introducing mathematics or simulations can often do more harm than good by clouding the essential issues with irrelevant detail. If, on the other hand, the problem is one of choosing among a number of well-defined alternatives whose behavior can be stated in the form of equations, nothing can match the power of a mathematical model. If the behavior of the chain can't be reduced to familiar equations, or if the problem at hand concerns the effects of variability on performance, a simulation is usually the best choice.

Choose the model to suit the problem

Because the three kinds of models have complementary strengths, many problems are best attacked with two or more models in combination. Conceptual models are usually the best place to start because they require the least amount of training to use, and they can be indispensable in developing a shared understanding of a problem and its possible solutions. The best starting point is usually a conceptual model because it provides a quick way to identify the key information required for building a formal model. Once the

Combining the types increases power

formal model has been explored, the results can be mapped back to the conceptual model, with appropriate modifications, to communicate the key insights to other managers.

The ideal is to use all three together

If it isn't clear based on the problem which kind of formal model to use, consider using both (Figure 5.10). One option is to use a mathematical model to find an optimal solution, then use a simulation to make sure the results are robust across the many kinds of variability that can affect the performance of the system. The other option is to use a simulator to get a better feel for how the supply chain works, then use the results to formulate a mathematical model suitable for optimization. The ideal is to move fluidly among all three kinds, using each to gain insights about the other until the best solution emerges.

Hire modelers who are fluent in all three

All three kinds of models—including conceptual models—require special training in order to use them effectively. Unfortunately, training in the use of models almost always focuses on one type to the exclusion of the others, or even on a single method within a type. Systems analysts are commonly trained in the use of structured conceptual models such as entity-relationship diagramming, financial analysts and operations analysts are usually trained to use mathematical models, and so on. In looking for specialists to help you in your own modeling efforts, it's important to find people who are fluent in all three types. To paraphrase the old saying, if you

Figure 5.10
Combining the Types

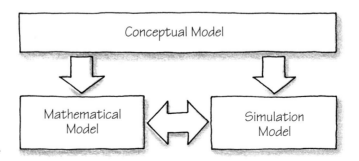

hire someone who only has a hammer, all your problems will look like nails.

Regardless of who constructs your formal models, you should be careful about delegating conceptual models. At this level, the most important modelers in the company are you and your fellow managers. You are the ones with firsthand knowledge of how the supply chain is constructed, the real-world experience in how well it's working, and the responsibility to make it work better. The best way to start any effort to model the supply chain is by gathering together the managers who make the chain work, bringing in a professional facilitator, and building a conceptual model. Once you have that model in hand, then you can bring in specialists to translate it into a formal model and analyze it in further detail.

Do the most important modeling yourself

Many managers find themselves reluctant to tap the power of business modeling, often in the mistaken belief that they aren't qualified to do it. After more than 15 years of facilitating business design sessions, I can say with confidence that not only are operational managers competent to do the work, they are the only ones who understand the business well enough to do the job. Once they get started, most managers find that, despite the hard work and contentious debates that group modeling efforts may involve, they love the process because it taps their natural abilities for organizing resources and solving problems. So don't resist the idea of modeling just because it's foreign to you; it's foreign to most managers at first. And remember that the only way to gain a competitive advantage is by doing the things the other guy isn't willing or able to do. Leveraging the power of business models is one of the most direct, cost-effective ways of improving your ability to win the new competition between supply chains.

6

Supply Chain Software

Fifty years ago, supply chains were designed and managed using the time-honored tools of paper and pencil, with a little help from calculators. Today, it would be almost unthinkable to operate a large supply chain without extensive software support. But there is a bewildering array of software to choose from, and picking the wrong package can bring your supply chain to a standstill. This chapter provides a guided tour of supply chain software, starting with classic manufacturing systems and winding up with specialty applications designed for specific supply chain problems. The tour concludes with a look at how the Internet is changing the way trading partners coordinate the flow of demand, supply, and cash across the supply chain.

The Manufacturing Platform

The easiest way to understand the many forms of supply chain software is to view them in the context of the business processes they support. The matrix in Figure 6.1 categorizes these processes in a way that reflects the structure of this book. The rows of the matrix correspond to the operational, planning, and design levels of management, and the columns reflect processes concerned with supply, production, and demand. All of the processes shown in the matrix are discussed in the appropriate chapters in Parts III through V. In the present chapter, I take the processes as given and focus on the software.

A management matrix provides the context

Because supply chains are concerned with moving manufactured goods, the functions of supply chain software are a natural extension of existing manufacturing systems. Today, the dominant software in manufacturing companies is the **enterprise resource planning (ERP)** system. Although the emphasis of ERP is on the internal

ERP is the dominant manufacturing system

Figure 6.1
The Supply-Chain
Management Matrix

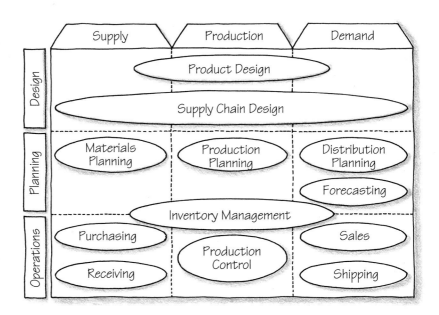

operations of a manufacturing organization—the activities that take place "inside the four walls"—many of the applications included in ERP packages are directly relevant to supply chain activities.

The heart of ERP is production planning

ERP systems can be difficult to understand because they have become so large and complex over the years, incorporating a tremendous array of functions and touching almost every area of a manufacturing company. However, the essence of ERP can be understood by placing a handful of key modules in the context of the management matrix, as shown in Figure 6.2. The heart of an ERP system is a set of planning modules that translate anticipated demand into plans for managing supply, production, and distribution. The other modules help a company implement these plans by providing computerized support for purchasing, receiving, sales, and other operations.

Planning works backward from distribution

The basic flow of ERP-based planning is shown in Figure 6.2. Using historical and expected sales as input, the distribution requirements planning (DRP) module builds a distribution plan that indicates

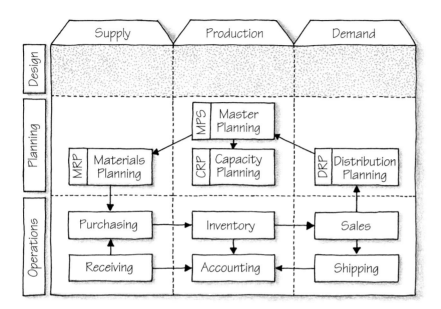

Figure 6.2
Modules of an ERP System

how many products of each type need to be at each location in each period. The resulting plan is passed as input to the master production scheduling (MPS) module, which works out when production will have to occur in order to meet the distribution schedule. The MPS module then calls on the services of two other modules to validate its schedule: The material requirements planning (MRP) module makes sure that all the necessary materials and components can be acquired in time, and the capacity requirements planning (CRP) module checks to see whether the available production facilities will be able to perform the work.

Although the focus of ERP is on production planning, several of the modules include tools for supply chain management. The material requirements plan generated by the MRP module can be fed directly into the purchasing system as a schedule of proposed purchases, and the distribution plan generated by the DRP module is used to choreograph shipments of finished goods through an echelon distribution system. In addition, the receiving and shipping

ERP supports several aspects of supply chains

modules handle the flow of materials in and out of the company, and the inventory control module monitors the current stocks of raw materials, work in process, and finished goods.

ERP is best suited for single plants

Although many companies use ERP systems to manage their supply chains, ERP by itself is rarely the best option. ERP was developed to manage the activities within a single production facility, and it doesn't lend itself to planning activities that span multiple facilities. Most ERP packages can, in fact, be used for more than one plant, but they plan the activities of each plant individually rather than developing an integrated plan that makes the best use of all the plants. Another concern is that, as explained in Chapter 11, the scheduling technique used by ERP was designed for the controlled environment of a manufacturing facility, and it lacks the flexibility necessary to handle the more dynamic requirements of supply chains.

Advanced Planning Systems

APS concentrates on design and planning

The most important application directly aimed at managing supply chains is the **advanced planning and scheduling (APS)** system. As with ERP systems, APS systems include a large number of modules that can be combined in various ways, and not every vendor offers the same selection of modules. However, the modules shown in Figure 6.3 are common to most APS systems, and they give a fair representation of APS capabilities. A comparison of this figure with Figure 6.2 quickly reveals the most important difference between ERP and APS: Whereas ERP supports the lower two layers of the process matrix, planning and operations, APS focuses on the upper two layers, combining planning with design.

APS can plan an entire supply chain

Unlike ERP, which is primarily concerned with production facilities, APS takes a network of supply chain facilities as its starting point. Setting up an APS system involves using the network design

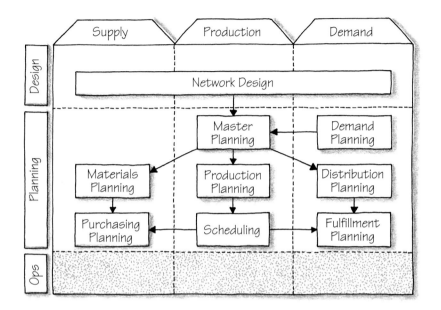

Figure 6.3
Modules of an APS System

module to enter a detailed description of the chain, including its facilities, transportation links, and other characteristics. Once this information is in place, the planning process follows the arrows shown in Figure 6.3. First, the demand planning module forecasts the demand for each product in each region. The master planning module then combines this forecast with the capabilities of the chain as described to the network design module, developing an overall plan for moving supplies through the chain. In order to develop that plan, it calls on the services of three specialized modules to analyze the impact of the master plan on materials, production capacity, and distribution requirements.

APS offers a number of advantages over ERP, including a more flexible scheduling system that can handle the more varied require-ments of supply chain management. The most compelling advan-tage of an APS system, however, is that it is based on mathematical models that support optimization, including the linear program-ming method described in Chapter 5. These models are used for

APS is based on optimizing models

design as well as planning, so an APS gives you the opportunity to optimize not only the schedule of operations but also the very structure of your supply chain. The optimization is done against any measures of performance you choose to specify, including cost, customer service, and profitability.

APS is usually linked to ERP systems

Although APS systems offer sophisticated planning and scheduling capabilities, they don't provide the operational modules necessary to translate these plans into action. The usual solution to this problem is to link APS systems into existing ERP systems. The most effective way to combine the two applications is to use a single APS system to plan the movement of goods across a number of production facilities, each of which is managed by a local ERP system (Figure 6.4). This approach offers the best of both worlds, combining the advantages of ERP and APS to provide a level of integration that isn't possible with either type alone.

APS is likely to merge into ERP

Linking APS and ERP systems is a substantial undertaking (see Chapter 11), and the cooperation between the two kinds of systems is still somewhat limited. However, this situation is already beginning to change for the better. ERP vendors have a history of absorbing new application categories that affect enterprise-level planning, and they are already hard at work rolling in supply chain software. Several vendors now offer APS modules that communicate with their existing ERP modules, and other vendors are likely to follow suit in order to remain competitive. In the meantime, be cautious

Figure 6.4
APS Integrating
Multiple ERP
Systems

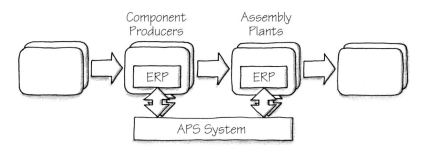

about ERP vendors that claim to support supply chains; they could be offering anything from a full suite of APS modules to an ad hoc collection of the supporting applications described in the next section. Chapter 11, which provides a more detailed description of how ERP and APS modules work together, should give you enough information to make an informed choice.

Supply Chain Applications

In addition to ERP and APS, there are several other kinds of applications that serve the needs of supply chain management. Figure 6.5 shows some of the key modules of a warehouse management system. As the diagram indicates, these packages focus primarily on operations, offering just enough planning functionality to smooth the flow of inventory through the facility. In addition, there are no modules for production because that's not a traditional function of warehouses, although this is beginning to change (see Chapter 15). The modules on the supply side are concerned with automating the process of receiving incoming goods and assigning

Warehouse systems focus on operations

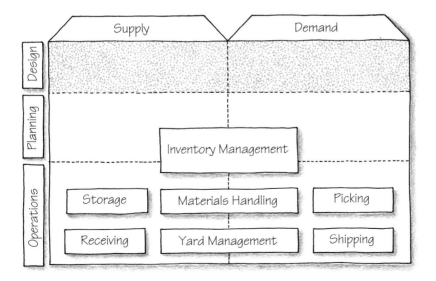

Figure 6.5
Warehouse Management Modules

them to the appropriate storage locations, and the modules on the demand side are concerned with assembling outbound orders and preparing them for shipment. The materials handling module bridges the gap between the two sets of modules, and the yard management module governs the movements of vehicles, containers, and inventory held in staging areas adjacent to the warehouse.

Transportation systems are highly specialized

Another important class of supply chain software is the transportation management system (Figure 6.6). A complete system includes everything from network design tools down to operational applications for tracking shipments, scheduling drivers, and determining how much it will cost to run a shipment between any two points. Because transportation requirements differ across industries and modalities—scheduling tanker ships is quite different from tracking the locations of rail cars—transportation systems are usually highly specialized for individual markets.

Figure 6.6
Transportation
Management
Modules

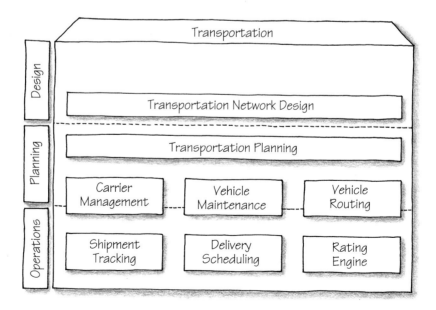

Warehouse and transportation management systems have been around for many years. The newest generation of software includes the applications shown in Figure 6.7. One of these, customer relationship management (CRM), is designed to integrate all customer-contact activities, including sales, service, and support. Newer still is the logical counterpart of CRM, supplier relationship management (SRM). CRM and SRM are usually limited to interactions with immediate trading partners, so they each span only a single link in the supply chain. However, some of the more advanced CRM packages include the ability to support relationships with customers' customers, and it seems likely that SRM packages will be extended in a comparable manner.

CRM and SRM help manage relationships

One of the most recent and exciting developments is the emergence of the supply chain visibility applications shown in the upper part of Figure 6.7. These applications track the movement of inventory as it flows through the chain, providing graphical displays that show expected and actual levels at each location. A closely related category is supply-chain event management software, which offers the ability to define business rules that trigger when specified events occur (or fail to occur). This software allows supply chain

The newest applications monitor movements

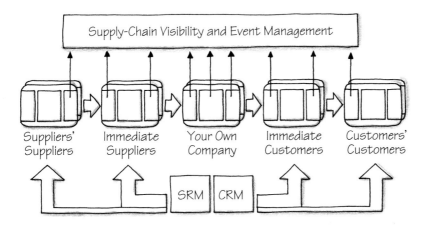

Figure 6.7
Emerging Applications

managers to focus their attention on managing exceptions rather than having to personally monitor every movement and compare it against plan.

Design tools aid in constructing the chain

Some of the most sophisticated systems for supply chain management are used in the design of the chain itself. Although this capability is built into APS systems, it is also available in stand-alone packages. Some of these systems use mathematical models to find optimal designs, and others use simulators to construct highly realistic models. The best systems offer a mix of these approaches, allowing each kind of model to compensate for the limitations of the other.

Implicit Business Models

Modeling is the foundation of these systems

A critical yet rarely understood aspect of the software systems described in this chapter is that these systems are all based on models of the supply chain. Some of the models are explicit and directly modifiable by users. Supply chain design systems, in particular, display a conceptual model of a chain in a graphical form to help designers understand and alter the structure of the chain. These systems then test the quality of a design by expressing it in the form of a mathematical or simulation model and evaluating that model to see how well it performs. Designing a supply chain is, in effect, an exercise in modeling.

Most of the models are implicit and fixed

Unfortunately, the explicit, modifiable models used in design systems are the exception rather than the rule. Although planning and operational systems also rely on models, these models are usually buried deep in the software and cannot be modified. ERP systems, for example, are based on a model in which quantities of goods are produced or transported during fixed intervals called time buckets, which are most commonly weeks. Production and distribution plans are constructed by working backward from the required quantities of finished goods to figure out how much purchasing and production has to occur in each time bucket. In this model, all work is done on the last possible date given the current constraints on materials and capacity.

How did this model come to be the standard technique for production planning? In large part, it is a historical artifact that has been codified in the architecture of manufacturing software. The model was developed back in the days before computers, when all planning was done on blackboards or large sheets of grid paper, and it reflects the limitations of human planners trying to cope with large matrices of numbers. The earliest planning systems simply translated the manual procedure into a program, relieving people of the need to move quantities from one time bucket to another by repeatedly erasing and rewriting numbers. This was a major breakthrough at the time because it greatly reduced the time necessary to construct a workable plan. But it did nothing to improve the planning process itself, which to this day is still based on doing everything as late as possible, and it has no ability to find optimal solutions based on business concerns such as cost. Compared to the power of contemporary models, the model underlying ERP scheduling is pretty simplistic. But once this model was transferred to a computer, it was never changed.

Some models are historical artifacts

A weak model wouldn't be so bad if it could be modified, but systems with implicit, hard-wired models don't offer that option. The result is that using one of these systems requires a company to adapt its business to the software rather than the other way around. This problem is most apparent with ERP systems because they automate so many core business functions, but it's also true of more recent systems such as the CRM packages, which are based on implicit models of how companies interact with their customers. Many companies insist that vendors modify their software to conform to the way they actually do business, but these customization

Lack of modifiability can be crippling

efforts often lead to failed installations and maintenance nightmares. The spectacular failure of Nike's customized APS system described in Chapter 1 illustrates the perils of this approach.

Be aware of models in choosing software

The presence of implicit business models in supply chain software is a problem without a good solution. Minor tweaks may help, but deep customization is rarely successful. In most cases, the choice comes down to "their way or no way," and that's not the kind of decision you should have to make when buying a multimillion-dollar system. But what are the alternatives? Supply chain software is now so large and complex that building your own system is rarely a viable option, and trying to run a large chain without software is a nonstarter in today's fast-paced markets. The best you can do is to be aware that implicit business models are lurking inside all commercial software packages and carefully choose the model that comes closest to fitting the way you do business. Once you've found the closest match, be prepared to change your operations to conform to the model. It may be a galling choice, but the alternatives are worse.

Internet-Based Systems

The Internet accelerates communication

The biggest change taking place in supply chain software today is the move to the Internet. The Internet does not, as was widely believed at the end of the last century, lead to a fundamentally different economy, nor does it alter the basic dynamics of supply chains. Physical goods still have to get from place to place, and the Internet doesn't alleviate the need to choreograph that movement as precisely as possible. What the Internet does do is provide a vastly improved communications medium for coordinating this movement of goods. Like the telegraph, the telephone, and the fax machine before it, the primary impact of the Internet is on the speed, and not the nature, of business processes. As with these earlier technologies, this impact is proving to be both deep and pervasive.

Boiled down to its essence, supply chain management consists of choreographing the flow of demand, supply, and cash. Two of these flows—demand and cash flow—can be moved entirely to the Internet (Figure 6.8). Orders consist entirely of textual data that is readily transmitted in electronic form, and payments can be made using electronic funds transfer (EFT). Moreover, all the supporting information that is passed up and down the chain—forecasts, plans, notices, and the like—can be shifted to the Internet as well. With the exception of actually shipping the goods, every function of the supply chain can be performed faster, cheaper, and more accurately using the Internet. The advantages are profound, and the Internet is rapidly becoming the standard medium for supply chain management.

Two of the three flows now use the Internet

For products that consist primarily of information, it is possible to move the flow of supply to the Internet as well, creating a fully electronic supply chain. Newsletters, books, designs, pictures, software, music, and other information products can be packaged as pure data and delivered almost instantly anywhere in the world. Not only is **electronic distribution** faster and cheaper for such products, it promises to change the very definition of what it means to deliver a product. For example, music can be delivered

Some products can be shipped electronically

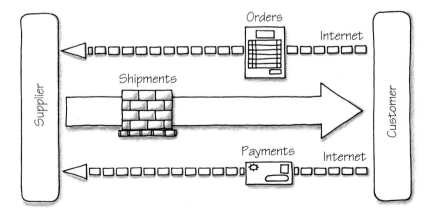

Figure 6.8
Moving to the Internet

each time it is listened to rather than being stored by the consumer between uses, and software can be continuously updated by a vendor to reflect bug fixes and enhancements. These kinds of changes are already taking place in many information-based products.

XML adds meaning to raw data

To date, the use of the Internet to communicate information about the supply chain has been hampered by a lack of standards for packaging data. It's relatively easy with today's technology to send an e-mail requesting information about a product, or to place an order by selecting that product on a Web site. But consider a company like Ingram Micro, which handles 60 million transactions a day. To move even a fraction of that traffic onto the Internet requires a lot more than human-readable messages and Web pages; it requires taking people out of the loop entirely and letting machines do all the work. The key technology for making that happen is now in place with the advent of **XML**, the *extensible markup language*. What XML does, in essence, is embed tags in data to identify each element of the data and give it meaning.

XML can be read by machines

Using XML means prices can be tagged as prices, discount terms as discount terms, and so on. XML can be used to make Web pages readable by machines, and it can be used in messages to allow machines to communicate directly with each other. For example, a price list with standard quantity discounts might be posted on the Web in XML form, whereas an order requesting a particular quantity might be sent as an XML-formatted message. In neither case is it necessary for human beings to be involved in the process. Because XML is easy to code and decode, applications software can easily handle tasks like preparing price lists, reading these lists to find the best quantity break, generating purchase orders, and so on. Given its simplicity and clarity, XML is rapidly becoming the lingua franca for data exchange over the Internet.

In addition to placing labels on individual pieces of information, XML allows data to be assembled into nested structures. For example, an order can be defined as a nested structure consisting of a header, a body, and a footer, as shown in Figure 6.9. Each of these elements can, in turn, be defined in terms of more basic elements, until the structure reaches the level of simple text. Moving in the opposite direction, orders can function as elements in still larger structures, such as contracts, and so on.

XML supports complex data structures

Of course, two companies have to agree on all these structures before they can start sending orders back and forth, and that's where standards bodies come in. It's a slow process to achieve agreement even on a seemingly simple structure like an order, and in many industries two or more groups are proposing conflicting standards. Many companies have avoided the wait by just transferring the conventions of the electronic data interchange (EDI) standard over to the Internet. But EDI is overkill for the Internet, and

XML-based standards are emerging

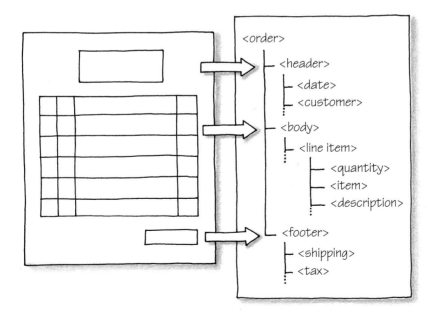

Figure 6.9
An XML Order

despite years of standardization it still has at least a dozen distinct dialects. For truly universal communication, simpler formats are called for, and these are now beginning to emerge.

Web services allow applications to interact

XML can be used today in Web pages and messages, but its greatest potential lies in allowing applications to interact over the Internet without any human involvement whatsoever. In order for this to happen, applications need to be able to "call" each other over the Internet, ask for particular services, and receive the results of their requests. That capability requires another layer of protocols on top of XML to handle such tasks as locating the appropriate application, discovering its capabilities, submitting a request in the required manner, and making sense of the response. The desire to link applications over the Internet is strong, and protocols have come into existence surprisingly quickly. The essential capabilities, collectively known as **Web services**, are already operational in real systems, and their use will likely skyrocket over the next five to ten years.

All three levels of management are changing

The Internet is changing supply chain management at every level. To date, most of the changes have come at the operational level, with more and more transactions taking place electronically. At the planning level, companies are already exchanging forecasts and production plans over the Internet, and XML will soon become the common format for these exchanges. At the design level, the Internet is widely used to exchange files containing product designs, and the eventual conversion of those files to XML will gradually make the design process more interactive.

The Internet will transform supply chains

As these changes take effect, supply chain management will be transformed in a profound way. As XML and Web services become widely adopted, all the routine interactions required to run a supply chain will shift to the Internet. Because programs will communicate directly with other programs, these transactions will occur below the level of human awareness and they will happen faster than a person could even follow. Freed from the mundane tasks of placing orders and updating schedules, the people who run supply chains will be able to operate at a much higher level, setting goals for the chain and analyzing its performance. In effect, running a supply chain will become as automatic as walking; instead of thinking about how to get every muscle to move in just the right way, you'll be free to focus on where you are going and how to get there. It's not quite the vision of the marathon runner clicking off six-minute miles, but it's a long way from Frankenstein's monster struggling down the village lane.

There's a lot of software out there for supply chains, and assembling the best system for your chain is no small task. The most important decision you'll make is the choice of design and planning systems, and acquiring the optimizing capabilities of APS—either as part of an ERP package or separately—should be a high priority. Whether you need systems to manage warehouses and transportation systems depends entirely on your chain, but you should definitely look into the new visibility and event management packages. Be cautious about customer and supplier relationship systems, however, as they take a rather provincial view of the supply chain, and they seem to be particularly prone to the implicit-model problem. Finally, make sure that any systems you buy are ready to operate over the Internet, using as many of the advanced services as possible. Otherwise, you are likely to find your systems crawling rather than running against the competition.

PART

III

Operations

7

Meeting Demand

This chapter marks the transition from supply chain concepts and tools to an examination of how chains are actually managed, beginning with their daily operations. The most basic operation is fulfillment, the process of satisfying the immediate demand for products. As shown in Figure 7.1, the **fulfillment cycle** begins with an order from a customer and ends when payment is received for the delivered goods. In effect, fulfillment represents a complete cycle of demand, supply, and cash flow across a single link of the chain. This chapter examines each of the component processes from the supplier's perspective, including processing the order, assembling the goods, shipping the order, and getting paid.

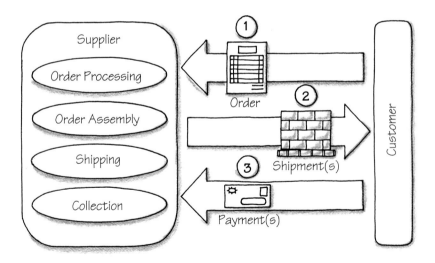

Figure 7.1
The Fulfillment Cycle

Communicating Demand

Demand is communicated through orders

The way orders are transmitted from customers to their suppliers has changed many times over the years, constantly moving toward faster media, but the information contained in orders is as old as business. Essentially, an order answers the classic W questions: Who is doing the buying and selling, what is being requested, where is it to be delivered, and when is it supposed to arrive?

There may be many parties involved

Although simple to state, all of these questions can have complex answers. In the case of *who*, there may be just two parties—the customer and the supplier. As described in Chapter 2, however, the three different flows involved in an order—demand, supply, and cash flow—are usually handled by different groups within the buying and selling organizations, so there can easily be six or more parties involved in a transaction, each of which must be treated as a different operational or legal entity. Even for a relatively simple transaction, just uniquely identifying the various parties is more than many order systems can do.

An order can cover multiple products

Specifying the *what* of an order can also become complicated. A single order usually requests a variety of different products, and it's not sufficient to simply name these products. Off-the-shelf goods must be specified using unique identifiers such as part numbers, universal product codes (UPCs), or stock-keeping unit (SKU) numbers. Some of these identifiers have been standardized within particular industries, but many are unique to each organization, requiring one or both parties to perform a translation between the two identification systems. Orders for customized goods must contain very detailed specifications regarding dimensions, composition, material quality, and the like. Stipulating the quantities of these products—normally a matter of just specifying a number and a unit—can also be a challenge when the two companies measure the same goods in different ways (pounds vs. bales, for example) or use different measurement systems (metric vs. customary).

The answer to the *where* question can also be complex. It may be a single location, or it may be multiple locations, with a different mix of products going to each destination. These destinations are more than just addresses—each can have its own receiving capabilities, hours of operation, and other characteristics. A further consideration is that, for companies that operate multiple plants, products can come from multiple locations, so shipments of these products may need to be split or merged in transit. In that case, the products will have to go by way of a common intermediate destination such as a cross dock or distribution center. Figure 7.2 illustrates a distribution center that merges shipments from three factories then breaks them out for delivery to two assembly plants.

Deliveries can go to multiple locations

Even the question of *when* can introduce complications. Although usually specified as a simple date, delivery targets are actually intervals of time. Historically, the interval was implicit, with the date indicating the last acceptable day for delivery. Given the current emphasis on minimizing inventory, however, the date often specifies an actual day on which delivery should occur, and delivery

The delivery time is usually an interval

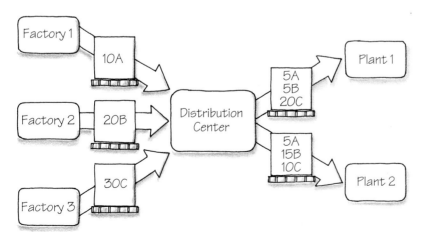

Figure 7.2
Merging and Splitting Shipments

prior to that date may be no more acceptable than delivery after it. With JIT operations, the interval is usually specified more precisely by adding a time to the date, and the supplier may be penalized if a delivery arrives as little as 30 minutes late. Then there's the question of whether all the goods have to meet the same delivery date. At one extreme, a customer can stipulate that the order is **ship complete**, meaning that all the items must arrive in a single delivery, without the option to backorder items that are currently out of stock. At the other extreme, each item could have its own schedule of deliveries, causing a single order to be spread out over many deliveries.

Orders can also address *how* and *why*

In addition to answering the *who, what, where,* and *when* questions, an order can also address *how* questions: how the goods are to be packaged, how they are to be shipped, their form and quality on receipt, and so on. Finally, although not normally included in an order, *why* information is becoming increasingly important to maintaining synchronization in a supply chain. For example, many manufacturers now share their production schedules with their suppliers. Instead of simply requiring that materials arrive on their dock at a specified time, they let their suppliers know what they are building and when, allowing the suppliers to make better decisions about priorities in the event that deliveries fall behind schedule.

Orders have a common structure

This is clearly a lot for a single document to communicate, and orders have evolved a common structure for packaging this information. As shown in Figure 7.3, an order consists of three basic parts: a header, a body, and a footer. The header specifies such generic information as the parties involved, the critical dates for the transaction, and the terms of payment. The body contains line items, each of which specifies a quantity of product to be delivered together with the price per unit and the extended price for the quantity requested after any discounts are applied. The footer

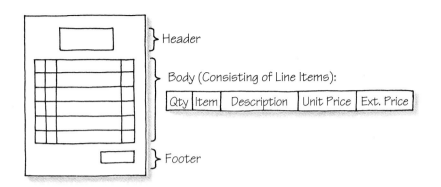

Figure 7.3
The Structure of an
Order

contains financial information that depends on the content of the
line items, such as the total price, taxes, and delivery charges.

Not all of this information appears on the order that initially triggers demand. The order transmitted by the customer usually takes
the form of a purchase order, which doesn't normally include prices
and other financial terms. This information is added by the supplier
and returned to the customer in the form of a sales order, which
represents a commitment on the part of the supplier to provide the
goods on the indicated terms. If the customer agrees with the terms
added by the supplier, including any changes in the products, quantities, and dates, the order becomes binding on both parties. If not,
it becomes the subject of negotiation.

*Orders are
created
interactively*

Although the basic structure shown in Figure 7.3 is sufficient for
most orders, it often requires extension to handle multiple deliveries. The most common form of extension is to add another level of
structure underneath the line items to specify separate deliveries,
as shown in the left panel of Figure 7.4. In some industries, this
nesting is inverted to place line items below delivery dates, as
shown in the right panel of Figure 7.4. This form, commonly
known as a **customer schedule**, is usually found in JIT environments, where it is important to see at a glance what items are
arriving in each delivery.

*Orders can be
nested for
multiple
deliveries*

Figure 7.4
Three-Level Orders

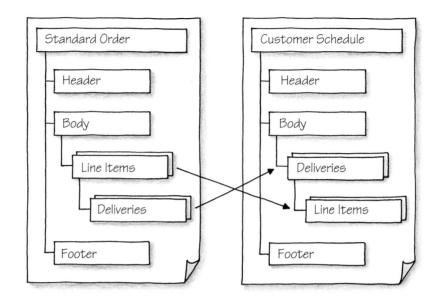

Processing an Order

Orders can
arrive in
many forms

Orders can be transmitted in a variety of forms and can make use of several different media (Figure 7.5). Historically, orders were either sent in the mail or dictated over the telephone. With the invention of the fax machine, paper orders could be sent over telephone lines,

Figure 7.5
Receiving Orders

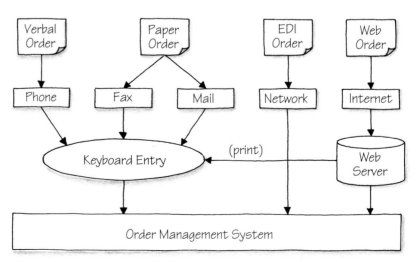

greatly speeding the delivery process. Similarly, the development of the electronic document interchange (EDI) protocol allowed companies to transmit orders in seconds over private networks. However, EDI technology was expensive, and only large companies were able to afford it. The Internet now makes electronic orders easy and affordable for companies of all sizes.

Because all these techniques are still in use, companies must be able to handle orders received in most if not all of these modes. The first challenge is to get all the orders into a common form, a task that is best handled by order management software. In the case of mail, phone, and fax orders, there is little choice but to key the orders in manually, as shown in Figure 7.5. Companies that use EDI are able to accept orders directly into their order management systems without manual entry, but Internet orders are not yet sufficiently standardized to permit full automation. Many companies continue to accept orders over the Internet, print them out, and manually re-enter them into their order management systems. The advent of XML and Web services, as described in Chapter 6, should remedy this problem, but it will take a few years for the remedy to work.

Manual entry is still a common practice

Once an order is "in the system," a supplier begins a sequence of activities that can range from the merely complex to the truly Byzantine. Figure 7.6 illustrates the major steps in order processing, shown in the sequence they would most commonly be carried out. But every company operates a little differently, and the sequence can vary even within a company. If a supplier received a million-dollar order from a relatively small customer, it would very likely move the credit check up to the front of the process.

Order processing can be slow and complex

Ordinarily, the first step in the process is to check all the entries in the order, to make sure they are reasonable and valid. Many of these checks are handled automatically by the order management

Validation checks the individual entries

Figure 7.6
Major Steps in
Order Processing

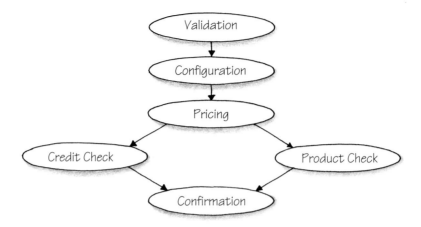

system, which filters out such basic errors as letters in fields that require numbers, and values that lie outside of typical ranges. The system can also make sure that the customer is already known to the supplier and has a line of credit to back up its orders. Most systems can review the individual line items to make sure that all products are properly identified and quantified, and some can assist with any mapping that might be required between the product identifiers or units of measure used by the customer and the supplier. Once this automatic validation is complete, orders are usually given a "reasonableness" check by an account representative to see whether the goods requested are of the same type and quantity this customer normally orders.

Configuration
checks product
compatibility

The next step, configuration, is required only if the mix of products on an order is intended to be used together. This process typically involves two different checks, one for compatibility and the other for completeness. As the names suggest, the first check makes sure that the components will work together properly, and the second ensures that the customer receives everything necessary for the assembled system to function as expected. Because configuration isn't required in most industries, order management systems only include configuration checking capabilities if their target market requires them. With highly sophisticated products such as large computers or telecommunications switches, suppliers often construct specialized knowledge-based systems that use business rules to check configurations for compatibility and completeness.

The pricing step is often a complex process in its own right, involving a sequence of sophisticated tasks. Although order management systems provide support for many of these tasks, pricing can still involve considerable time and effort, and it's the source of many errors and complaints in large transactions. The major tasks are:

Pricing requires its own sequence of steps

1. **Determining the correct unit price**—If the supplier prices its products according to region, market, and other factors, selecting the appropriate price to use can require the application of multiple rules, some of which may conflict with each other.

2. **Applying appropriate discounts**—Once the unit price is determined, it is reduced by any discounts that might apply based on company policies, customer contracts, product promotions, and other considerations. Discounting is itself a dark science; multiple discounts may be applicable, and some discounts can be combined with each other according to various formulas, while others are mutually exclusive.

3. **Computing the extended price**—This step can be as simple as multiplying the discounted price times the quantity requested, but it usually requires the use of one or more quantity discount schedules, with discounts being applied either to all the units purchased or just to those beyond each price-break quantity. The order total may be subject to yet another discount based on the dollar amount and/or the current cumulative purchases of the customer.

4. **Calculating additional charges**—Determining the appropriate shipping fees, taxes, tariffs, and other charges can add another layer of complexity, particularly in the case of

international sales. Simply determining how to ship the order may require checking the cost of several different transportation options and picking the one that best conforms to company policies and customer contracts. The application of additional charges also tends to vary by industry and by company practice, making it difficult to use off-the-shelf order systems to compute these charges.

Credit checks may be limited by software

Once the order total is known, the next step is to make sure that the customer has enough credit to cover the purchase. In a full-featured credit management system, each customer is assigned a maximum amount of credit, and outstanding purchases are subtracted from this maximum to determine the available credit for new purchases (Figure 7.7). Although simple in principle, this approach requires an integration of accounting and order management systems that is still the exception rather than the rule, and suppliers may have to be content with simply checking to see whether a credit flag has been set for the customer. An additional feature that's lacking in many systems is the ability to use a separate party, such as the customer's parent organization, as a credit source, accruing all outstanding charges against that common source.

Figure 7.7
Checking Credit

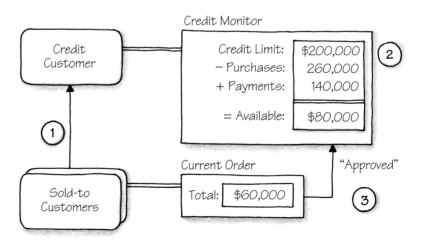

Although the practice is far from universal, most companies like to be sure they can deliver on an order before committing to it. In the case of products made to stock, current and planned inventory may be checked to make sure that the product is **available to promise** (**ATP**) to the customer. For products that are made or assembled to order, the plant is checked to ensure that it is **capable to promise** (**CTP**) the products. In either case, the supplier has the option to reserve the inventory or capacity in question or simply to take a chance that it won't also be promised to another customer. Although earmarking inventory is certainly preferable, it requires an exceptional level of integration with production and inventory management systems.

Availability checks can use ATP or CTP

At present, the best tools for performing real-time ATP and CTP checks are the advanced planning and scheduling (APS) systems described in Chapter 6. Unlike ordinary inventory management systems, APS systems can evaluate alternative sources for a product and determine the best source based on business rules. For example, they can check several different warehouses to see which one can deliver a product by the required date at the lowest total cost to the chain, or compare several different plants against outsourcing options to decide where to have a product assembled. Not only does this real-time ATP and CTP capability keep you from defaulting on your commitments, it also allows you to make more aggressive commitments when you have capacity to spare, improving your ability to win bids against competitors that lack this information.

APS systems offer good availability checks

The last step in order processing is getting the order approved. Depending on the size of the order, it may go through an internal review and approval within the supplier before being sent to the customer for approval. Once the order has been confirmed by the customer, the demand phase is complete, and the process of filling the order begins.

Customer confirmation is the final step

The goal is fully automated processing

Even with a good order processing system, the sequence of events described in the preceding paragraphs is often slow, labor intensive, and prone to errors. One of the enduring goals of product companies has been to fully automate order processing, reducing the time, cost, and mistakes associated with this activity. Now that orders can be transmitted over the Internet in standard XML format, it will soon be possible to perform many of these tasks by sending the order to existing systems and requesting services from them. For example, an incoming order could be sent simultaneously to an inventory management system for an ATP check, to an accounting system for a credit check, to a contracts system for a compliance check, and to a pricing system for appropriate unit and volume pricing. Because XML allows any application to read the order directly, it is not necessary for all of these functions to be carried out in a single, stand-alone order management system.

Assembling the Goods

Orders go to fulfillment locations

The supply phase of the fulfillment cycle begins with the selection of one or more facilities to fill the order. This is usually an easy decision; the supplier just ships the goods from the storage facility closest to the customer. But, as always, there are variations to take into account. One variation has to do with production strategies; make-to-order products, by their very nature, are created on demand at a production facility, so they won't be found waiting in a warehouse. Another variation arises from the centralization of order management, in which a company provides a single order point for two or more of its operating divisions. In this case, an order might be dispatched to several different locations, each of which would ship its portion of the order independently. If the customer has requested that the order be shipped complete, this may require that the various shipments be merged in transit and combined in a single delivery.

A complex sequence of activities is required to prepare an order for shipment. For clarity, I'll describe these activities in the context of a warehouse. The same activities occur when pulling inventory from factories, stockrooms, and other storage locations, but they are more easily understood in the specialized environment of the warehouse. All of these activities are supported electronically by warehouse management systems.

Supply activities follow a standard sequence

The layout of a typical warehouse is illustrated in Figure 7.8. Although not all warehouses are arranged in the linear fashion shown here, most are organized into the five different areas shown: a receiving dock, a bulk storage area, a picking area, one or more assembly areas, and a shipping dock. Each area is dedicated to a different function and has specialized equipment to support that function. A common variation of the structure shown is to bend the linear form into a U shape to allow a common set of docks to support both receiving and shipping. The most important consideration in the layout is maintaining a high rate of flow among the areas. It is not unusual for a warehouse to have 50,000 pallets in storage and to move hundreds of pallets through the system every hour.

Warehouses are laid out by product flow

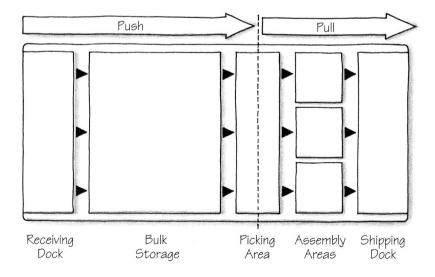

Figure 7.8
Layout of a Warehouse

Warehouses push stock in and pull it out

As shown in Figure 7.8, warehouses use both push and pull dynamics to control the flow of stock from the receiving dock to the shipping dock, with the push-pull boundary located at the picking area. When stock arrives at the warehouse, most of it is unloaded and placed in bulk storage, but a portion of it may be unpackaged and placed in trays, shelves, or bins in the picking area. These movements are all push activities because they queue up product in advance of demand. Subsequent activities are pull-based because they do not occur until the warehouse receives an order.

The first operation is picking the order

When it is time to ship an order, the warehouse management system generates a pick list indicating the quantities of each item included in the order. An employee called a picker takes this list and retrieves the items in the sequence they appear on the list, which is designed to take the picker on the shortest path that touches each of the items. This is an important optimization: Picking can account for as much as half the labor costs in a warehouse, and pickers spend up to 70% of their time moving from one location to the next. Even small improvements in the picking process can yield major savings.

Picking can be manual or automated

With relatively small, lightweight items, picking is usually done by hand. For larger products, pickers use hand trucks, motorized loaders, or other equipment to gather and move stock. In some facilities, conveyor systems move the stock, automatically routing packages to their destinations. In others, pickers stand in place and the stock is brought to their position by carousel-style dispensing systems. Regardless of how the gathering is done, the outcome is the same: The picked stock is deposited with the picking slip in its designated assembly area.

Order assembly follows picking

Once the stock is in the assembly area, other workers perform any final operations that might be needed prior to shipment. These operations are usually minor, often consisting of a quick visual inspection and the addition of a label. However, it is becoming increasingly common to perform final product assembly at warehouses, a practice that makes it easier for producers to customize their products to local requirements (see Chapter 15). For companies using this practice, the assembly area looks more like a miniature plant than a staging area.

After the order is assembled, it is packaged for shipment. Depending on the product, there may be up to three levels of packaging (Figure 7.9). The **primary package** is the box, can, blister pack, or other container that holds the actual product. The **secondary packaging** is usually a carton that groups a standard number of primary packages together for convenient handling. Except where warehouses perform final assembly, most products come prepackaged with these two levels of protection. The third layer, the **transport packaging**, is usually a pallet in combination with a protective covering such as a polyurethane sheet. Large shipments of a product are normally loaded onto **full pallets**, which contain only one kind of product. For smaller shipments, the various products going to a single destination are loaded onto **mixed pallets**.

Orders are packaged in three levels

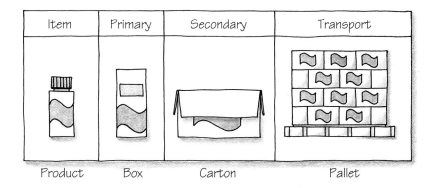

Figure 7.9
Three Levels of Packaging

Shipping the Order

Shipping is simple if carriers are used

What happens next depends on whether the supplier uses a carrier for its shipments or operates its own fleet of vehicles. If a carrier is used, there is nothing much to do once the vehicles are loaded but wait for confirmation that the delivery was made on time. In the case of a private fleet, there is a good deal of planning to be done even before the loading begins. This section describes how a supplier operates it own vehicles, assuming for the sake of clarity that these vehicles are trucks. This assumption is realistic given that trucking accounts for 70% of all shipping in the United States by dollar volume, and trucking presents some interesting problems that don't normally arise in transport by other modes.

The core problem is choosing a route

The basic problem to be solved is finding the best route to take from the supplier's warehouse to the destination facility. When customers order in full truckload (FTL) quantities, routing is usually a simple matter of finding the shortest path between two points. However, with deliveries in metropolitan areas slightly longer routes can sometimes yield shorter driving times, and certain routes may become particularly slow during peak traffic periods. The main problem with FTL shipments, however, is figuring out what to do with the truck once it has made its delivery. Because driving it back to the warehouse empty is a waste of fuel and driver time, companies are constantly looking for **backhauls**, which are shipments in the opposite direction that make use of the capacity provided by the truck. In the absence of a backhaul, trucks usually go to the nearest distribution center rather than returning to their origin.

Cross docking merges shipments in transit

A special problem arises when orders require shipments from multiple facilities. The simplest solution is to make the shipments independently but coordinate them such that they arrive on the same day. But this approach just transfers the cost of combining shipments to the customer, and many customers object to the practice. The alternative is a **merge in transit**, in which the multiple shipments are sent to a distribution center close to the customer site, reloaded onto a single truck, and sent on as a single delivery. The most cost-effective way to achieve this is to use a technique called **cross docking**, in which goods are moved directly from a receiving dock to a shipping dock without intermediate storage. Cross docking was originally developed by Wal-Mart, which uses it with great effectiveness in transporting goods to its national chain of discount stores. Cross docking is usually performed in specialized facilities of the sort illustrated in Figure 7.10.

One of the biggest challenges of shipping is tracking orders while they are in transit from a supplier to a customer. Suppliers often transmit an advance shipping notice (ASN) to let a customer know when its order goes out, but getting information on the progress of

Shipments can now be tracked in transit

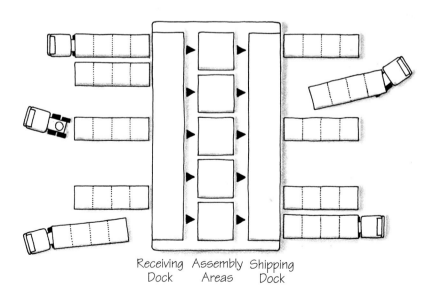

Receiving   Assembly   Shipping
Dock   Areas   Dock

Figure 7.10
A Cross-Docking Facility

a shipment has been difficult if not impossible. Federal Express showed the way of the future when it added barcodes to all its packages and scanned those codes each time a package moved from one facility to the next. Today, anyone with a tracking number and access to the Internet can track a FedEx shipment anywhere in the world. More recently, global positioning systems (GPS) and radio frequency (RF) transponders allow continuous monitoring of vehicles and containers right down to the level of individual boxes. These technologies can also be used to detect breakdowns and reroute vehicles to avoid congestion or synchronize deliveries.

Automated entry is essential for tracking

Part of an efficient tracking system is automating the entry of information regarding each shipment. Not only does this save time, it dramatically reduces errors. Figure 7.11 shows the results of a U.S. Department of Defense study of error rates for different techniques of data capture, including handwritten, keyboard entry, optical character recognition (OCR), barcoding, and RF (radio-frequency) transponders. The rates shown are the average number of errors for each 30 million characters entered. It is immediately clear from the table why barcodes and RF transponders are the techniques of choice for shipment tracking.

Figure 7.11
Error Rates for
Data Capture

Entry Method	Errors
Written	250,000
Keyboard	100,000
OCR	1,000
Barcode	10
Transponder	1

Collecting the Cash

Once an order has been delivered to the customer, the third and final phase of the fulfillment cycle begins—getting paid. The first step in this process is determining the actual amount due. In most cases, this is simply the total at the bottom of the supplier's sales order, which represents the amount the customer agreed to pay. However, the figure on the order may not be final, in which case further computation is needed to determine the amount due. For example, many bulk goods are sold by weight or volume, and the quantity of the shipment isn't finalized until the shipment is weighed or measured at the receiving end.

The cash phase begins with the amount due

Once the amount due has been determined, the supplier generates an invoice for that amount. Invoices have to reference the customer's purchase order, the supplier's sales order, or both. If multiple orders have been shipped to the same customer during a relatively short interval, they are usually covered under a single invoice to reduce paperwork. Most invoices are still sent by mail, but the same technologies that allow orders to travel over the Internet are now being applied to invoices, so invoices should start to move a little faster over the next few years.

The next step is generating an invoice

In an ideal world—at least from a supplier's point of view—all invoices would be paid promptly and accurately. In the real world, customers usually take as much time to pay as they can get away with because this gives them the use of the cash in the interim. As an inducement for prompt payment, invoices usually include payment terms along the lines of "2% 10 Net 30," which requires payment in 30 days but offers a 2% discount if payment is received within 10 days. This discount for prompt payment usually produces two batches of payments, one averaging 15 days and claiming the discount, and the other averaging 45 days.

The last step is receiving payment

Invoices may require a collection effort

In most cases, the only requirements for getting paid are an invoice and a modicum of patience. If the customer doesn't pay within the time allowed, the next step is to include the balance due on a monthly statement with a reminder of past due amounts. If that fails to produce results, one or more friendly phone calls to the bill-to customer may do the trick. If not, the supplier may place a hold on the customer's credit until payment is forthcoming. In supply chains with established trading partners, it is rare for payment problems to escalate beyond this point, but the next step would be to initiate legal action or turn the account over to a collection agency.

Cash flows at a leisurely pace

Compared to the urgency that usually accompanies the first two phases of the fulfillment process, the payment phase can be a rather leisurely interaction. Figure 7.12 offers a typical fulfillment timeline to illustrate this point. In the example shown, a supplier spends an average of three days processing each order, and it takes about a week to deliver the goods. The average time for it to fill an order—called the **fulfillment lead time**—is therefore 10 days. The accounting department generally invoices completed orders in

Figure 7.12
Fulfillment Cycle
Timeline

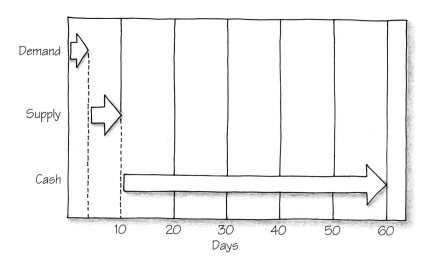

about 5 days, and the average age of the company's accounts receivable is 45 days. For this company, the process of getting paid consumes 50 of the 60 days that make up the fulfillment cycle.

Historically, the cash portion of the fulfillment cycle has not been viewed as a critical aspect of supply chain management. The task of collecting payment is simply delegated to the accounting department, which applies its own policies and procedures for collecting payments. But cash flow isn't merely the last of the three flows—it's the one that motivates the other two. Many suppliers are beginning to question whether compressing fulfillment lead time without accelerating the flow of cash is an entirely balanced proposition.

Payment isn't given the priority of shipment

Profit depends on the effective use of all resources, and cash is the ultimate resource because it is the primary means of acquiring other resources. As described in Chapter 9, tying up cash in any area of a business inflicts an opportunity cost because this cash could be used for other purposes. In the present instance, having cash sitting in receivables for four to six weeks inflicts a tremendous penalty on a company. To get a feeling for the magnitude of this penalty, suppose the supplier in Figure 7.12 does $600 million dollars in sales and has an opportunity cost of 14%. With 45-day receivables, the company floats $75 million to its customers, with an opportunity cost of $10.5 million a year. Depending on its margins, this company could be devoting as much as a 20% of its operating profits to financing its customers' purchases.

Receivables inflict a high opportunity cost

Of course, suppliers can easily justify this float because they make it up by floating the costs of their own supplies. This is just the way the game is played. But this is another example of the kind of zero-sum game described in Chapter 3; there is only so much cash flowing up the supply chain, and there can't be any net gain across the chain from trading partners slowing down its movement. In fact, this game slides down into the lose-lose region because none of the

Slow payments reduce supply chain profits

activities involved in billing and collecting contribute any value to the end product. From the perspective of the supply chain as a whole, these are wasted dollars, pure and simple.

Accelerating Fulfillment

Fulfillment has become very complex

In light of all the operations necessary to fill an order, it should come as no surprise that so many companies have trouble with fulfillment. Many of the practices, including the ritual exchange of similar but slightly different documents at each stage, date back to the early days of commerce. On top of this traditional foundation, many complications have been constructed in the name of improved sales and customer service, including tiered pricing, quantity discounts, revolving credit, special terms, custom configuration, and specialized packaging. The result is a complex process that takes a long time to carry out, incurs a great deal of expense, and provides lots of opportunity for errors.

The normal process is routinely violated

These problems tend to frustrate everyone involved in fulfillment, including not only your customers but also the people in your company who serve those customers. To reduce the frustration and meet their objectives, sales staff and customer service representatives often find ways to subvert the process to better serve their own customers. For example, if there isn't enough stock on hand to fill an order, a service rep might call a friend at the warehouse and arrange to have his customer receive goods originally intended for another customer. In a more extreme case, the service rep might convince a plant manager to push a production run forward in order to meet a customer requirement. Such practices, sometimes sanctioned under the name of expediting, provide an excellent example of local optimization hurting the chain as a whole. They may speed up delivery of a single order, but they do so by throwing off other orders and creating additional work to resolve the conflicts and confusion they produce.

Expediting individual orders is clearly not the best way to solve the fulfillment problem, but finding a better way to fix these problems can be a challenge. Many companies have applied the techniques of business process reengineering to improve their fulfillment process, but usually with limited success. The problem they ultimately come up against is that the practices that make fulfillment slow and complex are difficult to change, in part because customers have come to expect a certain way of doing business. Simplifying the flow of paper, eliminating pricing tiers, or skipping the confirmation step on routine orders may all make perfect sense from your point of view, but convincing your customers to accept these changes is another matter. And even if you do bring your customers around, the savings you realize from such incremental improvements may be outweighed by the cost of bringing about the change.

Incremental improvement often fails

The alternative to incremental improvement is radical change—simply throwing out the old way of doing business and coming up with a dramatically streamlined process. It may seem paradoxical, but radical change is often easier to achieve than incremental change. For example, rather than asking your customers to alter the way they place their orders, it may be simpler to eliminate orders altogether in favor of automated replenishment. This is the approach taken by JIT, vendor managed inventory, and several other programs described in Chapter 3, and it has worked quite well in practice. In a sense, orders still exist, but they have become so simplified and standardized that they bear little resemblance to the orders of old. In a JIT environment, for example, the "order" may take the form of a plastic bin that holds a particular set of parts. Processing this order couldn't be simpler: When a bin arrives, you return it full.

Radical change may be a better remedy

Another example of radical change is the move toward instant payment. Many companies that have adopted JIT practices are now applying the same techniques to the billing and payment cycle. As each shipment of supplies arrives at the customer site, scanning in

Instant payment eliminates billing

the delivery automatically triggers an electronic deposit in the supplier's bank account. No invoices, no statements, no payment terms, no collections, no credit checks, and no float. Instant payment not only eliminates a great deal of cost on both sides of the transaction, it wraps the business up a lot faster. Given the sluggish pace with which cash normally flows up the chain, the fulfillment cycle can be accelerated by a factor of 5 or 10 with this technique.

Radical change requires new relationships

Making radical changes of this sort clearly requires deep changes in the nature of your relationship with customers. You can't just call them up one day, welcome them to your new instant-payment plan, and read off an account number. Changes like these have to come as part of a larger package that redefines the relationship, and the package has to be attractive to both parties. For example, instant payment is one way to compensate JIT suppliers for the extra cost associated with making frequent, small deliveries.

Looking back at the slow, complex, labor-intensive processes that go into filling a single order, it may be hard to imagine getting from where we are today to the ideal of automatic supply chains described in the last chapter. The problem isn't figuring out a better way to handle fulfillment; that's mostly a matter of stripping away much of what's there and streamlining the rest to the point where it can be carried out by software. The hard part is cultural; the complexities of fulfillment are woven into the very fabric of your organization, and your relationships with customers are predicated on the maze of discounts and buying options they've come to expect. It would be nearly impossible to dismantle this entire system and still keep your company in business. But you can set up a parallel system, one that offers lower cost and faster service to customers who opt for automated orders and payments. Then let the two systems compete, and natural selection will do the rest.

8

Maintaining Supply

Just as fulfillment delivers products to meet customer demand, so replenishment acquires the materials necessary to build those products. The **replenishment cycle,** shown in Figure 8.1, involves the same activities as the fulfillment cycle, but views them from the perspective of the customer rather than the supplier. Given this perspective, the chapter focuses on three key questions that drive purchasing decisions: when to place an order, how much to buy at a time, and how much inventory to keep on hand. The answer to the last question reveals a disturbing truth: There is no amount of inventory that will prevent stockouts, so setting inventory levels is basically a matter of risk management. The final section turns to the question of how you can improve replenishment by removing time and cost from the process.

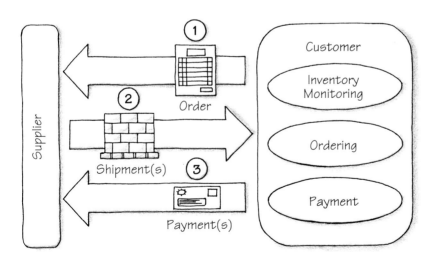

Figure 8.1
The Replenishment Cycle

Triggering Replenishment

Replenishment policies answer three questions

Each time a facility fulfills an order, it reduces its inventory of finished goods. Sooner or later, that inventory has to be replenished. Behind this self-evident truth lie three key questions:

1. When should inventory be replenished?
2. What quantity should be ordered with each replenishment?
3. How much inventory should be maintained on site?

The answers to these three questions constitute what is known as a **replenishment policy**. The first three sections of this chapter address the three questions in turn, starting with the question of when to place an order.

Running out is one possible trigger

There are several options for deciding when to replenish inventory. One solution is simply to wait until the current inventory is exhausted. This practice is usually the result of inattention rather than intention, but it is actually the best policy for items that have shorter lead times than "need" times. If a supplier can buy or build a product in a week and its customers are happy with 10-day lead times, then that supplier has the very attractive option of operating with no stock on hand. It would only maintain inventory of the product if there were other benefits, such as reducing costs by ordering or building in quantity.

Running low is a more common trigger

Attractive as it might be, the zero-inventory solution is rarely an option because customers want to take delivery faster than the replenishment lead time. Ordinarily, then, a facility has to order stock in advance of demand and keep enough on hand to fill orders from its inventory. To do this, it has to monitor its inventory levels and place a new order while it still has enough stock to avoid running out before the order arrives. This monitoring can take one of two forms, called periodic review and continuous review. With a

periodic review policy, inventory is counted at fixed intervals and an order is placed whenever the count falls below a preset **reorder point** (**ROP**). Under a **continuous review** policy, the count is monitored at all times and an order is placed as soon as the count hits the reorder point.

Under both review policies, inventory levels describe a sawtooth pattern over time, with gradual declines as inventory is consumed followed by sudden jumps when replenishment stock arrives. With continuous review, a new order is triggered whenever the stock reaches the reorder point, as shown in Figure 8.2. Stock continues to diminish during the **replenishment lead time**, but the reorder point is set high enough to minimize the frequency of **stockouts**, in which sales are lost due lack of inventory. The periodic review policy produces a similar pattern, but orders wait until the next inventory count occurs rather than being placed immediately. The facility continues to deplete its inventory during this additional wait, so it has to set the reorder point higher to compensate for the delay. The result: Periodic review requires more inventory than continuous review.

Periodic review requires more inventory

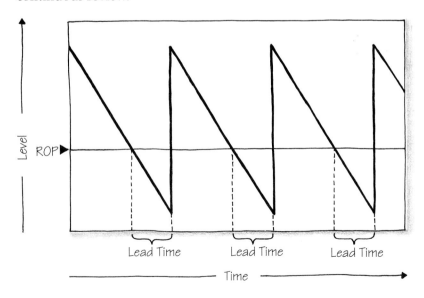

Figure 8.2
Inventory Levels Under Continuous Review

Bin systems provide continuous review

Although continuous review is more efficient than periodic review, it is also more expensive because it requires an accurate inventory count at all times. Historically, periodic review was the preferred method because it avoids this added expense. However, there are ways to get the benefits of continuous review without the cost of constant counting. A simple example of this is the two-bin system used in factories to maintain a supply of parts at a workstation. In this scheme, an operator draws parts from one bin while the other is being refilled by an upstream workstation. As each a bin is emptied, it is sent back for a refill, triggering another cycle of the replenishment process. It's a simple, elegant way to monitor counts without counting, and it's easily extended out to suppliers. In the automotive industry, specially shaped, reusable bins are sent to suppliers to trigger the replenishment of parts kits at assembly stations. In addition to creating a precise flow of parts from suppliers, these bins facilitate assembly by presenting the parts to assemblers in a standard manner, and they eliminate the waste associated with temporary packaging.

Inventory systems automate stock counting

With the advent of computerized inventory control systems, the task of counting has become trivial, so continuous review is now the method of choice. In order for these control systems to work, however, they must be notified every time inventory is reduced. In retail facilities, this is usually handled by point-of-sale (POS) systems tied to the cash registers. In factories, it may be accomplished by putting barcodes on components or punching counters at stock cages. These techniques don't eliminate the need for manual counting altogether; inventory is always subject to **shrinkage** through theft or loss. But manual counts are used only for verifying and adjusting the computer counts, which fully automate the process of triggering orders.

Information is cheaper than inventory

The ability to switch from periodic to continuous review is a good example of how information can replace inventory, producing substantial savings. In this case, the information is nothing more than a single number indicating the current count. But this number can be worth a lot: In one comparison, converting from periodic to continuous review reduced required inventory from 1,570 to 906 units. Given the escalating costs of inventory, it's usually a good deal cheaper to hold the count than to hold the inventory.

Determining Order Quantity

The preceding section answered the question of when to replenish inventory, and this answer provides the basis for tackling the second question: What quantity should be ordered with each replenishment? That quantity hinges on the relative costs of placing an order and holding inventory. The **order cost** is the basic cost of placing and receiving an order, independent of the quantities involved. The **holding** (or **carrying**) **cost** is the cost of stockpiling inventory in advance of consuming it. It includes the costs of storage and handling, the opportunity cost of the capital tied up in the inventory, the loss of value due to obsolescence or spoilage, and the cost of insuring against risks such as fire and theft.

Order size depends on two kinds of cost

These two costs tend to push the order quantity in opposite directions. Increasing order quantities reduces order costs because fewer orders are required to buy a given amount of inventory, but it also drives up holding costs by increasing average inventory levels. Conversely, ordering in smaller quantities reduces holding costs at the expense of order costs. Finding some sort of balance between the two is important because neither cost is trivial. Manufacturing companies usually have a significant percentage of their capital assets tied up in inventory, and they want to bring that percentage down. But placing an order generally costs $100 to $150, and that adds up fast given the volume of orders required to keep a plant running.

The two costs produce conflicting pressures

The obvious question at this juncture is whether this tradeoff has a sweet spot, a quantity at which the sum of these two costs is mini-

EOQ finds the lowest total cost

mized. It does, and the spot can be found using a mathematical model known as the **economic order quantity (EOQ)**. The equation for this model is simple, but it's easier to see how the model works by looking at a graph. As Figure 8.3 indicates, holding costs increase linearly with quantity, while order costs decrease inversely with quantity. The total of these two costs, shown in the top curve, drops with increasing quantity and then rises again. The lowest point on this curve is the EOQ, and it is easily calculated using standard formulas. For any given combination of order cost and holding cost, the EOQ gives the exact size of the order that should be placed to minimize the total expense of buying and holding inventory.

The EOQ model shows the rogues in action

The EOQ model provides a good example of how the kinds of relations described in Chapter 4 show up in real-world problems. The relation for holding cost over quantity is linear (the first rogue in the rogues gallery of relations shown in Figure 4.4), and the relation for order cost is monotonic (the second rogue). Combining these two produces a third relation that is continuous (the third rogue), so three of the five rogues in the gallery appear in this one

Figure 8.3
Inventory Cost
Curves

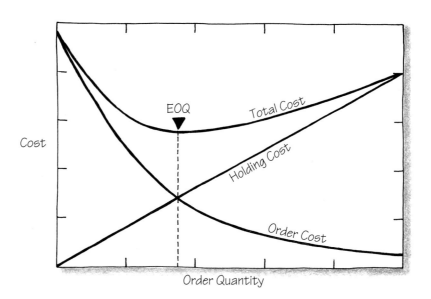

model. In real-world applications of EOQ, the fourth rogue also pops up when quantity discounts introduce discontinuities in the total-cost curve, changing it from a smooth line to a scalloped one that jumps downward at price breaks. These discontinuities complicate the EOQ model and make it tedious to calculate; most buyers just run the regular EOQ calculation and bump the quantity up if it's close to a price break.

The EOQ model was developed more than 80 years ago and has been in continuous use since. In recent years, however, its usefulness has been called into question because it doesn't take into account fluctuations in demand, incentives for buying inventory in advance of need, the effects of requesting multiple products on a single order, and a host of other factors that can influence order quantities. More important, this kind of local optimization overlooks higher-level opportunities for reducing costs, such as simplifying the order process or eliminating orders altogether. But the EOQ model is still around for the simple reason that, in the absence of a more comprehensive plan, it gives a quick and reasonably good answer.

EOQ is a limited solution

Maintaining Safety Stock

The two preceding sections dealt with the questions of when to replenish inventory and how much to buy on each order. The present section tackles the third question: How much inventory should a facility maintain on site? The quantities calculated in the EOQ model provide a lower bound on this number; there should always be enough stock on hand to satisfy demand during the replenishment lead time. But these calculations are based on average figures for demand and supply. In reality, the number of units sold varies from day to day, shipments are delivered late, goods arrive in an unusable condition, and so on. If any of these events causes a stockout, customer orders go unfilled. There is no margin for error in the basic EOQ model.

There's no margin for error in the EOQ model

The solution lies in holding safety stock

The standard solution to this problem is to hold excess inventory—safety stock—that is used to avoid stockouts when demand is greater than expected or supplies arrive late. The role of safety stock can be seen graphically in Figure 8.4, which adds a dose of realism to Figure 8.2 by illustrating some variability in demand and supply. In the example shown, safety stock is needed in the first cycle to cover a higher level of demand, as reflected in the steeper consumption line. It's also needed in the third cycle to compensate for a late shipment, as reflected in the extended lead time.

Safety stock can't eliminate stockouts

In short, a company needs to maintain enough inventory to support its normal operations—a quantity known as the **cycle stock**—plus enough safety stock to cover variations in supply and demand. Using the EOQ model causes the cycle stock to vary between zero and the EOQ level, averaging out to half the value of the EOQ. That leaves the question of how much safety stock is required to avoid stockouts. The answer, unfortunately, is "more than you could possibly afford." Managers usually hate answers like that, so it's important to explore the reason behind this conclusion. It

Figure 8.4
Adding Safety Stock

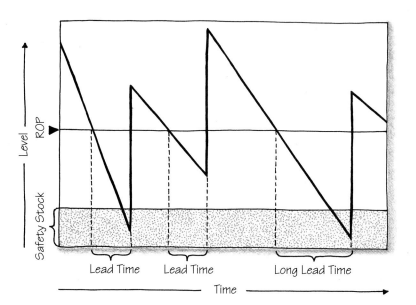

turns out to be the work of one of the two core problems of supply chains: variability.

As described in Chapter 5, variability in most quantities conforms to the normal distribution, a recurring pattern that describes how far values are likely to deviate from the average. As you may recall, this distribution is described by just two parameters: the mean and the standard deviation. Given those two parameters, the normal distribution predicts the number of times each possible value is likely to occur. For example, Figure 8.5 shows the likelihood of each level of demand for a product with a mean demand of 100 units a week and a standard deviation of 10 units. Just looking at the curve, it's clear that demand is rarely going to be less than 70 units a week or more than 130.

Variability follows the normal distribution

The problem with that conclusion is the word *rarely.* The normal distribution has the unfortunate characteristic that the ends of the distribution never quite drop to zero. No matter how far out the value, there is always some probability of that value occurring. In Figure 8.5, the likelihood of experiencing a demand of 140 units is

Extreme values can't be eliminated

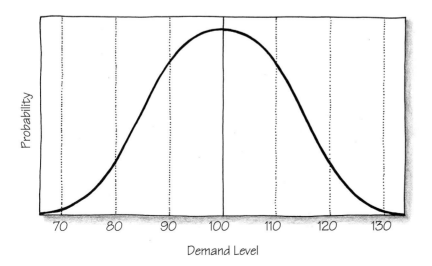

Figure 8.5
Distribution of
Weekly Demand

very small—only a fraction of a percent—but it's not zero. Neither is the probability of 150 units, nor even 200. Which means that no amount of safety stock is enough to entirely eliminate the possibility of a stockout. This isn't a failure of the normal distribution as a model; it's an accurate description of what happens in the real world. The normal distribution simply reflects the profound impact of variability on planning and performance throughout the supply chain.

Customer service level measures availability

Given that stockouts can't be eliminated altogether, the best that safety stock can do is reduce stockouts to an acceptable level. The standard procedure is to set a target level of product availability, called the **customer service level** (**CSL**), then adjust the safety stock to meet that level. Naturally, higher CSLs are better, but setting them too high can be very expensive because safety stock rises exponentially with the service level. Figure 8.6 illustrates the rapid rise in safety stock required to hit item fill rates in the high 90s, which is where most companies would like to keep them. For this particular product, simply increasing the fill rate by a half a point,

Figure 8.6
Required Levels
of Safety Stock

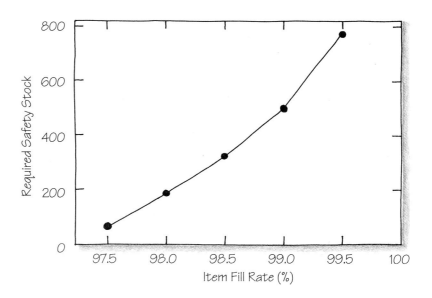

Item Fill Rate (%)

from 97.5% to 98%, requires holding nearly three times the safety stock. This is a high price to pay for such a small improvement given the high costs of holding inventory.

Given that increasing inventory yields such rapidly diminishing returns on service level, how should you go about choosing the right level? The ideal would be to have a formula comparable to the EOQ to tell you the level at which the cost of holding extra inventory just offsets the cost of stockouts. But how do you calculate the cost of a stockout? If a customer is willing to accept a backorder, the cost is the expense of the backorder. If the customer turns to another supplier for this one purchase, the cost is the loss of the revenue from the sale. If the customer turns to another supplier and never comes back, the cost is the lost revenue for all future sales to that customer. Few companies have a good handle on the likelihood of these various outcomes, much less an accurate way of estimating lost revenue from future sales. Most simply set a service-level target somewhere in the high 90s and adjust safety stocks accordingly.

> Safety stock involves an economic tradeoff

Using fill rate as the measure of the customer service level doesn't quite resolve the matter because fill rate can be measured in more than one way. In the example above, it was implicitly defined as the ability to fill orders for a single product from stock—what is often called the **item fill rate**. But business customers rarely order just one product; they generally place multi-line orders that cover a number of products. Although this reduces the cost of order processing on both sides of the transaction, it also makes it harder for suppliers to fill the orders because the probability of filling an entire order—the **order fill rate**—is roughly the numeric product of the item fill rates for all the lines on the order. Figure 8.7 illustrates graphically how quickly the order fill rate drops as the number of items on the order goes up. Even with an item fill rate of 95%, the order fill rate drops to 60% with as few as 10 line items. With 20 items, barely a third of outgoing orders ship complete.

> Multi-line orders have lower fill rates

Figure 8.7
Predicting Order
Fill Rates

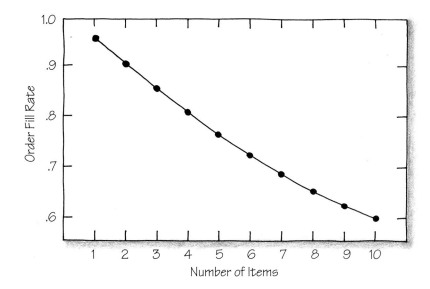

**Variability can
lead to vicious
cycles**

Let me put this another way: When customers require complete shipments, suppliers have to maintain much higher inventory levels than they would otherwise require. For example, to hit an order fill rate of just 90% on 10-line orders, a supplier would have to have an item fill rate of 99%, and that calls for a great deal of safety stock. This safety stock is entirely devoted to coping with variability in customer demand. But there is a vicious cycle at work here: Receiving incomplete orders is one of the sources of variability on the customer side that these customers are trying hard to control, so they are increasingly insistent on complete shipments. This is why the problem of variability is so insidious: Trying to reduce it at any one link in the chain may just push it up or down the chain, often amplifying it in the process. The only real solution to this problem is for trading partners to work together to remove variability across the chain rather than trying to cope with it through point solutions such as added safety stock.

Streamlining Replenishment

Like the fulfillment process described in Chapter 7, replenishment has become increasingly complex over the years, producing corresponding increases in the time, cost, and errors associated with the process. These problems, in turn, often lead people within a company to try to beat the system by speeding up their own orders, usually at the expense of other orders that may be equally urgent. In addition to slowing down the replenishment process as a whole, these expediting battles lead to extra work and may also incur surcharges for rush orders.

Replenishment has become overly complex

As in the case of fulfillment, the solution is not to bypass the fulfillment system but to improve it, and radical change in this system may produce better results than attempts at incremental refinement. Here again, radical changes require the cooperation of trading partners, but that cooperation is usually easier to obtain in the case of replenishment because you have a lot more clout in your dealings with suppliers than you do with customers. In general, the further upstream you can push the changes, the more likely you are to remove time and cost from the chain as opposed to just pushing it around within the chain.

Radical change may be easier to achieve

The actual changes should, of course, be closely aligned with the changes used on the fulfillment side so that the flow through your own company is as smooth as possible. If your customers are demanding smaller, more frequent shipments for JIT production, then it makes sense to move replenishment in the same direction, accelerating the flow of goods through your facilities rather than becoming the point at which batch shipments convert to a flow mode. By making the same changes on both sides of your supply chain, you have the best opportunity to create an arrangement that is more economical for everyone.

Replenishment should match fulfillment

Radical change alters supply economics

The shift to frequent, small shipments is a good example of how this balancing act works. If all you do is reduce the size of shipments to and from your trading partners, everyone will get hurt because you will all lose economies of scale. The tradeoff expressed by the EOQ model still applies—there is no escaping it—so, unless you make other changes, the savings in holding costs don't offset the increased cost of placing additional orders (see Figure 8.3). The trick to making the economics work is to reduce the order costs by simplifying and standardizing the order process, preferably by eliminating orders altogether. In a chain that uses returnable bins, for example, processing an "order" amounts to little more than refilling the bin. It's only by reducing order costs to an absolute minimum that you bring the EOQ down to where frequent deliveries are cost-effective for everyone.

Collaboration isn't required for commodities

Collaborating with suppliers to integrate operations and streamline replenishment is a significant undertaking, and the effort should be reserved for suppliers that provide critical materials, such as custom components and standard items that are subject to shortages. For widely available commodities, such as nuts and bolts, the classic approach of dealing with several qualified suppliers and shopping for price may still be the best option. This is the area where the Internet is having the greatest impact on the replenishment process.

Electronic catalogs simplify selection

Historically, commodity suppliers were selected by digging through stacks of catalogs to find out who offered the required products, checking price books to compare costs, sorting through flyers to see whether anyone had a promotion in progress, and calling the supplier to check availability. Today, searchable **electronic catalogs** on the Web reduce the time and tedium of this process to a fraction of its former level, significantly reducing order costs for catalog purchases. Some of these catalogs are hosted by suppliers and are specific to their products, but others are more like distributor catalogs, merging products from multiple suppliers and organizing them by type.

These catalogs become even more useful when they are incorporated into **electronic exchanges**, Web-based marketplaces in which buyers and sellers conduct business without having to leave their desks or even pick up their phones. Suppliers post their products on the exchange, which merges them into a common catalog and provides tools for searching and comparison (Figure 8.8). Customers browse the catalog, add their selections to a "shopping cart," then fill in a short form to place their orders. In addition to handling transactions, exchanges often provide added services such as qualifying buyers and sellers, providing information on the state of the market, and even supporting collaboration among supply chain partners.

Although most exchanges work from the prices set by suppliers, some host **electronic auctions**, in which supplies are sold to the highest bidder (Figure 8.9). In a normal auction, suppliers post products on the exchange, and customers post bids indicating how much they are willing to pay for those products. At the end of the bidding period, the exchange automatically compares the bids and notifies the bidders of the outcome. In a **reverse auction**, the roles are switched: Customers post requests for quotes (RFQs) for specific products, suppliers submit bids, and the sale goes to the *lowest* bidder rather than the highest. While normal auctions tend to push prices up, reverse auctions generally have the opposite effect and are often favored by customers for that reason.

Electronic exchanges come in a variety of forms, depending on their access and ownership structures. **Public exchanges** require only that participants be qualified to buy and sell the materials

Electronic exchanges mediate transactions

Some exchanges support auctions

Exchanges can be public or private

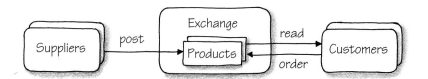

Figure 8.8
An Electronic Exchange

Figure 8.9
Electronic Auctions

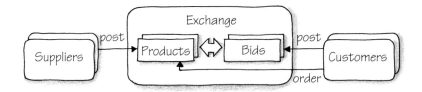

handled by the exchange, and they are usually hosted by independent organizations that specialize in managing a market. **Private exchanges** are accessible to companies that have been approved for membership, and may charge a fee for use of the exchange. Private exchanges can be independent organizations, or they can be hosted by one or more of the trading parties. In the latter case, they are sometimes referred to as **captive exchanges**. In several industries, there has been a rapid evolution of structure from public to private exchanges, then to captive exchanges as a few dominate players extend their market control to include the electronic channel. A recent Forrester Research report indicates that 42% of companies are now doing business on private exchanges, compared with only 11% doing business on public exchanges.

Exchanges are alive and well

Exchanges—like so many technology innovations—have fallen victim to the hype-and-snipe cycle, in which analysts make grossly exaggerated forecasts for new product categories and then declare these categories to be failures when their predictions aren't met. In the case of exchanges, the only thing that failed was the idea that venture-funded start-ups could insert themselves between established trading partners and take a piece of the action. As soon as the potential of exchanges became apparent, the major buyers and sellers set up their own captive exchanges, bypassed the start-ups, and took their markets back. A good example of this is Covisint, the purchasing exchange launched by U.S. automakers in the last quarter of 2000. The exchange handled $129 billion worth of purchases in the first half of 2001.

It's clear that replenishment has become just as complex as fulfillment, which isn't surprising given that the two are really the same process viewed from different perspectives. In addition to working with suppliers to set up a fully auto- mated order system, as suggested at the end of Chapter 7, there are several other things you can do to improve your replenishment process. One is to drive down your order costs to make it more economical to place smaller, more fre- quent orders, thereby reducing your required levels of both cycle stock and safety stock. Another is to reduce variability in your consumption, further reducing your need for safety stock. But the most powerful technique is to substitute information for inventory wherever you can, automating inventory counts and constantly updating your suppliers so that they can anticipate your needs and help you minimize your inventories.

9

Measuring Performance

One of the keys to improving supply chain operations is having a solid set of measures in place to monitor performance. The challenge here is making good choices among the dozens of measures available. Some companies try to measure too much, overwhelming themselves with data that never quite form a coherent picture. Others measure too little, relying on one or two indicators that don't reflect the full spectrum of performance. This tendency to focus too narrowly is exacerbated by management fads such as cycle-time reduction in the 1990s and the current obsession with inventory velocity. Just as there is no easy answer to all supply chain problems, there is no magic measure for improving performance. This chapter introduces a framework for understanding and selecting supply chain measures based on four broad categories: measures of time, measures of cost, measures of efficiency, and measures of effectiveness. You will need at least one and probably several measures from each category if you want to get the best performance out of your chain.

Measuring Time

Time is the easiest measure to capture because it involves nothing more than taking two readings and performing a subtraction (Figure 9.1). The times of greatest interest in supply chains are process times, which measure the amount of time required for key business processes to run from initiation to completion. As the examples in Figure 9.1 suggest, the processes involved can be measured on any scale from seconds to months.

Time is the simplest measure

Figure 9.2 illustrates some of the process times involved in the fulfillment activities of supply chains. The overall fulfillment process, shown at the top of the figure, can be broken down into

Lead time is the key measure in fulfillment

Figure 9.1
Measuring Time

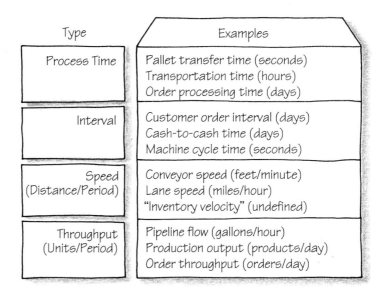

component processes dealing with the supporting flows of demand, supply, and cash. Although the total duration of the fulfillment process is critical to cash flow, it is rarely measured directly. Rather, the primary concern is with the **fulfillment lead time**, which is the sum of the first two phases. The third phase is usually handled

Figure 9.2
Fulfillment Times

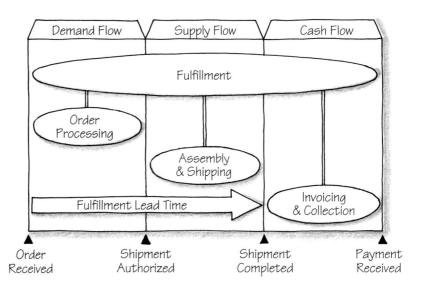

by the accounting department, where it is measured indirectly in the aging of accounts receivable. Fulfillment lead times vary considerably across industries, but a typical lead time for an order that has not been previously scheduled is in the range of two to three weeks. Of that time, several days might be spent processing the order, several more days assembling the order, and the remaining time taken up by transportation.

Figure 9.3 shows a breakdown of the replenishment process into the same three phases. In this process, the primary concern is with **replenishment lead time**, which is measured from the time a request for goods is submitted for purchasing to the time those goods are available for use. Of necessity, this time includes the supplier's fulfillment lead time, which to the customer is simply a waiting period. Because the supplier's lead time is such a visible part of the fulfillment lead time, companies often equate the two and attempt to reduce lead times by demanding faster fulfillment from their suppliers. However, it is rare that a customer's purchasing and receiving processes can't be accelerated as well.

Replenishment lead times span more steps

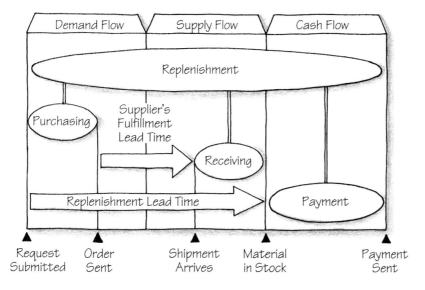

Figure 9.3
Replenishment Times

Intervals are as important as process times

Times that aren't directly tied to a single business process are usually referred to as intervals. As indicated in Figure 9.1, one such interval is the time that elapses between orders from a particular customer, a measure that might range from hours in a JIT environment to weeks in a traditional production operation. Another interval of interest is the **cash-to-cash time**, which is usually measured in days. As can be seen in Figure 9.4, this interval doesn't correspond directly to any one process. Rather, it begins when raw materials are paid for, which happens late in the replenishment process, and ends when payment is received for the finished goods, near the completion of the fulfillment process.

Cash-to-cash time is an important measure

Historically, cash-to-cash times have not received as much attention in supply chains as other, more visible time-based measures such as lead times. However, companies now recognize cash as a vital supply chain asset that needs to be recovered and put back into play as quickly as possible, so this measure is being used with increasing frequency. Cash-to-cash times typically run about 70 to 90 days, but efficient companies get this number below 60 days, and the best keep it under 30. As described in Chapter 1, Dell has

Figure 9.4
Cash-to-Cash
Times

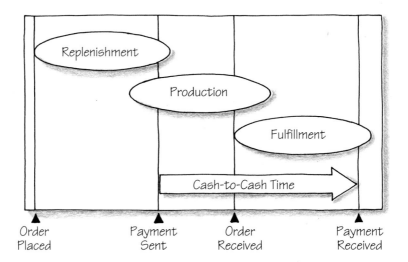

actually driven its cash-to-cash time into the negative range, receiving payment from its customers before paying its suppliers.

The third example of an interval shown in Figure 9.1, machine cycle time, raises the question of how the popular measure of cycle time fits into this framework. Originally, **cycle time** referred to the interval between repetitions of a periodic process, which is not necessarily the same as the duration of that process. For example, a production line with a cycle time of 30 seconds would produce two products a minute, but the time required to assemble any one product—the time it takes materials to get from one end of the line to the other—might be 20 minutes. Contemporary usage confounds these two measures, applying the term *cycle time* to process durations as well as repetition intervals. Given this confounding, you may want to be cautious when you see the term *cycle time* to be sure you understand exactly what is being measured. In this book, I avoid confusion by avoiding the term.

Cycle times are ambiguously defined

Another approach to measuring times is to invert them and express them as **speed**, which is a distance divided by a unit of time. In supply chains, speed is used mostly for assessing the transportation function, reflecting either actual performance or lane characteristics. Speed values range from the leisurely pace of ocean freighters to the blur of parts flying through pneumatic tubes.

Speed is an alternative measure of time

When speed takes on a particular direction, it is called velocity. Recently, **inventory velocity** has become the term of choice for describing the speed at which material flows through a supply chain, and the current emphasis is on finding ways to increase that velocity. This is an excellent goal (see Chapter 15), but inventory velocity is more of a metaphor than a measure. People who talk about inventory velocity—most notably Michael Dell—aren't really describing the speed at which inventory is transported. Rather, they're referring to the amount of time it takes to transform raw

Velocity is not a separate measure

materials into finished goods. If you look for actual measurements of inventory velocity, you'll come up empty-handed; what you'll actually find are reports of such traditional measures as inventory turns or days on hand, as defined later in this chapter.

Throughput reflects the speed of operations

The last type of measure shown in Figure 9.1 is throughput, which is defined as units of work divided by a unit of time. This type of measure is really a variant of speed, but it's concerned with how quickly work is performed rather than how quickly something moves. For supply chains, throughput is usually of much more interest than speed. Examples of throughput include products produced per week, orders processed per day, gallons of output per hour, and items picked per minute.

Measures of time are usually aggregated

As with all measures, measurements of time can reflect a particular instance of a process or interval—the time to deliver an important order, say—or they can summarize a number of these instances, such as the time required to deliver all the orders received at a given facility during the prior month. When measurements are aggregated, they are usually reported as a single number—sometimes a total, but usually an average value such as the mean. This is a dangerous practice because reducing a group of measurements to a single number masks the variability among those measurements, and coping with variability is one of the deepest challenges in supply chain management.

Variability in process time is important

Figure 9.5 illustrates this point by showing the distributions for the fulfillment lead times of two suppliers. Supplier A requires an average of 17 days to fill its orders, whereas Supplier B requires 19 days on average. Based on these average values, Supplier A clearly offers better performance. But the actual measurements underlying these averages tell a different story: A is much less consistent in its delivery times than B, with lead times as little as 9 days and as long as

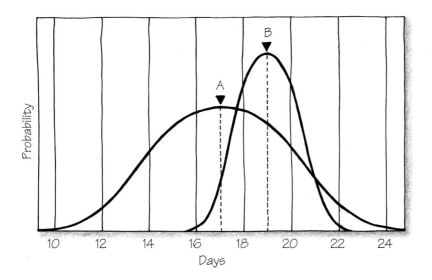

Figure 9.5
Two Lead-Time
Distributions

25 days. Early deliveries cause you to hold inventory longer than necessary, and late deliveries require you to increase inventory levels to avoid stockouts, so any deviation from the requested delivery date requires you to hold more inventory. Depending on your holding costs, you may find that the consistency of Supplier B makes it a better choice even though it's a little slower than A on average.

It's also important to understand what happens to variability when you combine processes to form larger processes, as shown in Figures 9.2 and 9.3. Do the variations in the component times cancel each other out, making the total time a more stable measure? Or do they add up, making it less stable? If the times for the component processes are reasonably independent of one another, the variability in the distribution of the total time is the sum of the variability in all the component times. In effect, all the variability that is picked up along the way is accumulated in the distribution for the total time. The business message is this: If you want to minimize variability in your supply chain, you have to minimize it in every single process along the way.

Variability adds up along with mean times

Measuring Cost

There are many kinds of costs

The second major category of measures deals with costs, which come in a wide variety of types. Compared to the simplicity of measuring time, measuring cost is considerably more difficult, and complex issues can arise when you try to mix or combine different types of cost. Figure 9.6 provides examples of five different types, but these are only meant to illustrate some of the ways in which costs can arise. There are certainly other kinds of costs you will need to consider, and the ones shown are not mutually exclusive. For example, most periodic costs are also indirect costs, and the expense of correcting an error might include costs of every other type in the list.

Direct costs go directly into products

Direct costs, the first type, are those you can attribute directly to the production of finished goods. As shown in Figure 9.7, this category includes the cost of raw materials together with the cost of the processes necessary to acquire these materials, transform them into finished goods, and deliver them to customers. Measuring direct

Figure 9.6
Measuring Cost

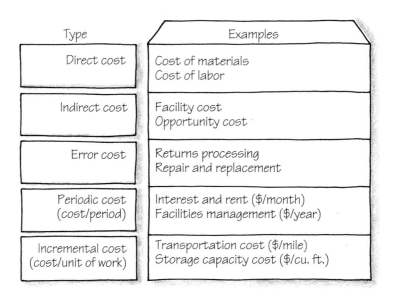

Type	Examples
Direct cost	Cost of materials Cost of labor
Indirect cost	Facility cost Opportunity cost
Error cost	Returns processing Repair and replacement
Periodic cost (cost/period)	Interest and rent ($/month) Facilities management ($/year)
Incremental cost (cost/unit of work)	Transportation cost ($/mile) Storage capacity cost ($/cu. ft.)

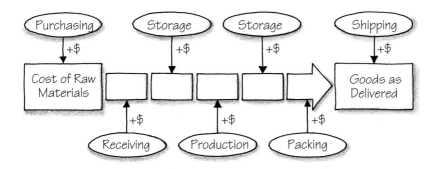

Figure 9.7
Direct Costs

costs accurately is difficult because few accounting systems provide the necessary information, but most manufacturing companies have a reasonable handle on their direct costs.

Indirect costs, the second type, are those that are necessary to run your company but that can't be attributed directly to the creation of a particular product. As shown in Figure 9.8, these include the costs of purchasing and maintaining the equipment used in producing goods, the costs of building and operating the facilities that house this equipment, and the costs of running all the support organizations that are essential to a manufacturing enterprise. Indirect costs are relatively easy to measure because they usually correspond to major accounting system categories. The challenge lies in figuring out how to allocate these costs to finished goods. If you are going to

Indirect costs pay for support systems

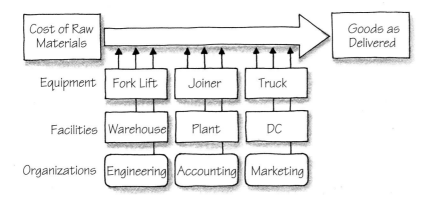

Figure 9.8
Indirect Costs

make money on your products, the selling price has to recover not only their direct costs but also their fair share of the indirect costs.

Activity-based costing allocates indirect costs

The most systematic approach to allocating indirect costs is **activity-based costing** (**ABC**). In this approach, indirect costs are allocated to products by way of activities and the resources they require. Translating slightly to match the terms I use in this book, the idea is that all costs are ultimately due to the use of resources by processes. If you can trace back all the resources required by a production process, therefore, you can determine its actual cost. Resources that are fully consumed by a process appear as direct costs, and the process absorbs their costs in full. Resources that are required for the process but that aren't consumed by it appear as indirect costs, and a pro rata portion of these indirect costs is charged to the process. In Figure 9.9, a printing process consumes ink, paper, and labor, so it pays the full freight for these resources. It requires the press but does not consume it, so the process only accrues a cost proportionate to the time it monopolizes the press. Similarly, the printing process makes use of a print shop and requires the office to manage the paperwork, so those resources also pass on a portion of their total cost.

Figure 9.9
Costing a Printing Process

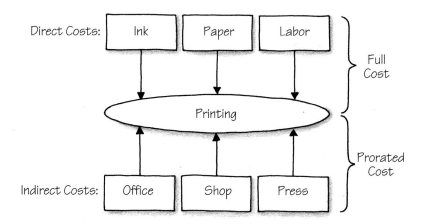

In effect, activity-based costing seeks to translate indirect costs into direct costs. This task becomes increasingly problematical as access to resources becomes more indirect. Working out the cost contribution of equipment may be difficult, but allocating the cost of facilities is even harder, and figuring out how to allocate the overhead of back-office staff functions can be a highly creative endeavor. Despite these obstacles, activity-based costing has proved quite useful in assessing the profitability of individual product lines, and it often yields surprising insights. So much of product cost is hidden by indirection that, without the kinds of analysis called for by activity-based costing, it's hard to know which products are actually generating a profit.

Indirect costs are translated into direct costs

A particularly important kind of indirect cost is opportunity cost, which is the loss of revenue that could have been realized from an alternative use of the funds invested in a process. If you invest $200,000 in a production run and don't recover that investment until six months later, you have lost the opportunity to use that money for some other area of the business. Opportunity cost is logically equivalent to paying interest on the money that's tied up in the process, but it uses a higher rate because opportunity cost is based on the return you could get from the best use of the money in your operations, and companies commonly put this figure in the range of 10% to 15%. At these rates, the production run in the example would incur an opportunity cost of up to $15,000, and you would have to recover that cost along with the original $200,000 before you could realize a profit.

Opportunity costs come from tying up cash

A third kind of cost is the expense attributable to errors in supply chain processes. These errors include incorrect quantities, invalid product substitutions, inaccurate prices, inventory stockouts, late shipments, deliveries to the wrong location, damaged goods, and missing items, to name just a few. The most obvious error cost is the expense of running corrective processes, such as handling returns,

Error costs are due to process failures

expediting replacements, reworking defects, and handling settle-
ments. Because these corrective processes are usually ad hoc and
time intensive, they are generally more expensive than the original
process, causing the total cost of a transaction to more than double.
Less obvious error costs include such long-term consequences as
the loss of future business from customers who change suppliers
due to process failures, as well as damage to the company's reputation if these failures become frequent. These kinds of costs are, of
course, much harder to measure.

**Ratios capture
relative costs**

Like all measures, costs can be expressed either as a simple number
or as a ratio to some other number, usually a measure of time or
work. As shown in Figure 9.6, cost measures based on time include
such periodic costs as annual interest and monthly rent, while costs
based on work include measures like transportation cost per mile,
cost per order processed, and cost per cubic foot of space. The
advantage of stating costs in absolute terms is that they all have
the same units and can be added and subtracted, as they are in
financial statements. Relative costs, on the other hand, are more
useful for comparing performance on the same process across organizations, or across time periods within the same organization,
because they factor out the effects of volume. Some typical cost
ratios used in supply chains are selling costs as a percent of sales,
transportation cost per mile, and cost per cubic foot of storage.

Measuring Efficiency

**Efficiency
reflects resource
utilization**

Costs, although critical to supply chain performance, fail to
capture an important aspect of supply chains: the efficiency with
which a chain utilizes its resources. If facilities, vehicles, equipment,
and other assets are not used at or near their full capacity, their
indirect costs must be spread across fewer products, raising the cost
of each. Similarly, supplies must be consumed as quickly as possible
to minimize holding costs, which are a major component of direct

cost in supply chains. The purpose of the third category of measures is to assess the efficiency with which a chain utilizes its assets (Figure 9.10).

Of the many assets required for supply chains, inventory usually receives the most attention because it inflicts such a heavy financial burden. Several measures are used to monitor inventory levels, including current and average counts, but the most widely used measure is the **inventory turnover ratio**, also called **inventory turns**. The turnover ratio for a product is the annual sales of that product divided by the average quantity on hand. For example, a product selling 60 units a year with an average inventory of 10 units has a turnover ratio of 60/10 = 6. Industries differ greatly in their inventory turns, but a turnover ratio of 6 is fairly typical. Within industries, turns can vary by a factor of 4 or 5, so if 6 is the average it would be common to see some companies turning their inventory only 2 or 3 times a year while others were turning theirs 10 or 12 times a year.

Inventory is usually measured using turns

Although the turnover ratio is the most common measure for conventional production, companies that have adopted JIT production usually find that the measure becomes unwieldy. For example, Lear Corporation, which builds automotive interiors for U.S. carmakers,

Days on hand is an equivalent measure

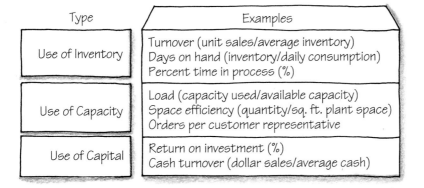

Figure 9.10
Measuring Efficiency

Type	Examples
Use of Inventory	Turnover (unit sales/average inventory) Days on hand (inventory/daily consumption) Percent time in process (%)
Use of Capacity	Load (capacity used/available capacity) Space efficiency (quantity/sq. ft. plant space) Orders per customer representative
Use of Capital	Return on investment (%) Cash turnover (dollar sales/average cash)

turns its inbound inventory between 120 and 214 times a year. When turns get this high, it's both easier and more precise to measure inventory in terms of **days on hand**, which is the number of days the inventory would last given normal consumption. In the case of Lear, the company is operating with one to two days of inventory on hand. Although the two measures provide the same information, the days-on-hand measure puts the information in a more meaningful form for companies that go through inventory as quickly as Lear does.

Time in process is a revealing measure

If you reduce the amount of inventory you keep on hand for a given product, individual items in that inventory move through the chain faster. This is what is meant by increasing the velocity of inventory, and it's an excellent idea even though, as noted earlier, velocity doesn't actually represent a new measure. One interesting approach to quantifying the notion of velocity is to measure the amount of time products spend being processed in some way, including transportation as well as transformation, then divide that by the total time the products spend in the chain. This ratio indicates the relative amount of time the product is actually moving through the chain rather than just sitting there taking up space.

Products spend most of their time waiting

A number of studies indicate that, despite attempts to accelerate inventory movement, products in the pipeline still spend the majority of their time sitting around. It's not uncommon to find time-in-process results in the range of 10% to 20%, and one study of the automotive industry in England found that steel parts for cars spend only about 3% of their time in process. A related study of the automotive assembly process found that, of the 40 days required to manufacture a car, only one and a half days—less than 4% of the total time—are actually spent assembling and testing the vehicle.

To most managers, these figures seem shockingly low. Where does all the time go? One way to answer this question is to plot the time in process against the passage of calendar time and look for the flat spots. Figure 9.11 illustrates this technique by showing the movement of a product through two links of a supply chain. As you can see, the product spends a large percentage of its time sitting in raw materials or finished goods inventories, and the bulk of the remaining time is spent in transit. Most of the active processing of this product takes place in two spurts, in the third and ninth weeks, while the product is actually on the floor of a production facility. But even in these periods the product spends most of its time waiting, getting no more than an hour's worth of attention in the course of a day. A detailed chart of those periods would reveal a miniature version of the pattern in Figure 9.11; the product would be seen to spend most of its time sitting in queues or moving between workstations, with relatively little time in process.

Charting time-in-process reveals the problem

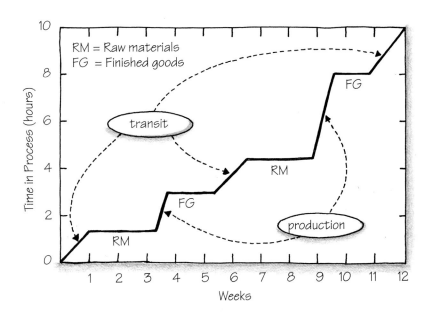

Figure 9.11
Mapping Time in Process

Capacity usually includes a reserve

The second type of efficiency measure shown in Figure 9.10 deals with the use of fixed capacity such as facilities and machinery. The most important measure is the load, which represents the percentage of capacity that is in use at any time. Since capacity represents a fixed cost, you'd like to keep the load high so you can amortize this cost over as many products as possible, reducing the cost per unit. But if you want to retain some flexibility to handle varying levels of demand, you can't run your chain at 100% capacity except for brief spurts. Finding the right balance point—whether it's 80% or 98%—depends in large part on the degree of variability you need to cope with in your chain.

Ratios are used to compare efficiency

Other measures of capacity utilization are expressed as the work performed by a unit of capacity, such as the quantity of product created per square foot of plant space, or the number of orders processed per customer representative. As with other measures, expressing the use of capacity in terms of ratios is helpful when making comparisons across facilities, or across time within a single facility. Unlike absolute measures of capacity, these ratios automatically adjust for any differences in the volume of work across facilities or over time.

Cash should be turned over frequently

The third kind of efficiency measure shown in Figure 9.10 is concerned with the use of capital, which is particularly important because it is the medium for acquiring other resources. The most common measure for assessing the efficient use of capital is the return on investment (ROI) ratio, obtained by dividing net profit by the capital required to produce that profit. An alternative measure is the cash turnover ratio, defined as annual sales divided by cash in use. The turnover ratio is directly analogous to inventory turns, and it measures the efficiency with which a company moves cash through the business. Another important measure for tracking the use of cash is the cash-to-cash time described earlier in this chapter.

Measuring Effectiveness

While efficiency is critical to profitability, it is of little value unless it is accompanied by another quality: effectiveness. Unlike efficiency, which is concerned with the economical use of resources, effectiveness reflects how well a process achieves its business objectives. The two qualities are often confused, but the distinction is simple: Efficiency measures how well you use what you have, and effectiveness measures how well you get what you want.

Effectiveness measures process success

Effectiveness is a concern for all the processes involved in replenishment, production, and fulfillment, but the fulfillment end of the business usually receives the most attention because it's the most visible to customers. To put the matter bluntly, it doesn't matter how good you are at purchasing and production if you can't deliver products to your customers in a timely, reliable manner. Given this focus, the most important measures of effectiveness are concerned with customer service levels (Figure 9.12).

Fulfillment receives the most attention

Customer service can be measured in a variety of different ways. In years past, customer service level (CSL) was usually defined in terms of proximity—the percent of customers within 400 miles of a warehouse, say—under the tacit assumption that holding inventory close to the customer was tantamount to good service. A more

Customer service has many measures

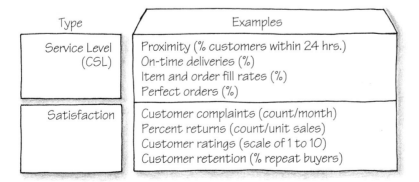

Type	Examples
Service Level (CSL)	Proximity (% customers within 24 hrs.) On-time deliveries (%) Item and order fill rates (%) Perfect orders (%)
Satisfaction	Customer complaints (count/month) Percent returns (count/unit sales) Customer ratings (scale of 1 to 10) Customer retention (% repeat buyers)

Figure 9.12
Measuring Effectiveness

common measure today is the **on-time delivery** rate, the percentage of orders that arrive at the customer site within a certain time limit. That time limit can either be a fixed period, such as next-day delivery, or it can be the promised date on the order; the choice depends on what it takes the keep the customer happy. Item and order fill rates, described in Chapter 8, are also common measures of CSL; in this case, the choice between the two is determined by whether customers require complete shipments or find partial shipments acceptable. Best-in-class companies generally keep both their on-time delivery rates and their item fill rates in the high 90s. For average to poor companies, both figures can drop down into the 70% to 80% range.

CSL can be a measure or a constraint

However it is defined, the CSL metric can be applied in two ways: Sometimes it is a measure, and other times it is a constraint. Some companies simply measure their CSL and use it to monitor their performance across products, regions, and time. Others specify a target CSL and use this target as a constraint on the supply chain, improving the chain until the target level is reached. For example, you might set a target CSL of having 97% of your orders ship complete by the promised date, then work on your chain until you hit that target. Of course, any measure can be used as both a target and an outcome, but this dual usage is particularly common in the case of CSL because it plays such a defining role in supply chain performance. Before you can interpret a CSL figure for a competitor, you need to understand not only how they define the measure, but also whether the reported value is a result or an objective.

The standard for service continues to rise

Maintaining good fill rates and delivering orders on time are vital to good customer service, but it's possible to hit target levels for these metrics and still have problems with fulfillment: Items may be shipped that weren't ordered, products may be incorrectly labeled or packaged, the order may be priced incorrectly, supporting documentation may be missing, goods may be damaged in transit, or the entire order may arrive precisely on time in perfect condition at the wrong location. To help control these kinds of errors, many firms are now adopting a **perfect-order** measure as their standard of customer service. This metric records the percentage of orders that ship complete, arrive on time, contain the correct goods, are free of damage, and have accurate paperwork. The perfect-order measure is a demanding standard, but it's the right measure for a company that aspires to excellent service.

The other way to measure effectiveness is to measure customer satisfaction, which can be monitored either passively or actively. Passive measures consist mostly of counting complaints, returns, requests for adjustments, and other indications of trouble. Active measures solicit feedback from customers who might otherwise remain silent. Passive measures are the most common, but active measures are the most effective. It doesn't take much; getting your customers to rate your service on a 10-point scale or even to mark a checkbox on delivery forms asking "Are you satisfied with this order?" can produce a good baseline for tracking satisfaction while requiring a minimum of effort on the customer's part. When more informative measures are needed, customer surveys and interviews are the appropriate instruments. Caterpillar, which is renowned for its customer service, sends out nearly 90,000 surveys a year—and pays very close attention to the results.

> **The ultimate measure is customer satisfaction**

The ultimate measure of effectiveness, of course, is customer retention. If you have a growing base of loyal customers that buy your products in ever-increasing quantities, you're clearly doing something right. If a lot of customers try you once and then move on, or if you start to see increased turnover in your customer base, it's time to call some former customers and ask them for honest feedback on why they took their business elsewhere. This can be hard to do, and many managers never get around to picking up the phone. But the information is absolutely vital to improving your

> **Customer retention is the ultimate measure**

supply chain, and just asking the question may be enough to convince a customer to give you another try.

Given all the different ways you can measure your supply chain, how should you go about choosing the best set of measures? There is only one good answer to that question. Measures are pointless unless they help you move toward specific objectives, so the correct way to choose your measures is to work backward from your objectives. But a discussion of objectives lies in the realm of planning, not operations, and planning is the focus of Part IV. After discussing the planning aspects of demand and supply in Chapters 10 and 11, I will return to the subject of performance in Chapter 12, and explain how to use objectives to unify planning, operations, and measurement into a consistent program for improving supply chain performance.

PART

IV

Planning

10

Forecasting Demand

Managing a supply chain requires planning the production and movement of goods many months into the future. That's a difficult process in itself (see Chapter 11), but the deeper problem is that you can't know in advance how many products customers will buy, so all of your plans are based on guesswork. The first step in planning a supply chain, therefore, is to use the techniques of demand forecasting to make your guesses as accurate as possible. For stable products with a long sales history, you can use standard models that identify trends and project them into the future, as described in the first section of the chapter. You can also group similar products together to improve the accuracy of your forecasts, using techniques described in the second section. But if you're trying to forecast sales of an innovative product with no sales history, you'll need a different set of techniques, as explained in the third section. Regardless of how you arrive at your forecasts, the best way to improve them is to work with your trading partners to develop integrated forecasts spanning every link in the chain. That topic is covered in the final section of the chapter.

Projecting Trends

For a product with a known sales history, the best guide to future sales is past performance. Using the techniques of **time-series analysis**, you can apply standard formulas to analyze a sales history, extract information about recurring patterns, and use those patterns to project sales into the future. To see how this works, look at the upper panel in Figure 10.1, which plots monthly sales figures for a particular product over the past three years. There are clearly patterns here: There is an overall increase in sales from one year to

Statistical models project future sales

Figure 10.1
A Time-Series
Analysis

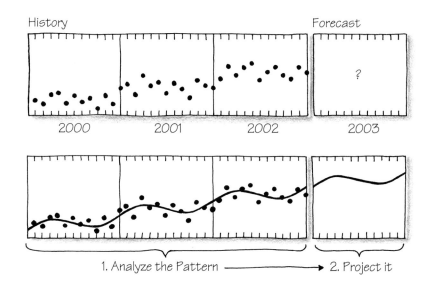

the next, but the sales appear to be relatively flat within each year, and the amount of variability from one month to the next appears to be roughly constant over time. The time-series analysis of these data shown in the lower panel confirms these impressions and reveals that demand actually varies in a systematic way over the course of each year, with higher sales in the spring. The analysis also makes a clear prediction about the sales you can expect in each month of the coming year.

There are four components of demand

Time-series techniques can be as simple or as sophisticated as you like. For a product with a flat sales curve, your forecast is just the past month's sales. For products that show a simple trend over time, it may be sufficient to use a **moving average** to predict the next month's sales. But if the product's history shows a more complex pattern of the sort seen in Figure 10.1, or if you want to forecast sales further into the future than the next month, then you need to use the full model. This model analyzes a sales history into four distinct components, as shown in Figure 10.2:

1. The **level component** is a single value that represents average sales. All other components are variations around this level.
2. The **trend component** is a straight line that reflects the overall tendency for sales to increase or decrease.
3. The **seasonal component** is a curve that captures the rise and fall in sales over the course of each year.
4. The **random component** represents all other variation in demand, regardless of its cause, and has no systematic pattern over time.

The first three components are called the **systematic components** of demand because they behave consistently over time and can be predicted. Each of these components is represented by a parameter in the time-series model. When you run a time-series analysis, the model first estimates these parameters by adjusting them to fit the historical sales data as closely as possible, then uses its estimates to project future sales.

Forecasting predicts systematic components

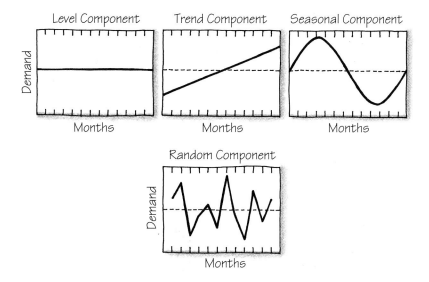

Figure 10.2
Components of Demand

Confidence intervals show expected variation

By definition, the random component can't be predicted, but the model does estimate the magnitude of that component and project it forward as well, allowing you to anticipate the range of demand you are likely to encounter. Most forecasting tools illustrate this range visually by drawing **confidence intervals** on the forecast plot, as shown in Figure 10.3. In the example, the likelihood of actual demand being within the range indicated by the two bars is 90%, with only a 10% probability that it will fall either above the top bar or below the bottom bar. So you can be pretty confident that actual demand will fall within the interval shown.

Forecasting has a limited range

The most distant period for which you generate a forecast is called the **forecast horizon**. Given the way the time-series model works, you can set the forecast horizon as far in the future as you like. However, the accuracy of the forecast falls off dramatically as you look further out, as you can see from Figure 10.3. For the coming month, the expected demand is 130 units, and will most likely fall

Figure 10.3
A Forecast with Confidence Intervals

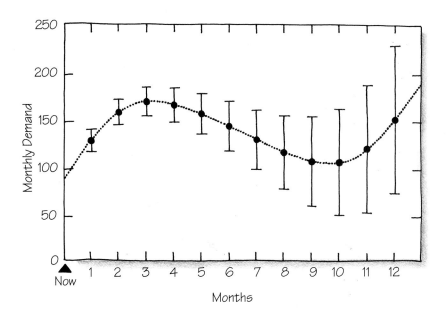

between 120 and 140. By contrast, the confidence interval out at the horizon runs from 75 to 230 units, a range of more than 3:1. In practice, it rarely makes sense to set the forecast horizon more than 12 to 18 months in the future.

You can increase the accuracy of your forecasts substantially by updating them continuously based on current sales, a technique known as **dynamic forecasting**. In years past, when forecasting was done by hand, the more common practice was **static forecasting**, in which a forecast was generated and then used as is through the forecast horizon. Now that forecasting is fully automated, most companies use dynamic forecasting. To see the advantage of this approach, imagine the forecast in Figure 10.3 scrolling to the left each month, with the confidence interval for each month shrinking dramatically as the month gets closer to the present.

Dynamic forecasting constantly updates values

The business advantage of forecasting is that it eliminates predictable variability from your future demand stream, allowing you to plan production much more precisely. To see this advantage in action, consider two firms trying to predict the same flow of demand over the course of the coming year (Figure 10.4). The demand exhibits a great deal of variability, as evidenced by the spread of its distribution, but most of that variability is due to a pattern of increasing sales combined with seasonality, as shown in Figure 10.3. Company A doesn't use forecasting, so it has to be prepared to handle the full range of possible demand levels across the entire year. This is an expensive proposition, requiring both increased safety stock and reserve production capacity. Company B uses forecasting to eliminate the known sources of variability, placing narrow constraints around the actual demand it will have to cope with in any given month. This allows Company B to get by with very little safety stock and no reserve capacity, giving it a substantial financial advantage over Company A.

Forecasting confers a competitive advantage

Figure 10.4
Removing
Uncertainty from
Variability

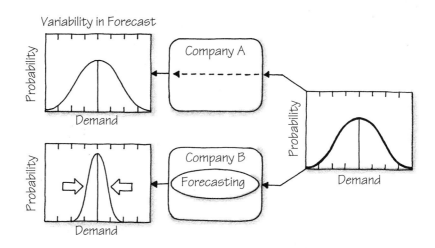

Aggregating Demand

**Companies
rarely forecast
individual
products**

The preceding section explains how to forecast demand for a
single product, but in practice you would generate forecasts for
individual products only in special situations—for example, when
you are deciding whether to introduce a new product or enter a
new market. Setting those situations aside, the cost of generating
separate forecasts for thousands of different products would be pro-
hibitive, and the standard procedure is to group similar products
together when making forecasts. This technique—called **aggregation**—might seem like it would degrade the quality of the forecasts
because it would ignore differences among the individual products.
In fact, just the opposite is true: These **aggregate forecasts**, as they
are called, are actually more reliable because they are based on
larger samples of customer behavior.

**Forecasts
improve with
larger samples**

Why does sample size make a difference? Whenever you use a
small number of samples to generate predictions about a larger
population, you run the risk of sampling error—that is, of picking a
sample that doesn't happen to represent the population as a whole.
One of the basic laws of statistics is that the likelihood of sampling

error goes down as the sample size goes up. To cite a familiar example, a sample of 10,000 voters provides a far more reliable forecast of an election result than a sample consisting of only 10 voters. The same reasoning holds for forecasting demand. If you sell 200,000 products a year from a catalog of 10,000 SKUs, each product has just 20 sales a year on average, and that's not enough to support a reliable forecast. But if you group those SKUs into 100 categories, then each category will have 2,000 sales on average, and that gives you enough data to make solid forecasts.

In addition to aggregating demand across products, forecasts also aggregate demand across customer type, geographical region, and other factors. Also, the fact that forecasts are based on the number of sales within each forecasting period means that sales histories are automatically aggregated across time. Seen in this light, the choice of forecasting period takes on new importance. When a forecast is based on large quantities of data, it is possible to get reliable forecasts down to the level of weeks or even days. Forecasts with sparse data, on the other hand, should use months or even quarters as their time period. There are standard formulas for determining the most appropriate period to use with any given sample size.

Aggregation is essential for reliability

One of the most important considerations for aggregating products into groups is the overall level of sales. It has long been recognized that in most companies, a handful of products account for the majority of sales. This phenomenon is known informally as the "80:20 rule," which states that 80% of sales come from 20% of the products. A more formal technique, called **Pareto Analysis**, uses three categories, with a breakdown of 80% A products, 15% B, and 5% C. In addition to reflecting the classic 80:20 rule, Pareto Analysis also expresses the observation that half the products of a company usually account for 95% of the company's sales (Figure 10.5). There's no particular reason why the percentages should come out this way, and the sales of your products could certainly follow a

Use Pareto Analysis to help group products

Figure 10.5
Pareto Analysis of
Demand

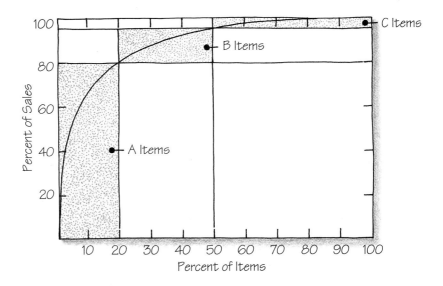

different curve. But Pareto Analysis produces the results shown in
Figure 10.5 with remarkable consistency across companies in many
different industries, so you shouldn't assume that your company is
an exception until you do the analysis on your own sales.

**Forecast
fast-moving
products
separately**

Given that a small number of products account for the majority of
your revenues, you should invest much more effort in forecasting
products in the A category, either by forecasting them individually
or by aggregating them into small groups with similar A products.
Demand for these products is critical to the success of your company, and having sufficient data at the item level is rarely a problem
with these products because their sales numbers are so high. Conversely, you should aggregate the 50% of the products that account
for only 5% of sales into large groups to reflect their relatively small
contribution to sales and their correspondingly low data density.

**Combine
products with
similar sales
patterns**

When combining products for aggregate forecasts, be careful not
to mix products with different sales patterns, as reflected in their
time-series components. For example, don't pool seasonal products
with nonseasonal products because that would underestimate the

effects of season on the seasonal goods, and it would forecast seasonal patterns for products that do not exhibit them. By the same token, you shouldn't combine seasonal products with different peaks; grouping bathing suits and parkas in the same aggregate forecast could cause both products to appear as constant, year-round sellers, missing the seasonal component altogether.

Many manufacturers use the techniques of group technology, in which similar kinds of products are made with the same core components and the same production operations. Often, the differences among products within a group aren't introduced until late in the production process, perhaps in final assembly. For such companies, aligning forecasting groups with production groups is quite beneficial because the aggregate forecasts automatically determine the material requirements for all shared components. Given that differentiation occurs relatively late, it may also be possible to put off buying the differentiating components until just before production is completed, when forecasts for individual product types are more accurate. This technique, known as postponement, is described in Chapter 15.

Groups may also be based on production

Aggregation across customers is usually done either by region or by type. Aggregating demand by region has the advantage that it tends to group customers that exhibit the same seasonality, style, and fashion preferences, as these variations usually have a strong regional component. In addition, it provides a head start on distribution planning because it groups expected demand according to its destination. The alternative to using customer region is to use customer segments defined by such characteristics as demand volume, required customer service level, order frequency, and other buying habits. This is another good place to apply Pareto Analysis, which often reveals that 80% of total sales come from just 20% of the customer base, and that half of the customer base accounts for only 5% of sales. As with products, you should try forecasting your sales

Group customers by region or type

to customers in the A group individually, and you can safely lump all of the customers in the C group together without sacrificing much accuracy.

Use percentages to make item forecasts

One concern you might have about aggregate forecasts is that they seem to throw away information about individual products, information that may be important to you. This really isn't the case, though—it just takes an extra step to get that information back. If you know that a product normally accounts for 12% of the sales of a group in an aggregate forecast, then you just multiply that forecast by 12% to get back the item forecast. Figure 10.6 illustrates this process for the first three items in an aggregate forecast spanning four quarters; as the total sales go up, forecasts for the individual products also rise in keeping with their percent of sales. At first glance, it may seem like this process is attempting to get back a level of precision that was given up when moving to an aggregate forecast. But there is no sleight of hand here. If the aggregation is done properly, all the item forecasts share the same demand pattern as a group, differing only in their overall levels. The percentages provide just the right information to pull out these levels.

Figure 10.6
Breaking Out Item Forecasts

	Item	Percent	Q1	Q2	Q3	Q4
Aggregate	All	100%	473	491	503	519
Breakout	001	17%	80	84	86	52
	002	10%	47	49	50	52
	003	8%	38	39	40	42
	...	...	...	...	...	...

Quarterly Forecast

Analyzing the Future

The techniques of time-series analysis described so far are powerful, but they aren't the answer to every forecasting problem. New products, which have no sales history, obviously require a different approach. If a product is similar to existing products, it may be possible to project its sales by taking a percentage of an existing aggregate forecast. If not, alternative techniques may be necessary to predict its sales. Similarly, it may be necessary to supplement time-series analysis with other techniques for products that are subject to changing market forces, such as increasing customer expectations or the emergence of new competitors.

Time-series analysis doesn't fit every product

In situations where time-series analysis isn't enough, forecasting requires the use of old-fashioned, cause-and-effect reasoning. This reasoning generates numbers, and it may involve a formula or two, but—unlike time-series analysis—it is much more art than science, and its methods are not nearly as well established. Accordingly, the techniques described in this section are known as **subjective** or **judgmental techniques**.

Forecasts often require cause-effect analysis

The general approach for subjective techniques is to consider all the business influences that might affect future sales, estimate their individual effects, and then combine them to form a prediction. Most of these influences are extrinsic factors, as defined in Chapter 4, because they lie outside your immediate control. As Figure 10.7 illustrates, the extrinsic factors include the state of the economy, the characteristics of the market for the product being forecast, and the needs and wants of the customers who will buy the product. Intrinsic factors, such as your own decisions about pricing and promotions, also play a role.

Subjective techniques analyze extrinsic factors

The major effect of general economic factors is to act as a multiplier on sales: A robust, expanding economy generally increases

Figure 10.7
Overview of
Forecasting
Factors

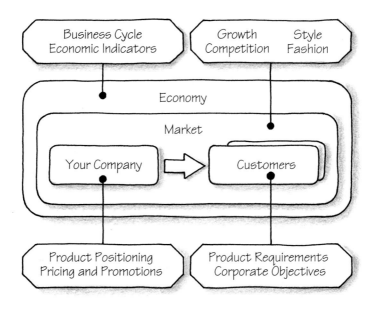

Economic factors are readily incorporated

sales, and a weakening economy reduces sales. Because the effect of the economy on sales is simple to model, it is relatively easy to incorporate into predictions. Usually, adjustments are made to forecast sales based on the current values of one or more economic indicators.

Market factors are harder to model

Market factors are harder to incorporate because they interact in complex ways. These factors include changes in the size of the market, the actions of competitors, and the effects of changing styles and fashions. The best way to predict changes in market size and share is to apply trend analysis techniques from statistics and use the results to adjust sales forecasts. Actions of competitors are nearly impossible to predict, so the best a company can do in this regard is to run a series of "what if" scenarios to determine how vulnerable its sales are to a variety of competitive maneuvers. Predicting the effects of style and fashion often comes down to sticking a wet finger in the air.

The most critical set of extrinsic factors shown in Figure 10.7 are the requirements and objectives of the target customers for a product. For established product categories, customers usually know what they want and can articulate their requirements if asked. For new or emerging products, where rapid innovation is occurring, customers may not have formulated their requirements in any systematic way. In this situation, it is usually better to focus on the customers' objectives to see which potential products would be most attractive to them. In either case, there is no substitute for asking the customer, using a combination of surveys, focus groups, and interviews.

The customer ultimately drives demand

The only intrinsic factors shown in Figure 10.7 are the actions of your own company with regard to the positioning, pricing, and promotion of your product. Because there are so few intrinsic factors compared to extrinsic factors, you need to use them to full advantage to influence demand. Exactly how you use them depends on your supply chain strategy. For example, if you seek to be the price leader in your industry, then your price has to be low enough to induce customers to bring their business to you. The use of intrinsic factors to influence demand is a major issue in supply chain design, and it is explored in detail in Chapter 13.

Company actions influence demand directly

The biggest challenge in demand forecasting is predicting the sales of a product that breaks new ground. As shown in Figure 10.8, innovative products go through a lifecycle that is characterized by slow sales as customers decide whether to adopt the product, then a period of rapid growth as the product catches on, followed by stable or declining sales after the product has established itself in the market. The difficulties in forecasting innovative products lie in predicting how soon a product will enter its growth phase, how quickly sales will take off, and how high they will eventually go. Forecasting these numbers is a high-stakes game. If you overestimate how

Innovative products are hardest to forecast

Figure 10.8
Lifecycle of
Innovative
Products

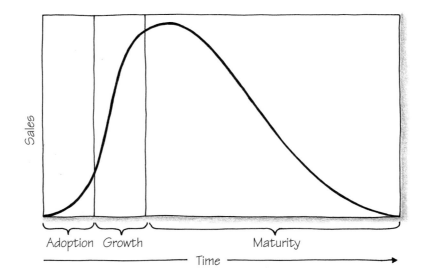

well a product will be received, you'll be stuck with excess production capacity and unsold inventories. Underestimate it and you'll be faced with angry customers, expensive measures to accelerate production, and opportunities for competitors to gain market share.

New products often have tipping points

One reason that predicting the sales of innovative products is so difficult is that the behavior of sales levels over time can be extremely complex. In Chapter 4 I introduced the kinds of relations that can be found in systems in terms of five "rogues," beginning with the well-mannered linear relation and ending with the nastiest rogue of all, the multi-valued relation (Figure 4.4, Panel E). Well, this is one place where that particular rogue is known to make an appearance, and it comes in the form of a phenomenon called the **tipping point**. The tipping point was originally discovered in the study of epidemics of contagious diseases, but it has now been shown to apply to many other kinds of "contagious" systems as well, including crime levels in big cities, trends in the stock market, and consumer buying patterns.

Tipping point behavior comes about through the interaction of people who communicate some kind of "germ" to each other, either the literal germ of a disease or the germ of an idea about crime, the economy, or a desirable product. Once a certain threshold of "infected" people is reached—the tipping point—the likelihood of infection rises precipitously and triggers an epidemic. Figure 10.9 illustrates how this works by plotting the sales of a new kind of product—a Web watch, say—against the number of people currently wearing the watch. Sales start out on the lower curve and increase gradually as more and more people start wearing the watch, just as you'd expect. But once a certain number of people are wearing the watch, the likelihood of others being "infected" with the desire to own this watch takes a sudden leap, and sales shift over to an entirely different growth curve. Stranger still, the sales stay on the upper curve even as the watch becomes passé, and they don't fall back to the lower curve again until the watch has almost disappeared from wrists.

Tipping points cause demand "epidemics"

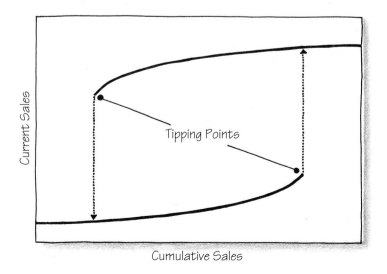

Figure 10.9
The Tipping Point

Be prepared for sudden leaps in sales

Tipping point behavior—for diseases as well as ideas—is now well understood and can be reproduced using a simple mathematical model of communication. What is not well understood is how to predict whether a particular outbreak of an infectious idea or disease will reach the tipping point and trigger an epidemic. The important thing to understand about tipping points, therefore, is simply that they exist, and that they can lead to totally unexpected leaps in demand, as well as to sudden failures of demand even after long runs of popularity. Tipping point behavior is most likely with highly innovative products, and it's seen most often when the decision to buy the product is heavily influenced by fashion—the classic recipe for fads. If you sell this type of product, don't be surprised if sales suddenly explode on you. And if they do, expect them to implode just as suddenly after a modest but steady decline in sales.

Integrating Forecasts

Reliability is higher with multiple forecasts

A good way to improve the reliability of demand forecasts is to have multiple analysts generate forecasts independently and then combine their results. The problem here is figuring out how to integrate the forecasts in a meaningful way. One solution is simply to average them all together, but this can be risky. Just as aggregating across seasonal products with different peaks can cancel out the effects of seasonality, averaging independent forecasts can mask patterns that are evident in each forecast but that don't align precisely across forecasters. The better approach is to try to understand the reasoning behind each forecast and somehow combine the reasoning rather than just the numbers.

The Delphi technique combines forecasts

The obvious solution—just get the forecasters together in a room and let them hash it out—doesn't always work well. Experience indicates that these discussions quickly become a contest of wills, and the "integrated" forecast usually turns out to match the forecast of the most assertive analyst. A better approach is to use the **Delphi technique**, in which analysts reach a consensus without ever meeting as a group. Instead, the analysts submit their forecasts and their supporting rationales in writing to a neutral party, who creates a summary comparison of the forecasts without revealing their authors. Analysts then modify their forecasts as they think appropriate given the views of their anonymous colleagues, and the process repeats until consensus is achieved. Although time consuming, research shows that this technique produces substantially more objective and reliable forecasts.

Combining forecasts to gain consensus is difficult within a single department, but the problem becomes harder still when forecasts are generated by different departments. Many departments have a stake in predicting demand, including marketing, sales, production, distribution, finance, and personnel. Unfortunately, these groups have different perspectives on demand, use different techniques for predicting it, and have different incentives for how high they'd like the forecasts to be. The Delphi technique can work here as well, but few companies make the effort to unify their forecasts. Instead, they just let each department forecast independently and plan accordingly, an almost certain formula for departmental discord and corporate confusion.

Departments usually forecast independently

If combining forecasts across departments is too difficult for most companies, it should come as no surprise that fewer still take the next step and integrate forecasts with those of other companies in the supply chain. Yet the failure to do so is one of the most pernicious problems in supply chain management because it impairs both the efficiency and the effectiveness of the entire chain. Here's why: When each of the suppliers in a chain forecasts the needs of its immediate customers, every company in the chain winds up forecasting someone else's demand, as shown in Figure 10.10. This leads to a lot of wasted energy because each company is forecasting a different version of the same underlying demand. Worse,

Companies also forecast independently

Figure 10.10
Link-by-Link
Forecasting

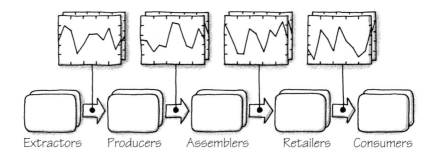

Extractors   Producers   Assemblers   Retailers   Consumers

link-by-link forecasts can introduce errors that cascade and amplify up the chain.

Only consumer demand should be forecast

A bit of reflection on where demand ultimately comes from suggests a much better approach. When a supply chain is viewed as a whole, there is only one true source of demand: the consumers of final products. All other demand—for raw materials, subassemblies, intermediate products, and the like—ultimately derives from consumer purchases. To reflect this distinction, consumer demand is known as **independent demand**. All of the purchases made by companies upstream of consumers depend in some way on consumers' choices, so these purchases are called **dependent demand**. The modern view of forecasting is that only the independent demand should be forecast, and that all other demand should be derived from these forecasts.

The best approach is to share forecasts

Having each company focus its forecasting efforts on independent demand does not, in itself, eliminate redundant forecasting. Case in point: It's common for manufacturers and retailers to each make their own forecasts of consumer demand, and both types of companies justify the practice by claiming that they have a better understanding of consumer buying habits. But the most powerful approach is for supply chain partners to collaborate to build a shared forecast, combining their differing perspectives on consumer behavior in order to obtain the most reliable predictions of future sales

(Figure 10.11). Here again, formal processes such as the Delphi technique may be required to make sure that shared forecasts truly reflect the predictions of all the participating companies.

Collaborative forecasting neatly addresses the problems described at the beginning of this section. First, duplication of effort is eliminated, often reducing the overall forecasting effort by 80% or more. Second, there is no cascade of errors up the chain to distort demand. The most dramatic benefit, however, is the improvement of forecasting accuracy that results from sharing knowledge about consumer behavior. There are sales patterns that manufacturers can see that distributors and retailers cannot, but there are other aspects of consumer behavior that can only be observed close up. When supply chain partners combine their unique perspectives to improve their understanding of independent demand, they can do a much better job of anticipating the needs of the consumers who keep the chain in business.

Collaborative forecasting improves predictions

There are many obstacles to collaborative forecasting. Sales forecasts are usually considered highly confidential, and sharing this data requires a degree of trust and openness that simply isn't compatible with the adversarial relationship that has long characterized

The technique requires trust and openness

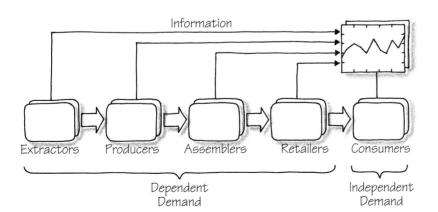

Figure 10.11
Joint Forecasting

customers and suppliers. But the competitive advantages of integrating the supply chain are driving deep changes, and the long-standing barriers to cooperation are crumbling in the wake of JIT, quick response, continuous replenishment, and other industry programs (see Chapter 3). The time for collaborative forecasting has arrived, and most companies seem ready to accept it.

Forecasting systems provide powerful tools for anticipating the demand that is about to be placed on your supply chain, but using these tools effectively requires that you know when to apply them. Time series analysis produces the most precise predictions, but all it does is look for patterns in the sales history and project those patterns into the future. For mature products in stable markets, that may be all you need. For other products, you need to look beyond statistical patterns and examine cause-and-effect relationships to predict sales. It takes a lot of work to generate good forecasts, but the ability to tune your supply plan to match future sales offers an excellent return on your investment in the process. The advantages can be amplified if you work with your trading partners and pool your insights to gain a better understanding of the ultimate source of demand, the buying habits of the consumers at the end of your chain.

11

Scheduling Supply

Once you have a demand forecast in hand, you need to figure out the most cost-effective way to satisfy the expected
demand. This chapter explains how you can use ERP, APS,
and simulation systems to plan the production and movement of goods across your chain. Although most companies
tend to rely on just one kind of system, the most effective
approach is to combine the three, using each system to solve
the problems it handles best. As with other areas of supply
chains, the biggest challenge is merging the plans of individual companies in order to achieve an integrated solution
for the chain as a whole.

Planning with ERP

Supply chain planning starts with a conceptual model of what
has to be done, determines the time required by each component
process, and then schedules each process in a way that completes
the sequence at the right time. At the broadest level, meeting
demand consists of three core processes: procuring the necessary
materials, producing the goods, and distributing them to customers
(Figure 11.1). To keep the discussion clear, I treat these processes as
strictly sequential, so that each process is triggered by the completion of the preceding process. This is a correct representation of
how scheduling works, but in practice there could be a fair degree
of overlap among these top-level processes. For example, production might begin as soon as materials start to arrive, even though
the procurement process is still under way. Similarly, the output of
production would normally be placed in the distribution channel
as it came off the line rather than waiting until the entire run
was complete.

*Scheduling
uses a simple
conceptual
model*

Figure 11.1
Scheduling the
Core Processes

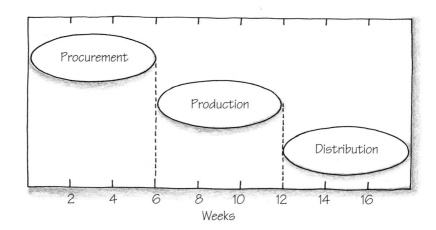

Planning
depends on the
software used

The actual techniques used and the goals pursued differ substantially depending on the software used to perform the scheduling. The first three sections of this chapter explain how production plans are constructed using ERP, APS, and simulation-based planning systems, in that order. As you read through these sections, bear in mind that these are complementary systems, not alternative solutions as they are often portrayed. Each has strengths and limitations, and the best practice is to use two or more systems in combination to perfect your plans.

There are
two main
approaches to
scheduling

There are two broad approaches to scheduling, called forward scheduling and back scheduling. **Forward scheduling** begins with a start date and adds processes in the order they will be executed, scheduling each process to start as the preceding process completes (Figure 11.2, left panel). This kind of scheduling is most appropriate when the start date is known and the completion date has to be determined from the results of the scheduling effort. When a company has a required completion date and needs to figure the necessary start date, the back-scheduling approach is the more natural choice. **Back scheduling** aligns the completion of the last process with the target completion date, then adds processes in reverse order of their execution (Figure 11.2, right panel).

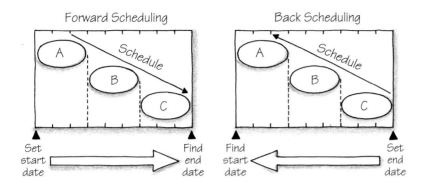

Figure 11.2
Forward and Back
Scheduling

Enterprise resource planning (ERP) systems, the operational foundation of contemporary manufacturing (see Chapter 6), are based on the back-scheduling approach. As shown in Figure 11.3, the first step of an ERP run is to feed a demand forecast into the DRP (distribution requirements planning) module, which works backward from the required delivery dates to figure out when finished goods need to be shipped. DRP passes the required shipping dates to the MPS (master production scheduling) module, which determines

**ERP systems
rely on back
scheduling**

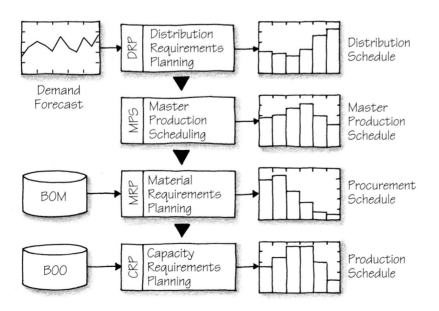

Figure 11.3
The ERP
Scheduling
Process

when production needs to start on each batch of products in order to be ready for shipment. MPS then passes these dates to the MRP (material requirements planning) module, which determines when the required raw materials have to be ordered. The last module in the chain, the CRP (capacity requirements planning) module, determines when the necessary labor and equipment will have to be available to perform the work.

ERP uses bills of materials and operations

The operation of these modules is complicated by the fact that each product in the demand forecast is normally composed of multiple raw materials. Moreover, the process of assembling these materials is usually not a single operation, but rather a sequence of operations in which the structure of the end product is built up out of subassemblies or intermediate mixtures. In order to handle these complications, products are described in terms of two documents, which are stored in electronic form by the ERP system and accessed by the planning modules as required. The **bill of materials** (**BOM**) is a nested list of all the raw materials that go into the product, structured according to the subassemblies of the product. Similarly, the **bill of operations** (**BOO**) uses its own nested structure to describe the sequence of operations necessary to create each component of the product. As shown in Figure 11.3, the MRP module uses the BOM to determine the timing and quantities of materials required for production, and the CRP module uses the BOO to determine the labor and equipment necessary to perform the work.

Planning may require several passes

The first two modules in the planning sequence, DRP and MPS, are entirely driven by requirements. That is, these modules work backward from the necessary completion dates to calculate when purchasing and production should begin without regard for the feasibility of those starting dates. Once the plan moves to the MRP and CRP modules, however, purchasing and production constraints enter the picture, and these modules may discover that the necessary resources can't be in place at the required time. If this happens, human planners examine the problem and look for ways to solve it. For example, they may be able to expedite some purchasing, add a shift at one or more plants, or outsource some of the production. If the planners are unable to relieve the constraints that keep the plan from working, they typically relax the original requirements by pushing out some due dates and then run the system again.

This description just scratches the surface of contemporary ERP systems. The amount of work performed by these systems in scheduling the activities of a manufacturing company is staggering in both its volume and complexity, and it's safe to say that much of modern manufacturing would be impossible without the aid of these powerhouse systems. There are, however, some limitations of ERP that affect the quality of its plans. In particular, the fact that ERP relies entirely on back scheduling means that the system schedules every activity at the latest possible time. Given the high costs of holding finished goods, that's often the best way to plan production. But there may be times when earlier production would be less costly, and an ERP system would miss those opportunities because it doesn't evaluate early production as an option.

ERP uses a single planning strategy

Similarly, ERP systems assume that you already know what you want to produce. This is certainly a reasonable assumption, but it means that ERP systems aren't much help when it comes to making decisions about how to prioritize production when demand exceeds supply, how to find the most cost-effective mix of products for each plant given local demand and selling prices, and other questions of this nature. Fortunately, the newer generation of APS systems can do these things and more, making them an excellent complement to ERP's powerful scheduling abilities.

ERP doesn't evaluate production alternatives

Optimizing with APS

APS uses hierarchical planning

Advanced planning and scheduling (APS) systems are similar to ERP systems in that they have separate modules for planning procurement, production, and distribution, but the way those modules interact to produce a master schedule is different. Rather than taking a demand forecast as an input, most APS packages include a demand planning module to generate that forecast for you (Figure 11.4). The demand planning module passes its forecast to a master planning module, which calls on the services of three subordinate modules to work up the best plans for purchasing, production, and distribution.

Iterative planning finds the best solution

All three of these specialized planners work on the problem concurrently, feeding tentative plans back to the master planner as those plans take shape. The master planner combines that feedback to reduce the set of possible plans, then requests a revised set of plans from its subordinates. This iterative process continues until the master planner identifies the most cost-effective plan for meeting expected demand. Once the human planners approve this master

Figure 11.4
The APS Planning Process

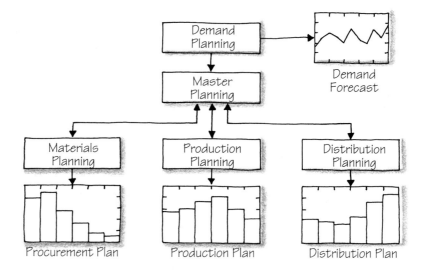

plan, the modules responsible for materials, production, and distribution pass their plans on to another set of modules (shown in Figure 6.3) that produce detailed schedules for purchasing, production, and distribution operations.

A powerful feature of the APS planning model is that changes can propagate in both directions. As with ERP, a change to the master plan can cascade down to lower-level modules, causing them to alter their plans. But unlike ERP, changes in the lower-level plans are communicated upward to the master plan, causing it to modify its own plan. This bidirectional flow can save a great deal of effort and guesswork. For example, it allows a purchasing manager to modify the purchasing plan directly and propagate the effects upward, which is much more efficient than having the master planner run the system repeatedly in order to produce the desired change from the top down. This capability also means that APS systems can be used to explore what-if scenarios to discover the potential effects of material shortages, strikes, and other disruptions to planned operations.

Changes can flow in both directions

The reason APS systems are able to find the most cost-effective production plan is that they use mathematical models of the sort described in Chapter 5 to calculate optimal solutions. Because these models are able to handle thousands of parameters, APS systems can take into account a huge number of constraints on production, including the cost and availability of materials, machinery, labor, and other key resources. For example, you could require that production be limited to certain plants, that 97% of customer orders be delivered on time, and that no overtime be used, then have the model find the plan that satisfies those constraints at the lowest possible cost. APS systems also use rules to determine preferences among plants when more than one can handle a production run, apply flexible criteria when choosing among transportation modes and carriers, and make countless other decisions based on business rules provided by human planners.

APS optimizes plans against objectives

APS takes planning beyond scheduling

Another attractive feature of APS systems is that they respond intelligently to situations in which there aren't enough materials, production capacity, or distribution options to handle the required load. APS allows you to automatically prioritize orders based on their size, their profitability, the importance of the customer, penalties for late delivery, and similar considerations. APS can also find the most profitable mix of products for any given plant, decide when to outsource production and distribution, and make other decisions that go beyond the basic scheduling of operations.

APS is normally coupled with ERP

Gaining the advantages of APS doesn't require giving up your existing ERP system. As described in Chapter 6, the two systems are routinely used in combination with each other, particularly in planning the operations of multiple plants within the same supply chain. To get the best of both worlds, use APS to work out the optimal solution for the portion of the supply chain you are planning, then pass that high-level plan to the ERP systems running in each plant. That technique lets the APS system use business logic to choose the best dates for the ERP runs, leaving the ERP systems to flesh out local plans based on these dates. Once the local ERP systems have generated their plans, the operational modules of the ERP system support the daily activities of each plant.

Coupling requires data linkages

In order to use APS in combination with ERP, you need to set up data linkages so that the systems can interact with each other (Figure 11.5). First, the material and production planning modules of the APS system must have access to the bills of materials and operations maintained by the ERP systems in order to identify all the component materials and tasks. Second, the master planning module on the APS side needs a way to pass dates to the MPS modules to give them targets for their local planning. Third, the order management modules of the ERP systems should to be able to access the ATP (available-to-promise) services of the APS system in order to uses its advanced ATP capabilities.

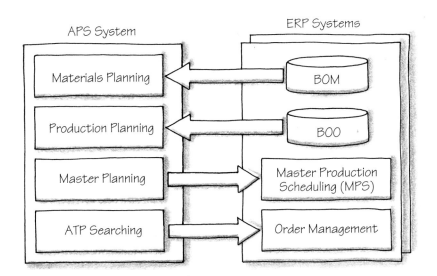

Figure 11.5
Linking APS to ERP

In years past, setting up these data linkages could be a major undertaking because of the closed nature of the systems. However, recent efforts to open up these systems and make their data available in standard formats have made integration substantially easier. The current trend of incorporating APS functionality into standard ERP packages should eventually make the linkages automatic.

These linkages are getting easier

Validating with Simulators

Although APS systems use more sophisticated models of the supply chain than ERP systems do, the APS models are still subject to some important restrictions. The ability of APS to generate optimized solutions is due primarily to the use of linear programming and related mathematical techniques. As described in Chapter 5, linear programming requires that all the relations in the model be linear in form—the best-behaved "rogue" in Panel A of the rogues gallery of relations (see Figure 4.4). In the extension of linear programming known as mixed-integer programming, this assumption is relaxed to allow some relations to take on the stepwise pattern shown in Panel D of Figure 4.4, but the other kinds of relations aren't permitted.

APS models have important restrictions

Linear approximations often work well

This restriction doesn't mean that you can't trust the calculations made by APS systems; it just means that you need to bear the limitations in mind when you look at the results. What the APS system actually does is approximate curved relations using the closest linear functions. If the curve is reasonably close to a straight line over the range of values used in a planning session, a linear approximation will have very little impact on the results. For relations that are highly nonlinear, it may be possible to break a relation down into simpler components (see Figure 8.3 for an example of how this works), or to approximate it by combining a sequence of linear segments. So the presence of nonlinear relations in a supply chain isn't a show stopper; it just means that the modelers have to be aware of these relations and handle them appropriately.

APS assumes parameters are fixed and known

Another assumption underlying linear programming and its kin is that all parameter values are fixed and known with certainty. This is hardly a realistic assumption for supply chains, which are characterized by uncertainty at every stage. Here again, however, violations of this assumption don't necessarily invalidate the results of an optimizer run; they just require caution in interpreting the output. If you have reason to believe that one or more of your key parameters is changing over time, or that there is enough random variation to make the results unreliable, you can compensate for this by making multiple runs using different values to determine the effects of variability in each parameter. This can be a slow process because it requires running the model many times, but it does provide a way of protecting against violations of the constancy assumption.

Simulations are free of these restrictions

In short, although the models used by APS are superior to those of ERP, they are still limited in important ways. Fortunately, simulation models are entirely free of these restrictions; they can represent even the most complex, nonlinear relations, and they can accommodate any degree or type of variability in parameter values.

For example, a simulator can explore the effects of allowing price, demand, supply, and other key parameters to change over time, including random variations in these parameters from one moment to the next. Because simulators incorporate variability by running a series of Monte Carlo trials, they produce distributions of expected values for each output rather than just a single number. In effect, all the known sources of variability are taken into account by the model, and the results can be trusted to hold across all possible variations.

The reason distributions are so important is that variability in supply chains translates directly into risk, and one of the goals of planning is to reduce risk. To see how a simulator can help manage risk, suppose your company is bidding on a multimillion-dollar production run of a custom product. Your APS system works out the optimal production plan, and your ERP system produces a detailed schedule that says the run can be completed in 100 days. But neither of these systems has taken variability into account, so you run a simulation of the production process to check the effects of variability. The result is the distribution of completion dates shown in Figure 11.6. This distribution reveals that, while the completion date produced by the ERP system is the single most likely outcome, your company actually has only a 50–50 chance of completing the run by that date. This result not only tells you that you should pad the date to reduce the risk of missing your deadline, it also tells you exactly how much padding you need. If you want a 97% chance of completing the job on time, for example, you should promise completion in 140 days rather than 100. Then see if you can negotiate a bonus for early completion.

Simulations help manage risk

In addition to helping you manage risk, simulations offer other important benefits. For one thing, simulation models generally stick much closer to the underlying conceptual model than do the more abstract models used in ERP and APS systems. Furthermore,

Simulations provide highly visible models

Figure 11.6
Uncertainty of a
Completion Date

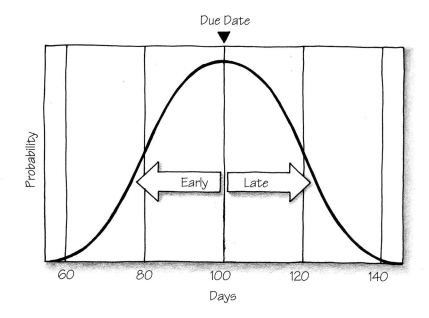

simulators include graphical animation tools that display the conceptual model on a computer screen during both design and execution. What this means to you as a manager is that your business model is directly visible to you. You can see how your facilities are laid out geographically, watch the materials flow among them, identify build-ups and bottlenecks, and make changes right on the screen to explore different ways to improve the chain. Given these advantages, simulators are excellent tools for understanding how the supply chain works, playing what-if with different configurations, and discovering the effects of business policies governing fulfillment, replenishment, and other operations.

Simulation complements ERP and APS

Despite these benefits, simulation is not a replacement for either APS or ERP. Although simulators can improve a supply plan using the techniques of hill-climbing described in Chapter 5, they lack the ability to seek out optimal solutions the way APS systems do. Simulators also lack the ability to generate the detailed schedules of ERP, and they offer none of ERP's support for day-to-day operations. As

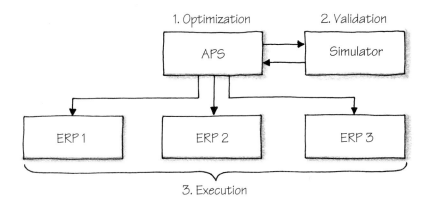

Figure 11.7
Using a Simulator
with APS and ERP

with other modeling situations described in this book, it isn't a matter of choosing the best tool, but of using the best mix of tools for a particular job. In the case of supply planning, one of the most effective strategies is to use a combination of ERP, APS, and simulation systems, as shown in Figure 11.7. In this approach, your planners use the APS system to develop an optimal plan, then use a simulator to fine-tune that plan to handle the effects of variability, nonlinear relations, and other factors beyond the scope of APS. They then pass this tuned version of the master plan on to the supporting set of ERP systems for detailed scheduling and operations. It's not the quickest or cheapest way to build a schedule, but the cost of this combined strategy can usually be justified given the huge impact of supply chain failures on both operating capital and corporate valuation.

Integrating Schedules

The techniques discussed in the preceding sections are designed to help a single company plan its production operations, integrating plans across multiple facilities as necessary to produce a coordinated flow of goods. There remains the problem of integrating production plans across multiple companies in the supply chain, smoothing the flow of goods *between* as well as within companies. This problem is

Internal planning is just the first step

directly analogous to the one examined at the end of the preceding chapter in the discussion of shared forecasting: When companies plan their production operations independently, they engage
in a great deal of redundant effort, and the likelihood that their
separate plans will mesh correctly when they are executed is
effectively zero.

**Independent
planning causes
supply failures**

Figure 11.8 brings the problem into sharper focus by illustrating the
plans each company generates for what it will buy, make, and sell
in the coming months. Because two of these three activities involve
interacting with trading partners, each company's plans include
implicit predictions about what those other companies will be buying and selling during those same months. In effect, each company
makes assumptions about the plans of the companies it deals with
and embeds those assumptions into its own plans, which are, of
course, the subject of the other companies' assumptions. This is
hardly an efficient way to do business, and it seriously impairs the
effectiveness of the chain as a whole. If Company A plans to buy
10,000 units of a product from Company B, but B only plans to sell
4,000 of its limited production run to A, these companies are going
to run into serious problems when they try to execute their plans.
In the old world of competitive purchasing this was just how business was done, but in the new world of chain-based competition,
it's a nonstarter.

Figure 11.8
Independent
Planning

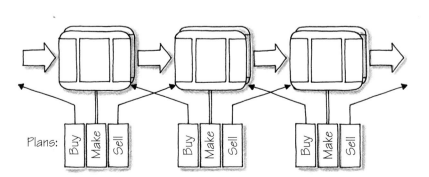

Supply chain breakdowns of this sort are expensive for all concerned, but the expense runs deeper than the obvious costs of lost sales and unsold inventory. As described in Chapter 8, companies all across the supply chain maintain safety stock to reduce the likelihood of supply failures. This safety stock is basically dead inventory. It doesn't move, it contributes nothing to the production process, and it adds no value to the final product. It just sits there taking up space, buffering a company against the uncertainties of supply and demand. Worse yet, it's redundant buffering because both parties at each link hold safety stock to hedge against the same supply risk. The supplier is holding extra stock of its finished goods to cover unexpected demand on the part of the customer, and the customer is holding extra stock of those same goods to cover unexpected shortages on the part of the supplier.

This redundant buffering is an example of how standard practices can lead to lose-lose situations between trading partners. Figure 11.9 illustrates the situation in terms of the tradeoff diagram introduced

Uncertainty is hedged at both ends

Redundant buffering raises total cost

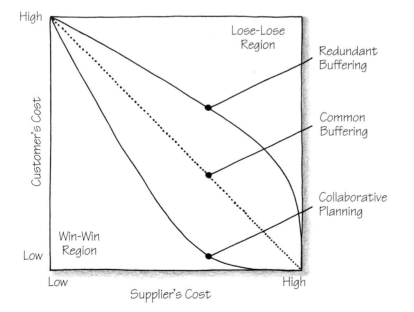

Figure 11.9
Tradeoffs in Safety Stock Costs

in Chapter 3; in this case, the lose-lose region lies above the line rather than below it because the diagram is based on cost rather than profit. In effect, the insurance represented by safety stock is being paid for twice over, which inevitably raises the total cost of the delivered goods. If trading partners did nothing more than agree on the total level of risk and divide the necessary buffer between them, they could at least get this aspect of their relationship back to the win-lose line. This may not be possible in an open-market situation, in which many customers are buying the same goods from many sellers, but it is a natural and straightforward way to pull cost out of a supply chain that is being planned and managed collaboratively. This cost reduction can be achieved even if there is no reduction of uncertainty in the quantity of goods that will flow across the link.

Collaborative planning reduces total cost

Although reducing redundant buffering is a good first step, trading partners can achieve much greater savings if they work together to reduce uncertainty rather than just doing a better job of coping with it. Because all of the demand in question is dependent demand, it can be predicted with high levels of confidence once independent demand is known. The level of independent demand can be predicted through collaborative forecasting, as described in Chapter 10, and it can be communicated in real time by transmitting consumer buying events upstream, as described in Chapter 3. A combination of these two techniques, in which joint forecasts are continuously updated based on emerging buying patterns, can resolve independent demand to a fairly narrow range of values, allowing planners to calculate dependent demand at each link.

Information brings down the cost of inventory

If this solution sounds easy, it's not; joint planning across a supply can be a time-consuming, frustrating, and error-prone process. But the potential savings from eliminating excess safety stock are tremendous, and the effort of collaborating on supply planning can give a trading relationship a solid push into the win-win region, as shown in Figure 11.9. This is another example of substituting information for inventory; collecting and communicating the information has a cost, but that cost is far less than the cost of holding the inventory. Moreover, the benefits of collaborative planning don't have to be taken on faith. There are standard techniques for calculating these savings, so it is relatively easy to justify the costs of joint planning based on near-term savings.

In one respect, collaborative supply planning is easier than you might expect because it uses the same tools and techniques as internal planning. In particular, APS systems provide an excellent platform for integrating plans across companies, and supply chain simulators give trading partners the ability to build shared models of how their supply chain works today and how they could work better in the future. One of the benefits of building shared models is that you can determine the most cost effective location for whatever safety stock needs to be maintained in the chain. The asymmetric tradeoff curve in Figure 11.9 illustrates a situation in which it is cheaper for a supplier to hold the stock than for the customer to hold it.

The same tools apply across companies

In the most basic form of joint planning, each pair of adjacent trading partners produces a common plan for the goods that will flow between the two companies. This link-by-link planning is a good start, but it requires a great deal of redundant effort. It can also lead to waves of change cascading up and down the chain, keeping the chain constantly off balance and out of synch. For example, if a company downstream needed to increase its planned orders for a particular week, it would work out that change with its immediate suppliers, who would then have to revise their plans and get together with their own suppliers, and so on. In the meantime, an upstream company might have to reduce its planned production for that same week due to problems at one of its plants, and its revisions would cascade down the chain. These waves of change

Link-by-link planning doesn't work well

hitting each other as they move up and down the change can cause havoc in the planning process.

Multi-link planning is much more efficient

A much better solution is to expand the joint planning effort to include multiple links in the chain, as shown in Figure 11.10. The critical information that all parties need to agree on is what materials will move across the links on what dates. All other planning factors—individual order quantities, internal production schedules, inventory safety levels, and the like—are subordinate to the overall information about supply movement and can be planned locally. If there is a change in the planned movements at any stage, such as reduced requirements downstream or projected shortages upstream, all trading partners learn of these changes at once and can begin to plan around them immediately.

Collaborative planning isn't easy

At present, collaborative planning across ownership boundaries is the exception rather than the rule. There is a growing recognition among supply chain planners that this is the next step in supply chain integration, but the challenges are formidable. At the technical level, posting and updating shared plans requires a common communication medium and standard protocols for exchanging production data. The Internet provides the necessary medium, and standards based on XML are beginning to emerge. But the

Figure 11.10
Collaborative
Planning

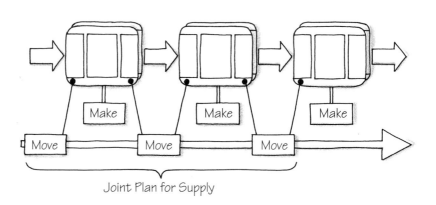

Joint Plan for Supply

challenges aren't limited to technical issues; the more serious obstacle is the problem of information sharing. Just as with collaborative forecasting, collaborative planning requires the exchange of highly confidential information, and sharing that information with suppliers and customers isn't easy. Given its competitive advantages, however, joint production planning is inevitable. Trading partners that manage to overcome the obstacles to this practice sooner rather than later will gain a first-mover advantage in the new competition between supply chains.

Unless you have a lot of experience with information technology, the array of software available for planning a supply chain can seem overwhelming. However, you don't have to have it all in place right away; you can start from where you are and gradually build up your corporate toolkit until you find that the right tool always falls to hand. The starting point is understanding the range of tools available and the proper uses of each. As vital as your ERP system may be to your company, you also need the ability to build realistic models of your chain, using APS systems and simulators to plan the most profitable flow of goods across the chain.

12

Improving Performance

The techniques of demand forecasting and supply planning offer many opportunities for improving the performance of a supply chain, but those improvements don't come automatically. The essential foundation of any improvement effort is a clear and consistent set of business objectives. Once you know where you want to go, you can figure out how to get there, then choose the best ways to measure your progress. However, objectives only work if they all pull the company in the same direction, so objectives have to be carefully aligned with each other. Finally, although most efforts focus on operational improvements, forecasting and planning are themselves learned capabilities that you need to monitor and improve over time.

Setting Objectives

Chapter 9 provided a framework for understanding the wide range of measures available for monitoring the performance of supply chains and organizing them into measures of time, cost, efficiency, and effectiveness. Although you might learn something useful from any of these measures, their real value comes from helping you track your progress toward specific objectives. Simply put, you need a clear and coherent set of business objectives to guide your attempts to improve your supply chain. Are you trying to reduce costs? Increase customer satisfaction? Get your products to market faster? Increase your market share? All of the above? If you don't know what you want to accomplish, no amount of measurement will solve your problem.

Measurement is driven by objectives

Once you have set your objectives, measuring progress toward these objectives is straightforward (Figure 12.1). The first step is to choose an appropriate set of measures for tracking your progress

Every measure needs a target

toward each objective. For each measure you select, you need to take a baseline reading to determine your current performance, set a target level for your future performance, and then take periodic readings to monitor progress toward that target. If you want to improve the efficiency of your fulfillment process, for example, you may decide to measure fulfillment lead time, order processing cost, and the number of orders per customer service representative. This would attack the problem from three different perspectives: time, cost, and efficiency. Each of these measures would go through the cycle shown in Figure 12.1.

Multiple measures validate improvements

As this example illustrates, using multiple measures for each objective can help ensure that your company is actually improving its performance rather than just making its numbers. Reducing fulfillment lead time is good, but if the cost per order goes up as well then there may not be a true increase in efficiency. Similarly, just measuring the productivity of customer service reps may not provide the full picture because it could be possible to hit the target for this measure by laying off a few reps and distributing the load over the remaining ones, thereby slowing down the fulfillment process. For that matter, even three measures might not be enough in this case; it might be possible to hit all three targets just by pushing

Figure 12.1
Measuring
Performance

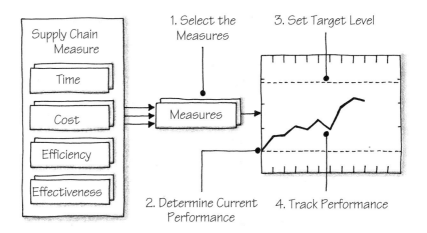

everyone to work faster, causing errors that cost more than the savings from the improvements. If that's a legitimate concern, you'd probably want to round out the set with a measure of order accuracy or customer satisfaction.

This example also illustrates the importance of looking for patterns in the way related measures change over time. As another example, suppose you are trying to enhance your competitiveness by improving your customer service level (CSL). If your measures of CSL go up but your measures of customer satisfaction don't go up with them, that tells you that something is wrong with either the objective or the measures. It may be that your customers are actually unhappy about something other than the service level, or it could be that you are using the wrong measures for CSL. But the unexpected pattern indicates that something isn't quite right, and you need to find out what it is.

Watch for patterns among measures

The fact that multiple measures may be required for each objective underscores the importance of tackling a reasonable number of objectives at any one time. Research has shown that most companies set too many objectives and take too few measurements, producing conflict about the company's direction and confusion about its progress. According to the results of one study, industry leaders in supply chain performance usually focus their efforts on three to five key areas, defining and tracking several measures of each. Another interesting characteristic of these leading companies is that they favor measures of effectiveness over measures of efficiency. For example, 85% measure on-time delivery, whereas only 75% measure supply chain costs and barely half (53%) measure inventory turns.

Keep objectives to a reasonable number

Another key to successful improvement is setting a realistic, achievable target for each measure. Suppose you decide to adopt a perfect-order measure and find that your current rate is 82%.

Targets should be achievable

Your goal may be to bring this up to 97%, but achieving that level of improvement in a reasonable time frame probably isn't realistic. A better approach would be to shoot for something like 90% after a year, 95% after another year, and 97% after a third. That way you have a series of controlled successes to build on rather than taking a single, wild shot at your ultimate goal.

There are three ways to set targets

There are three common ways of setting targets for objectives: going for a percentage improvement over the current performance, benchmarking yourself against the competition, and using formal models to discover opportunities for improvement. Targeting percentage improvements is by far the most common of the three, probably because it's the easiest, but there are important advantages to using the other two techniques in addition. For example, if competitive benchmarks reveal that you are among the best-in-class companies on a particular measure, an attempt to increase that measure by a large percentage is very likely to fail, and it might well take your best-in-class performance down with it.

Benchmarks reveal spreads in performance

Another attractive aspect of industry benchmarks is that they reveal the spread among the competition, and larger spreads generally translate into bigger opportunities. Supply chain benchmarks, in contrast to some other operational areas, often reveal substantial discrepancies in performance. Figure 12.2 illustrates a few results from one survey that compared companies ranked as having "good" to "excellent" supply chain performance with those ranked as "poor." The companies did not differ by a few percentage points; the companies at the lower end of the scale took almost 50% longer to fill their orders and cycle their cash, held their inventory nearly twice as long, and had twice as many late deliveries. These gaps are huge, and they translate into a tremendous financial and competitive advantage for the superior companies.

Measure	Class of Company	
	Good to Excellent	Poor
Lead Time	15 days	21 days
Cash-to-Cash Time	60 days	95 days
On-Time Delivery	95%	90%
Inventory Turns	10 turns	6 turns

Figure 12.2
Some Typical Benchmarks

The least common technique for setting targets is using formal models, which is unfortunate because this approach can be the most revealing of the three. If you use an APS system or a simulator to model your supply chain and search for optimal solutions, you may find that you have the potential to achieve breakthrough performance in an unsuspected area. Better still, rather than just giving you general feedback on how well you are doing against the competition, the model will show you exactly what you need to do to achieve the breakthrough. For example, it might reveal that outsourcing all your deliveries to Federal Express would double your performance on several key measures while also cutting your capital costs, even though individual deliveries would be more expensive than they are now. Of course, the model is only as good as the assumptions that go into it, but you can test the model by trying out the new idea on a small scale and refining the assumptions based on the results.

Models suggest breakthrough strategies

Avoiding Conflicts

Once you have chosen your measures and set their targets, the actual values you record will give you continuous feedback on how you are doing on your objectives. In principle, as long as each mea-

Objectives usually produce conflicts

sure is moving in the desired direction, you should be seeing steady improvement in your supply chain. In practice, however, objectives often conflict with each other, so that progress toward one objective takes you further away from another objective. This problem of conflicting objectives can be particularly hard to detect in supply chains because different groups within the company may set their own objectives without ever realizing that they are creating conflicts. However, if you fail to detect and eliminate these conflicts, your company will work against itself, exerting greater effort but reducing its ability to make any real progress.

Inventory levels are a common battleground

Figure 12.3 shows a simple yet common example of this kind of conflict. A manufacturing group is pursuing an objective to increase inventory turns from 14 to 18, so it is trying to reduce all three of its inventories. Meanwhile, the purchasing group is trying to meet an objective to reduce order costs by 10% by placing larger orders, which drives the raw materials inventory up rather than down. At the same time, the sales force is frantically shoving product out the door to earn bonuses for hitting their quarterly quotas, and it needs more finished goods so it can offer customers better selection and faster delivery. Rather than guide the company on a steady course of improvement, these incompatible objectives create a chronic

Figure 12.3
Conflicts Among
Objectives

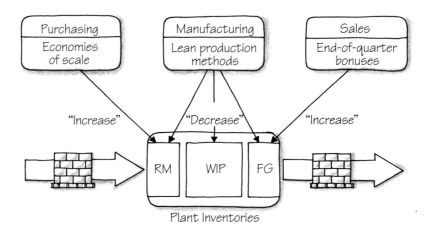

Plant Inventories

tension that pulls the company in different directions. The company wants to run, but, like Frankenstein's monster, most of its energy goes into fighting its own movements, and the best it can do is stagger forward.

Clearly, the only way to make any real progress is to align objectives across all the groups involved in managing the chain. Unfortunately, effective supply chain management involves almost every group in the company, and the long-standing motivations and practices of these groups makes alignment a difficult process. In many cases, it isn't even clear how to translate objectives into common units. How can sales incentives, which are revenue based, be aligned with production objectives, which are based on cost, quality, productivity, and other measures? And if aligning objectives within a single company is this hard, how can a group of independently owned companies hope to set and achieve shared objectives across a supply chain?

Objectives have to be aligned across groups

One approach to solving this problem is to find a single, common objective and map all other objectives back to it. The obvious candidate for this common objective is profit; if achieving an objective reduces profits rather than increasing them, then it may not be such a good objective. Of course, some objectives may reduce short-term profits in order to increase profits in the long run, but there are standard business formulas to handle that situation by taking into account the time value of money.

Profit provides a basis for alignment

In fact, it's helpful to think of objectives as being on three levels, corresponding to the three levels of management used to organize this book: operations, planning, and design (Figure 12.4). To justify operational objectives, you only have to show an increase in sales or a decrease in costs. For planning objectives, you might compare the net present value of future profits against the more immediate costs to demonstrate the expected real profit from meeting the

Objectives map to profits on three levels

Figure 12.4
Mapping
Objectives to Profit

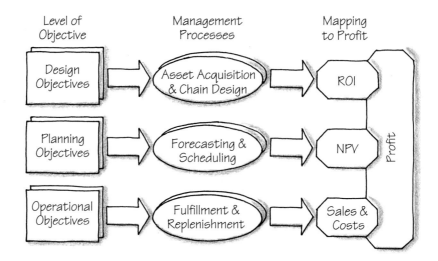

Level of Objective	Management Processes	Mapping to Profit

objective. Similarly, you would justify capital expenditures to improve the design of the chain by calculating the return on the investment in those assets. Once you have made these adjustments for the time value of money, you should be able to map all objectives into the common currency of profit, making it easy to compare their relative merits and ensure that they are all in alignment with profitability.

Profit mapping reveals conflicts

Mapping objectives to profit is simple in principle, but in practice it can quickly become so complex that the only way to understand the joint impact of objectives on profit is to model the chain with these objectives in place and watch what happens. To get a feel for how quickly the conflicts arise, consider the simple conceptual model of revenue and expense shown in Figure 12.5. This business system has four inputs, all under your control, and a single output, profit. As indicated by the two kinds of connecting lines on the right side of the figure, profit goes up with increases in revenue, and it goes down with increases in expenses. Revenue, in turn, can be increased by raising either unit prices or sales volume, and expense can be decreased by reducing the costs of either capacity

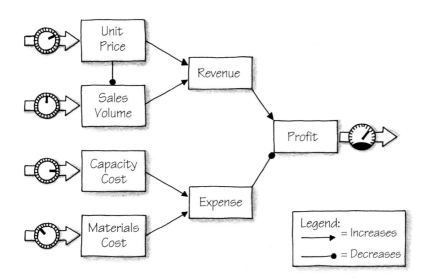

Figure 12.5
A Basic Revenue
and Expense
Model

or materials. So far so good; it's perfectly clear which way to turn
each knob to increase profits.

Well, almost—there is a slight conflict in that increasing the price
beyond a certain point discourages buyers and reduces the sales volume, as indicated by the negative link between price and volume.
This means price has conflicting effects on revenue: at low prices,
increasing the price increases revenue, and at higher prices, increasing the price decreases revenue. The point where the profits reach
a peak would, of course, be a good price to actually put on the product. But what is that price? It depends on the particulars of the
model: the values of the parameters, the shapes of the individual
relations, and so on. At least in this simple model, reducing the cost
of materials will always increase your profit, but there is no simple
rule that tells you how raising or lowering the price will affect profit.

**Price naturally
involves a
tradeoff**

This is not a particularly deep insight; every manager knows that
price involves a tradeoff between profit per unit and the number of
units sold. But the model gets a bit more interesting with the addition of a few objectives. Figure 12.6 shows the same basic model of

**Adding
measures
complicates
the tradeoffs**

Figure 12.6
Aligning Measures
to Profit

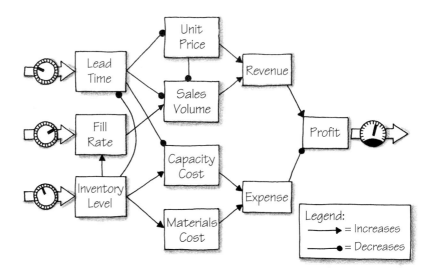

profit with three common measures of supply chain performance: lead time, fill rate, and inventory. It's obvious how these measures will appear in supply chain objectives; nearly every company would like to reduce its lead times, improve its fill rates, and bring down its inventory levels. But are these compatible objectives?

The effects on profit are hard to predict

Consider the effects of inventory levels. As you can see from the connections on the left side of the diagram, high levels of inventory increase both capacity cost and material cost, so reducing inventory would definitely reduce expenses. But having more inventory permits higher fill rates and shorter lead times, so there's a conflict among the objectives right there. Of course, there are other ways to improve lead times and fill rates. For example, you can reduce lead times by pushing inventory out closer to customers, but that drives up capacity costs because it requires more storage facilities. And so it goes. In short, there is simply no way to anticipate the effects of changing any of these measures without a detailed understanding of the system as a whole. Even though it's "obvious" which way to turn the knobs, any change you make could end up hurting profits rather than helping them.

There is a huge lesson to be learned from this tiny model: There are no simple formulas for improving your supply chain. Reducing lead times, improving fill rates, and increasing turns may produce dramatic improvements in performance, but they can also do more harm than good. Each of these measures has an optimal setting, and those settings interact in complex ways. The only way to reliably improve your supply chain is to model it and let the model seek out the settings that will produce the most profit. Then you can use those settings as your targets for each measure rather than picking arbitrary targets or just pushing as hard as you can in what seems to be the right direction. If the model says that you should increase inventory turns from 10 to 15, then stop at 15; cranking them up to 20 may be as bad for your company as staying at 10.

Only models can reveal optimal targets

This can be a difficult lesson to absorb. Throughout the history of business, managers have made subjective judgments about what would improve the performance of their groups, then worked to do as well as possible on their chosen measures. That time-honored formula for success has been shattered in the past few decades with the advent of information technology. Mathematical and simulation models now reveal the true complexity of business systems, making visible the intricate interdependencies among objectives and measures that once seemed to stand on their own merits. Today, the path to excellence lies not in improving individual measures of performance such as turns and fill rates, but using formal models to find the best balance among these measures.

Setting goals is a matter of balance

Aligning Incentives

In sum, improving the performance of your supply chain involves using formal models to find the performance levels that maximize profit, setting objectives for moving toward these levels, and taking systematic measurements to track your progress. This picture of success is nearly complete, but there is still a large piece missing:

Motivating change requires incentives

motivating your people to achieve the objectives. As any experienced manager knows, it isn't enough to set objectives and exhort people to strive toward them. You have to provide incentives that reward people for making the right kinds of choices, and the incentives have to be powerful enough to produce significant changes in behavior.

Incentives must be aligned with objectives

To date, incentives have not been handled very well in supply chain management. Employees often receive incentives that are at cross-purposes with corporate objectives, and their incentives are rarely tied to supply chain performance. One recent study produced some dismal statistics: Only 25% of companies in the United States use incentives based on supply chain performance; nearly all of these incentives are based on internal performance measures and are not tied to the performance of the chain as a whole; the majority of companies choose the wrong measures for their incentives; and their incentives are rarely aligned in a way that encourages consistent behavior. The use of incentives is clearly due for some profound changes.

Some incentives might change dramatically

Here's an example of how deep the changes may have to go. Instead of basing sales commissions on total sales, why not base them on contribution to profit? If all your products are equally profitable, it will work out to be the same thing. But if, like most companies, you make nearly all of your profit on 20% of your products (see Chapter 13), why not encourage the sales team to sell the products that actually make money for you? Not only would this improve the bottom line, it could help motivate your sales force to support profit-oriented initiatives that they might otherwise resist, such as raising prices on products that don't cover their costs, or keeping inventories of finished goods within reasonable bounds. Anything they can do to increase the profitability of the products they sell is money in their own pockets.

Once you accept profit as the common denominator across objectives, interesting opportunities open up for rethinking policies you may not even realize you had. Case in point: What's the policy governing the sequence with which you process incoming orders? Unless you are a highly unusual company, you have an unstated, implicit policy of processing them in the order in which they arrive. A recent study found that making one small change—servicing orders according to their profit potential rather than their arrival date—could increase average profits by 18% per year. Most managers would be thrilled to get that kind of jump in profit from such a simple change, but the idea would simply never occur to them unless they were already examining every policy for its contribution to profit.

No policy should escape examination

Incentive alignment is a complex discipline with robust mathematical foundations, but the business message is simple: You have to make sure that everyone's personal win is consistent with your objectives as a company. The good news here is that incentives really do work; with rare exceptions, the people in your company will behave in ways that maximize their personal rewards, however those rewards are defined. If you align your company's incentives so they all point in the same direction, you will create a powerful force that can drive the company to unprecedented levels of performance. If you allow these incentives to point in different directions, all that energy will work against itself and the opportunity for stellar performance will be lost.

Incentive alignment is a powerful tool

With the addition of this missing piece—alignment of incentives across the organization—the picture is complete; getting the maximum performance out of your company requires four distinct steps (Figure 12.7). First, use business models to identify the combination of performance targets that maximizes profits. Second, set achievable objectives that bring your company closer to its

Improving performance involves four steps

Figure 12.7
Improving
Performance

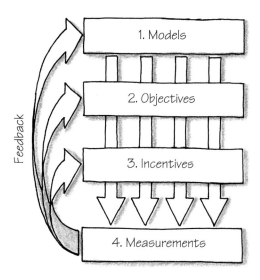

ideal configuration. Third, motivate your people to strive for these objectives by making their incentives contingent on hitting the targets. Fourth, set up a systematic program of measurement to track your progress on each objective. As shown in the illustration, the results of these measurements provide the feedback necessary to guide the entire program: They determine the sizes of incentive awards, they indicate how much progress you are making toward achieving your targets, and they provide vital feedback on the business model so that you can improve it over time.

Alignment has to span multiple companies

To improve the performance of a supply chain, the process shown in Figure 12.7 has to be applied not just to your own company but to the chain as a whole. One of the key insights of modern supply chain management is that improvements in a single link of the chain often harm the other links in ways that cancel out local benefits. The industry programs described in Chapter 3 illustrate this principle nicely in that they usually solve supply chain problems by displacing those problems onto other members of the chain. In order for the chain to improve as a whole, its members must be willing to sacrifice such local advantages for the greater good of being part of a successful chain. On the surface, this might seem to call for something akin to corporate altruism, but it doesn't; there are ways to make it pay for everyone to play, and finding those ways is the key to building a competitive chain.

This is where the idea of mapping all objectives onto profit really comes into its own. Simply put, making a profit may be the only objective that all the companies in a chain have in common. If their individual profits can be aligned with the total profits of the chain, then it is in the interests of each company to work for the good of the chain. If their profits aren't aligned, then they will inevitably pull in different directions and reduce the performance of the chain.

Profits align objectives across the chain

This is not to suggest that the competitive element of trade relationships can be eliminated altogether; the discussion of game theory in Chapter 3 made that clear enough. Rather, the goal should be to neutralize the competitive element by moving relationships into the win-win region and allocating the winnings equitably. It's harder to visualize this tradeoff function when multiple companies are involved because the two-dimensional graph shown in Figure 3.10 would have to be expanded into many dimensions, with a separate axis for each company. But you don't have to visualize the result; these diagrams are useful for explaining the concept, but they aren't actually used in practice. What you need to do is build a shared model of the chain, optimize that model to maximize the total profit across the chain, and then negotiate the allocation of this profit.

Sharing profits always requires tradeoffs

Improving Planning

Although the examples in the preceding sections focused on objectives for operational performance, this is only one of the three levels of objectives shown in Figure 12.4. The operational level usually gets the most attention when it comes to performance because the payoffs from improvement are immediate, but there is a danger of

Planning processes also need improvement

focusing so heavily on operations that you miss even better opportunities in the design and planning of your chain. Yes, you can increase your customer service level by holding inventory closer to your customers, but that requires higher inventory levels, so it just trades one operational objective off against another. On the other hand, if you can increase your ability to forecast your customers' requirements and schedule supplies to arrive just as they are needed, you may be able to improve customer service while *reducing* total inventory. That would be a win on both measures.

Forecasting needs to track errors

Forecasting provides an excellent case in point. As anyone in the business will be quick to tell you, the first rule of forecasting is that forecasts are always wrong. No matter how well you predict the systematic components of demand, there is always a random component that can't be predicted. Given this built-in limitation, getting better at forecasting doesn't mean eliminating error altogether. Rather, the goal is to make the residual error as small as possible while eliminating any bias toward under- or overpredicting demand. Meeting that goal requires two different measures, one to monitor the magnitude of forecasting errors and another to monitor their bias. Both of these measures are calculated from a set of comparable predictions, such as the set of forecasts for a particular product across different sales territories.

MAPE monitors the size of errors

Forecasting experts have several good statistics for analyzing the magnitude of errors, but for management purposes your best bet is probably the **mean absolute percentage error** (**MAPE**). Simply put, the MAPE tells you how many percentage points your forecasts tend to be off the mark, regardless of whether they are too high or too low. By monitoring the MAPE over time, you can see whether you are making any progress in reducing the size of errors, or make sure that a reliable forecasting procedure doesn't go bad on you. In Figure 12.8, Product A has a moderate but stable forecast

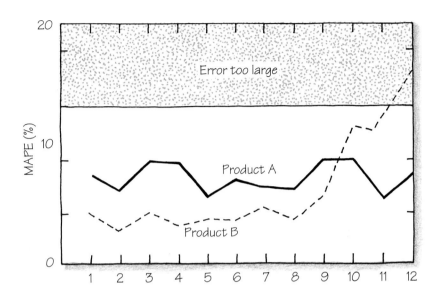

Figure 12.8
Measuring the
Magnitude of
Forecast Errors

error, whereas Product B has a lower error on average but now seems to be getting out of control. As this example illustrates, one of the advantages of using a measure based on percentages is that it translates error magnitudes into standard units, canceling out any differences due to the actual volume of sales.

For monitoring the *bias* of forecasting errors, the **tracking signal** is a good choice for managers because, like the MAPE, it expresses bias in standard units that don't depend on sales volumes. When there is no bias, the tracking signal is zero. A positive signal means that most errors occurred because demand exceeded the forecast, whereas a negative signal means that demand fell below the forecast. Figure 12.9 shows that Product A, which is stable in terms of error magnitude, is not doing so well on the MAPE measure because it's showing an increasing bias toward predicting more demand than is actually being realized. Product B, which shows increasingly large errors, does all right on the MAPE because it still shows no tendency to under- or overshoot the mark.

**The tracking
signal monitors
bias**

Figure 12.9
Measuring Bias in
Forecast Errors

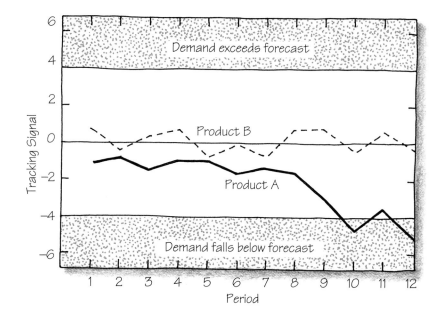

**Error measures
can have
automatic
thresholds**

The graphs in Figures 12.8 and 12.9 illustrate how forecasting errors are monitored, but it isn't actually necessary to draw these plots in practice. Instead, forecasters set thresholds on these measures, as indicated by the shaded areas in the diagrams, and let their forecasting systems call their attention to forecasts that go out of bounds. Using these automated thresholds makes it easy to track progress toward objectives for improving the forecasting process— you just set the threshold to the desired level and the software will let you know whenever you exceed it. The thresholds shown in Figures 12.8 and 12.9 are reasonably typical for volume products; it's good practice to keep the MAPE down in single digits, and a tracking signal that is more than four to six points away from zero is cause for concern.

**Handle
violations
according to the
technique**

What do you do when a measure of forecast error exceeds one of these thresholds? The answer depends on the forecasting technique you are using. If the magnitude goes out of bounds and you're basing your forecasts on market research, you may be able to improve the reliability of your data by increasing your sample sizes. If you are using the Delphi method and getting a consistent bias toward overforecasting, you should talk to the members of the forecasting team about where their optimism is coming from. If you are using time series techniques, then a breakdown in either magnitude or bias is telling you it's time to consider using a more powerful model.

The breakdown of a forecasting method isn't always bad news. Suppose you've been successfully forecasting demand for a product based on running averages for a number of years, but now the error component is getting larger each month and the tracking signal is up around 8. That just means that the demand for that product used to be static but is now increasing, and you need to add a trend component to your forecasting model to accommodate the increase. Having to adjust a forecasting technique because sales are taking off is the kind of problem most managers would love to have.

Forecast failures can be good news

In contrast to these well-established techniques for monitoring forecast errors, much less attention has been paid to measuring scheduling errors. However, the same principles apply, and the best approach is to systematically measure both the magnitude and the bias of scheduling errors, setting thresholds on both to trigger alarms when either kind of error grows too large. The most common problem is that schedules are routinely missed, sometimes with such regularity that planners—and their managers—become fatalistic about it. But fatalism is the wrong response to this situation. If there is a consistent bias in the scheduling process, it can and should be corrected, if only by adding a correction to whatever dates the planning process comes up with. This is a common practice, but it usually takes the form of covert "fudge factors" that planners attempt to hide from management. A much better approach is to treat completion dates as "forecasts" of future

Scheduling also needs performance monitoring

events that are inherently uncertain, and to develop systematic, public techniques for translating the output of scheduling systems into achievable forecasts of actual completion dates.

Forecasting flows naturally into scheduling

Forecasting and scheduling are usually treated as separate activities and are carried out by different groups, but there is a natural continuity between the two in which the forecasting process flows smoothly into the scheduling process. Instead of forecasting demand for a given time frame, then building schedules to meet that demand, a more effective technique is to do a rolling forecast that continuously informs the schedules that depend on it. This way, uncertainty can be removed from the forecast for each period as that period approaches, allowing you to fine-tune production runs as you get closer to their start dates.

Use forecast errors in building schedules

Although it's not common practice, another helpful technique is to use the analysis of forecasting errors to improve the quality of the scheduling process. If you know that there is a growing bias toward overestimating demand for a particular line of products, for example, it certainly makes sense to pare back scheduled production accordingly. More important, the magnitude of the forecasting error provides data for risk management in scheduling production. If you know that your forecasts for a particular product are typically off by 20%, you need to have substantially more safety stock and reserve capacity than you do for a product with a 5% forecast error.

Improving the performance of a supply chain is no small undertaking, but the new competition between chains means that it's a problem you have to solve. The most important point to take away from this chapter is that there are no simple answers, no magic formulas for pulling out excess time and cost. Efforts to reduce lead times, accelerate the flow of inventory, and other popular objectives may be part of an overall solution, but they can also make the problem worse. If you want a clear beacon to keep you on the path to success, here it is in a single sentence: The only sure way to improve your supply chain is to model it and let the model seek out the settings that will produce the most profit. If this is a hard message for most managers to accept, use that fact to your advantage: Embrace the idea and run with it while others are still mulling it over.

PART

V

Design

13

Mastering Demand

This chapter marks the transition to the highest level of supply chain management: making the design decisions that ultimately determine the capabilities and limitations of your chain. The first step in designing a supply chain is understanding the pattern of demand your chain has to serve. This demand pattern is formed by the intersection of customer requirements, as described in the first section, and product constraints, discussed in the second section. Although demand is usually taken as a given, the third section introduces a variety of techniques you can use to improve the shape of demand to better fit your chain, including a few techniques that actually improve demand by reducing it. The last section examines the phenomenon of demand amplification and reveals that most of this amplification is caused by standard practices in supply chain management that are easily modified to stabilize the flow of demand.

Knowing the Customer

With contemporary software, designing a supply chain is vastly easier than it used to be. Rather than laboriously calculating distances, costs, times, order sizes, and other quantities, planners can now use software to generate these values automatically, based on a geographical analysis of demand and supply. With these powerful new tools in hand, supply chain managers can focus their attention on the high-level tasks of analyzing demand, defining objectives, and identifying constraints.

Design is mostly done in software

The starting point for this process is performing a geographical analysis of demand. This analysis can be as simple as plotting customer locations on a map or as complex as combining consumer profile data

Customer location drives the design

with population density figures stratified by income and other characteristics. If your customers are large companies and you only have a few dozen of them, you can work directly with individual customers' locations. If your customers number in the thousands, you'll need to group them into service regions and use the data for the regions in the analysis. There are various techniques for allocating customers to regions, but the easiest way is to use postal codes. A common rule of thumb is to aggregate customers into about 150 to 200 regions, each of which is represented by a central service point. This is a manageable number of locations for planning purposes, and it doesn't introduce more than about a 1% error in the estimation of total transportation costs.

Customer buying patterns affect requirements

In addition to analyzing the volume and type of products that customers buy, it's important to examine their actual buying patterns. The analysis should focus on five major factors, as shown in Figure 13.1: the total volume of product that customers purchase per period, the frequency of orders, the lot sizes within each order, the variety of products included in each order, and the customer service level (CSL) required to keep them happy. To cite two extremes, just-in-time (JIT) production facilities may require daily deliveries of small lots of very specific product mixes, and they may place very tight constraints on fill rates and delivery times. At the other end of the scale, wholesale distributors may place infrequent orders for large quantities of products, require a different mix on

Figure 13.1
Customer Buying
Pattern

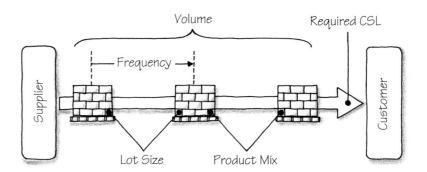

each order, and have much less restrictive requirements for time of delivery. These two kinds of customers would place very different demands on a supply chain. For example, the JIT customers would be best served by high-throughput distribution centers located close to their plants, whereas the distributors might be adequately served by a centralized, general-purpose storage facility.

Analyzing the customer service level (CSL) requirements of individual customers can help you identify opportunities for major savings in your supply chain. Some companies take pride in setting a high standard for CSL and applying that standard across the board, but providing a higher level of service than customers actually need can be wasteful given the tremendous expense of maintaining high CSLs (see Chapter 8). A more cost-effective approach is to vary CSL according to individual customers' needs, eliminating the waste of "over-serving" customers with low requirements while also avoiding unacceptable service for customers with high requirements (Figure 13.2). If you want to be recognized for excellent service, you will probably want to keep your CSL in the upper range of the acceptable zone, as shown in the illustration, but if you compete primarily on price then the "adequate service" range will help you keep your costs down.

Varying CSL by customer can be cost-effective

Once you have analyzed your customers with regard to their buying patterns, the next step is to look for correlations between how they buy and where they are located. For example, the common practice of defining regions based on the number of customers in each area works only if demand is fairly evenly distributed across customers. This is often the case when the customers are end consumers, but it's rarely the case when they are companies. As described in Chapter 10 (see Figure 10.5), the distribution of sales volume across corporate customers often follows the Pareto pattern: The top 20% of customers account for 80% of sales, and the bottom 50% accounts for just 5% of sales. If your customers display

Check to see if patterns vary by region

Figure 13.2
Setting the
Customer
Service Level

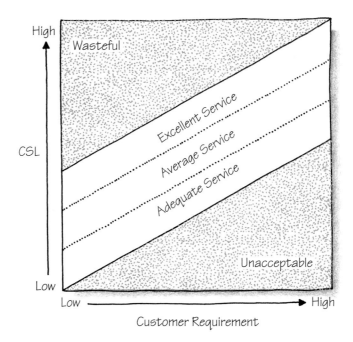

anything like this degree of skew, it may help to factor the location of your top customers into your geographic analysis of demand. If your biggest customers are all located in or near large cities, for example, that could mean that 90% of your demand is clustered in a relatively small number of locations. If it happens that those customers are also the ones that require high CSLs, you know right where to put your regional warehouses.

Customers should require only a few groups

In analyzing the buying habits of your customers, bear in mind that it's the broad patterns that you're after, not the detailed differences. It may be that your customer base is sufficiently homogeneous that a simple breakdown of demand by region captures all the information you need. If so, that's excellent news because it means you can engineer the entire chain to satisfy a single set of requirements, the best possible starting point for building a world-class supply chain. More likely, your customers will fall into a relatively small number of types based on their habits and requirements. In this case, you need to design a chain that is flexible enough to meet the different sets of needs without incurring unnecessary costs. In effect, you may need to design two or more supply chains that can operate across a common set of facilities.

For example, suppose your analysis reveals that your customers fall into three broad segments, which you designate as Types A, B, and C in keeping with their corporate personalities. Your Type A customers are JIT plants that buy specific parts kits and require one-day lead times with 30-minute delivery windows. They have demanding requirements, but they are willing to collaborate with you on forecasting and scheduling to help you meet those requirements. The Type Bs are mostly low-volume plants that purchase a range of non-kitted products with two- to three-day lead times, and the Type Cs are job shops that are comfortable with one- to two-week lead times.

The needs of the groups may be very different

If you design a single supply chain that treats all three groups the same, the most likely outcome is that you will be constantly expediting deliveries for your Type A customers in order to get those deliveries to move faster than the bulk of your goods, and you may well find that the cost structure of your chain makes you too expensive for many of your Type C customers. But if you set up specialized facilities and procedures of the sort shown in Figure 13.3, you may be able to keep everyone happy at a reasonable cost. In this particular design, Type A customers are served by small warehouses adjacent to their plants, making precisely timed deliveries in reusable parts-kit containers. Type B customers are served by having a package carrier such as UPS or FedEx deliver shipments from a central warehouse, and Type C customers are served by a conventional network of regional distribution centers.

Each group can receive specialized service

Figure 13.3
Overlapping
Supply Chains

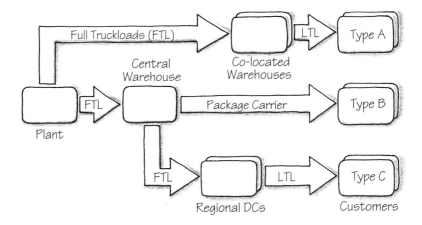

Analyzing the Product

**Intrinsic
qualities impose
constraints**

In addition to the requirements customers place on products and their delivery, the qualities of the products themselves impose constraints on how they are packaged, transported, and stored. As shown in Figure 13.4, these requirements can be understood in terms of three key considerations: form, density, and risk.

**Bulk materials
are cheaper
to ship**

With regard to form, the major concern is whether a product is shipped in bulk or packaged form. Shipping and storing bulk materials is much cheaper than handling packages; for example, it costs about 77 cents per ton to ship sugar from Hawaii to the mainland in

Figure 13.4
Intrinsic Product
Qualities

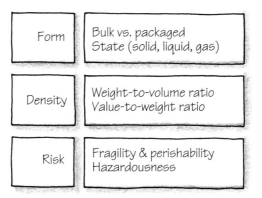

bulk, as compared to more than $20 per ton shipping it in bags. When materials are shipped in bulk form, the state of the material is a key consideration because solids, liquids, and gases differ greatly in the way they are transported. For example, some liquids and gases can move through pipelines, providing cheap transportation per unit shipped with constant, dependable throughput. State is important for packaged goods as well because liquids and gases generally require relatively expensive packaging such as tanks, barrels, bottles, or cans, and economic or environmental concerns may dictate that these containers be returned for reuse.

Density, expressed as the ratio of weight to volume, is also an important consideration in supply chain design. Low-density products are more expensive to ship because vehicles and containers "cube out" before they "weigh out," filling the available volume before they reach their full hauling capacity. When low density is the result of the way a product is constructed, as it is with lamps and lawnmowers, effective density is often increased by shipping products in a partially assembled state. A property closely related to density is the product's value-to-weight ratio; as this ratio increases, the relative cost of transportation drops and more options become economically feasible. When carbon travels in the form of coal, it usually moves by slow freight and goes no farther than it has to. When carbon travels as diamonds, it goes by plane and circles the globe.

Low density increases shipping cost

A variety of qualities related to risk can require special handling, packaging, transportation, and storage. Fragile items require additional packaging to prevent breakage during transport and storage. Perishable products risk spoilage, placing constraints on the length of time they can be in transit or storage, and some need constant refrigeration to preserve their freshness. Hazardous products, such as explosives and flammable gases, pose a more serious type of risk and usually require special handling to comply with government

Risk increases transportation costs

regulations. All of these kinds of risk increase the cost of transportation, and high-risk products are often shipped separately from other goods to isolate these added costs.

Customization shifts the push-pull boundary

In addition to these intrinsic qualities, the design of the chain has to take into account whether the products it handles are standard or custom. The degree of customization can vary from standard, off-the-shelf products to ones that are designed specifically for a single customer (Figure 13.5). In general, increased customization shifts the push-pull boundary further up the chain. Standard products allow the boundary to be set right next to the consumer, so these products can be made to stock and pushed all the way down the chain in anticipation of demand. At the other extreme, fully customized products can move the push-pull boundary all the way up to suppliers if the choice of materials depends on the design. Shifting this boundary upstream reduces the need for inventory because products are pulled by immediate demand rather than being pushed down the chain based on forecast (see Chapter 2), but it also increases the complexity of the fulfillment process and requires more flexibility in both upstream and downstream facilities.

Figure 13.5
Customization
Requirements

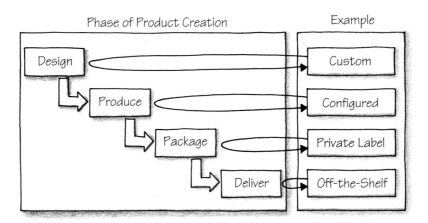

Another important consideration is the variability in demand for products over time. Products with steady, predictable demand are the easiest to handle because their requirements are well known and the chain can be designed around those requirements. If the demand varies but does so in a predictable way, this puts more stress on the chain but is still manageable. For example, seasonal products put a heavy load on their chains in advance of their peak season. It may be possible to handle these peak loads by leveling production across the year, building up inventory in advance of the season. This approach lowers the cost of production, but it does so by pushing the problem down the chain in the form of extra storage capacity to hold accumulated inventory.

Variability in demand stresses a supply chain

A better approach to coping with seasonable variability is to use products with different seasons to counterbalance each other, distributing the load on the supply chain as evenly as possible over the course of a year. This tends to happen naturally in the apparel industry, where summer and winter styles balance each other out over the course of the year. Other counterbalancing products may be less obvious but can still be identified. The classic example here is the plant that alternates between snow blowers and lawn mowers, taking advantage of common components and operations to minimize the cost of the semiannual changeovers.

Seasonal products can be counterbalanced

The most difficult products to handle are those with highly variable demand that can't be predicted with any consistency. This situation is most commonly encountered with innovative products, which have little or no sales history and whose sales are driven by trends or fashions. As described in Chapter 10 (see Figure 10.8), such products have a lifecycle that starts out with low demand and slow growth, goes through a period of rapid growth, peaks, and then slides into a gradual decline. As Figure 13.6 illustrates, the uncertainty of the demand for such products also changes systematically over the same time frame: Demand for newly introduced products

Innovative products are the hardest to handle

Figure 13.6
Demand
Uncertainty over
Product Life

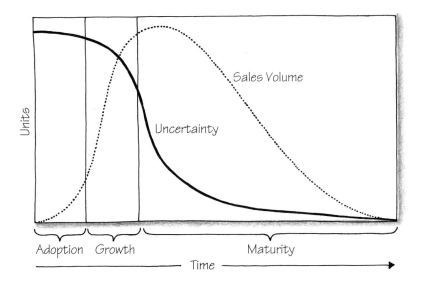

is highly uncertain, and this uncertainty starts to decline only as the full market embraces the product and the growth rate begins to fall off. It is only after the product is well into its peak sales period that sales become reasonably predictable.

Uncertainty requires excess capacity

Given the high uncertainty of demand for new products, it's hard to know how many to build or how much capacity to devote to production and inventory. Until a product approaches its sales peak and begins to exhibit a stable pattern, the supply chain for that product needs to maintain high levels of safety stock to handle higher-than-expected sales. In addition, considerable excess capacity must be held in reserve in order to ramp up production quickly in the event that the product takes off. Many a company has realized its dream of bringing a killer product to market, only to find its overnight success shattered by chronic shortages, cost overruns, and quality problems as its supply chain struggles to cope with the explosion in demand. But erring in the other direction can lead to equally devastating problems, including excess inventory, idle plants, and massive returns. Dealing with innovative products is one of the toughest problems in supply chains, and it's a core concern in the discussion of supply chain strategy in the next chapter.

In supply chain design, products are subject to the same constraint as customers with regard to how many products can be planned independently. In general, if you deal with more than a couple hundred different products, you need to aggregate those products in order to keep the numbers manageable. For example, a chain of discount stores with 20,000 products might organize those products into 100 groups averaging 200 products each. Unlike customers, which are usually grouped by region, product groups should be based on demand patterns, using the same groups that were used for aggregate forecasting and scheduling (see Chapters 10 and 11).

Aggregate products according to requirements

For some companies, the demand patterns that distinguish their product groups are sufficiently well aligned with conventional product families that these families can be used to aggregate products when designing the chain. However, this is not a foregone conclusion; product families are usually based on similarity of production or consumption rather than similarity in their demand patterns, and families often mix products with very different supply chain requirements. For example, marketing may choose to group products in ways that encourage cross selling, such as grouping accessories with the products they match—purses with shoes, say, or bits with drills. Often, these accessories have very different supply chains from the matching products and should not be grouped together in designing the chain.

Be wary of using marketing groups

In deciding how to aggregate products for design purposes, it is important—as always—to take the sales volume of products into account. If a Pareto Analysis reveals that 20% of your product line accounts for 80% of your sales, you should be able to take advantage of that fact in designing your supply chain. For example, you might be able to handle fast movers separately, gaining some

Analyze fast movers separately

economies of scale by shipping them only in full pallets or full truckloads. Alternatively, you might be able to convert the other 80% of your products to a centralized warehousing system, allowing them to bypass your regional distribution centers. That would slash the number of SKUs you have to track and queue at the regional distribution centers (DCs) to a fifth of what it would otherwise be, allowing you to streamline operations at your DCs while getting rid of inventories that don't turn over rapidly. Even if the centralized system required the use of faster shipping modes for some orders, the cost savings of skipping the DCs could yield a substantial net savings.

Shaping Demand

You can improve the quality of demand

The discussion of demand up to this point has taken a somewhat reactive point of view, stressing the importance of understanding the nature of demand and designing the chain accordingly. But it is possible to take a more proactive stance toward demand, actively shaping it to suit your purposes rather than working within the constraints it imposes. The obvious example of this is using marketing techniques to increase demand, but that's not the only approach to shaping demand, and it may not even be the best one. In fact, some of the most effective techniques for improving demand actually involve *reducing* it, at least in the short run.

Choose your customers to fit your chain

One of the most important things you can do to improve the shape of demand is make sure that you are serving the right customers. No matter how well you design your supply chain, it can't meet the needs of every kind of customer. If your primary objective is to pull time and cost out of your chain, then you are going to have a hard time meeting the needs of customers that require fast delivery and perfect fulfillment in response to unpredictable orders. If you try, you could find yourself expediting most of their orders, serving them at a net loss, and disrupting the rest of your supply flow in the process. Similarly, if you opt for a strategy based on flexible service and custom products, there's no point in trying to serve customers that buy a constant stream of standard products. You will never be able to match the prices of the low-cost provider and still make money on these customers.

The relentless pursuit of revenue often blinds companies to the harm that comes from serving customers at a loss. Indeed, most don't even know which customers are producing their profits. If you ran a Pareto Analysis on your own customer base using profits rather than sales as the measure, would it surprise you to learn that just 20% of your customers produced 80% of your profits? If so, get ready for a shock; the situation may be much worse than this. Unlike sales, profits can go into the negative range, allowing the skewing to be even more extreme. One firm discovered that the top 20% of its customers accounted not for 80% but for 225% of its profits. The next 60% of its customers hovered around the breakeven point, and the bottom 20% actually *reduced* profits by a stunning 125%. For this company, a supply chain design that led these unprofitable customers to take their business elsewhere would make a huge contribution to the bottom line, even if it didn't improve the performance of the chain at all.

Many customers are profit sinks

The idea of turning away customers may sound like heresy, but if it produces dramatic increases in profits it may be the only rational choice. Of course, it would be bad form just to call up certain customers and tell them you no longer wish to do business with them, but there are market mechanisms that can achieve the same end and may produce an even better result. If you can identify what is causing you to lose money with some of your customers, you may be able to change either your costs or your prices in a way that makes these customers profitable. Often as not, it is the customers who place the greatest demands on performance who also demand the biggest concessions on price. One way to counter this punitive

Tiered pricing can clear out the losers

behavior is to set up a tiered pricing structure based on service levels, then refuse to discount the premier service. This approach leaves your customers with complete freedom of choice: They can allow you to make a profit, or they can inflict their business on one of your competitors.

Use targeted selling to avoid future problems

Eliminating profit sinks from your customer base is only half a solution; the other half is avoiding such customers in the future. The simplest way to do this is to be sure your marketing and sales messages attract the right kinds of customers, and that means being clear about your distinctive competence. If you follow the time-honored practice of promising customers everything—the fastest service and the best products at the lowest price—then your customers are right to expect you to deliver on your promises no matter what it costs you. If you tell them honestly the ways in which you excel, they'll choose you for the right reasons and you'll both come out ahead.

You need to align incentives at every level

The idea of being selective about your customers will strike some managers as a radical notion, but it's no more radical than being selective about your suppliers. As described in Chapter 12, the key to getting sustained cooperation across the supply chain is to align everyone's incentives. If you bring in customers whose needs and expectations don't match the capabilities with your supply chain, aligning those incentives becomes extremely difficult. Unfortunately, the practice of selling to anyone who will buy is deeply entrenched, so it takes careful alignment of incentives within your own organization to alter this behavior. Basing sales commissions on profit rather than revenue, as suggested in Chapter 12, might be a good place to start. Another idea is to reward the marketing group based on the quality rather than the quantity of leads—and making the alignment of customer requirements essential to the definition of a qualified lead.

Just as serving the right customers is vital to shaping demand, being selective about the products you sell is also critical. In years past, decisions regarding new products were usually made without regard to supply chain constraints, since delivering the goods was a relatively low-level function. In the new chain-based competition, selling products that don't fit the supply chain is a hard decision to justify. It's not just a problem with moving those particular products through the chain cost-effectively; the deeper problem is that their requirements can keep the entire chain from reaching peak performance. If you have to maintain special equipment at all your facilities just to handle a small, low-margin segment of your product line, this would be a good time to consider divesting that line. If your goal is to compete with other chains based on cost, then you may want to rethink some of your more innovative products, which require excess safety stock and capacity.

Divest products that hurt the supply chain

As with culling out unprofitable customers, dropping products that don't fit your supply chain is only half a solution; the other half lies in making sure that all new products are well suited to your chain. If your goals include making your chain more flexible and responsive to changing needs, then you should take advantage of your ability to accommodate variable demand and seek out innovative products that other chains can't handle cost-effectively. Better still, use supply chain considerations to help shape the design of new products, allowing innovation not only in the product itself but in how you bring it to market. The sections in Chapter 15 dealing with design for supply and the use of postponement should give you some good ideas about how to do this.

Seek out products that match your chain

The current emphasis on improving the efficiency of supply chains can obscure the fact that the biggest opportunities still lie in innovation. As shown in Figure 13.7, most of the dollars devoted to improving the supply chain are spent on automating operations, a relatively

Innovation offers the greatest potential

Figure 13.7
The ROI Irony

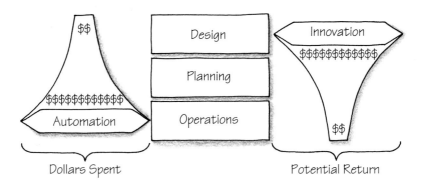

safe investment with an ROI that is easy to estimate. The fewest dollars are spent at the design level, where there is the most opportunity for innovation. The irony here is that innovation offers a far bigger potential for return. If you want to gain a few points of market share, by all means shave a few points off your costs. But if you want to dominate your market, you need to do something that the competition can't match just by increasing efficiency.

Stabilizing Demand

Stabilizing demand reduces cost

In addition to focusing on customers and products that fit your supply chain, you can also shape demand by stabilizing it. As described in Chapter 2, variability is one of the most costly problems in supply chains, particularly when it amplifies as it flows up the chain. Anything you can do to stabilize the flow of demand across the chain will improve your performance and give you a substantial advantage over chains that have to cope with higher levels of variability.

The biggest problem is demand lumping

The biggest source of variability in supply chains is a phenomenon called **demand lumping**, in which a steady flow of demand is divided up into arbitrary chunks that appear as sudden surges in demand. In Figure 13.8, a retailer sells products at a constant daily rate, but doesn't replenish its stock until it hits a fixed reorder

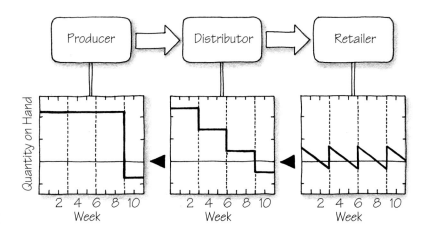

Figure 13.8
Demand Lumping

point. When it does reorder, it rounds up its requirements to the next level of packaging to avoid handling individual items, then rounds up a little further if it's close to the next quantity break in the distributor's discount schedule. The distributor follows a similar policy, but it waits longer and buys in larger quantities in order to get better prices. When it finally does place an order, the quantity is so large that it exhausts the producer's inventory of finished goods and triggers another production run.

As this example illustrates, lumping distorts the demand signal in two ways. First, it throws off the timing, delaying the demand signal as it moves upstream. If all the producer sees is this incoming demand signal, it doesn't even know that its product is selling until after nine weeks of sales. Second, it amplifies the apparent signal. When the producer finally does receive information about demand, it comes in such a large order that the producer may ramp up production to handle the surge. If the product continues to sell at a steady rate, the chain will gradually stabilize. But even the smallest variation in sales will continue to amplify up the chain, producing the infamous "bullwhip effect" that has such a devastating impact on upstream suppliers (see Chapter 2).

Lumping distorts both timing and amplitude

Lumping results from economies of scale

As this example illustrates, demand lumping is usually a by-product of such routine practices as quantity discounts, economic replenishment policies, volume packaging, and batch production runs. These are all sound business practices, having been developed to take advantage of economies of scale. The fact that these practices also create havoc in supply chains is a highly counterintuitive but deeply important insight. It seems that there is a fundamental tension between economies of scale and the smooth flow of demand up the supply chain.

Other practices can cause demand lumping

There are other causes of demand lumping that aren't related to economies of scale. One is **forward buying**, in which customers purchase supplies before they are needed in order to take advantage of favorable prices. These prices may be the result of natural fluctuations in the market, but they are usually caused by promotions on the part of suppliers. Another culprit is hoarding, in which customers buy more than they need in order to protect themselves against current or expected shortages. Hoarding can have particularly nasty effects on demand because it contains a positive feedback loop: Hoarding increases scarcity, which further increases hoarding, and so on. In some situations, such as chip shortages in the electronics industry, this self-amplification can escalate a relatively minor shortfall into a worldwide crisis.

Try basing discounts on total volume

Does this mean that you have to give up all your established business practices in order to stabilize demand? No, but you do need to modify those practices to reduce the incentive to lump demand. For example, try basing quantity discounts on total volume rather than the size of individual orders. This still encourages customers to buy in quantity, but it eliminates the incentive to inflate each order. The result will likely be a larger number of smaller orders, which will reduce your economies of scale in order processing. However, that problem can be solved by streamlining order management, as the industry programs described in Chapter 3 amply demonstrate.

Here are two more examples of how you can modify common practices to reduce the problem of lumping. Instead of basing promotional prices on the quantity purchased by your customers, base them on the quantity they sell to *their* customers. Using this **sell-through** amount reduces forward buying and helps ensure that promotions actually move product down the chain rather than just pushing it to the next link. Similarly, you can reduce hoarding with a **turn-and-earn** system, in which customers can only purchase scarce products in proportion to their outgoing sales. This discourages customers from "gaming" the system, inflating their orders in hopes of increasing their allocations.

Modify other practices to reduce lumping

One of the most effective techniques is to use promotions to stabilize demand rather than inflate it. Figure 13.9 shows a forecast for consumer demand with a serious dip over a period of about six weeks. Producers would normally respond to this kind of dip either by scaling back production during the slump or by holding production steady and stockpiling inventory. Both alternatives have their costs and benefits, but there is a third choice that may be preferable

Use promotions to stabilize demand

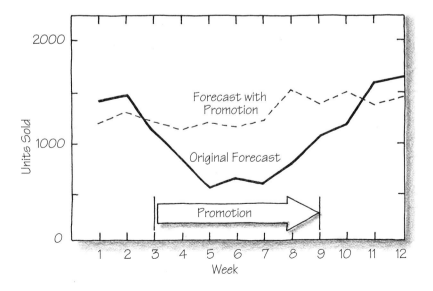

Figure 13.9
Smoothing Demand with Promotions

to both: Run a promotion during the slump, raising demand enough to consume the output of a stable production schedule. Even if most of this increased demand is due to forward buying, that's okay because, in this case, the forward buying is working to stabilize demand rather than distort it.

Mastering demand rather than just managing it is a powerful weapon in chain-based competition, but it's not an easy one to wield. In addition to knowing your customers and understanding how your products fit their needs, you have to be willing to make hard choices about which customers and products are right for your chain, and you have to modify business practices that are deeply ingrained in your corporate culture. But mastery is never achieved instantly, and these changes don't have to come all at once. If you can simply shift your thinking about demand from a conventional, reactive stance to a more proactive point of view, understanding that you can shape demand to fit the competitive advantages of your supply chain, you're already a step ahead of most managers.

14

Designing the Chain

The first step in designing a supply chain is to formulate a strategy for the chain. The most critical element of this strategy, described in the first section, is deciding how to make the tradeoff between flexibility and efficiency. Once your strategy is in place, the next step is to analyze your existing supply chain and identify options for improving it, as described in the second section. The third step is to use mathematical and simulation models to evaluate the options you've identified and produce the design that best satisfies your objectives. This last step is highly automated, but don't let that fool you—the most powerful tool for supply chain design is still your own insights into the nature of your business, and it's vital that you be actively involved throughout the process.

Choosing a Strategy

In the new, chain-based competition, success depends on formulating and executing a clear strategy for your chain. This is not yet a common insight; the very idea that supply chains require a strategy would come as a surprise to many managers. This is perhaps understandable; in years past, when logistics was viewed as a support function, managing the chain was primarily a matter of finding the best way to move whatever the company chose to sell. But in the new competition, the priorities are reversed: If you can't create and deliver products in a timely, cost-effective manner, it doesn't matter much how well you design and market them. This reversal places supply chain decisions at the very heart of corporate strategy.

Strategy is relatively new to supply chains

Supply chains have leapt from the backroom to the boardroom so quickly that most companies are just now beginning to formulate a strategy. Think back to the survey I mentioned in Chapter 1:

Few companies have a strategy in place

Ninety-one percent of executives in manufacturing companies ranked supply chain management as vital to their success, yet 59% of those executives stated that their companies *had no strategy* for improving their supply chains. The survey didn't ask how many executives in companies that did have a strategy believed it was a good one, or how many felt they were implementing their strategy successfully. However, it did find that only 2% of the executives regarded their supply chains as "excellent," so there can't be very many who were satisfied on either count.

The lack of strategy is a great opportunity

This widespread lack of strategy is what makes supply chain management such a hotbed of activity today. The stakes are high and the bar is low, so the business opportunity is huge. Simply put, you don't need to formulate the perfect strategy to win this game. If you can just put together a reasonably good strategy and implement it consistently, you will be well ahead of the competition. Moreover, formulating a supply chain strategy is not a particularly challenging task. The key issues can be described in a few paragraphs.

The central tradeoff is efficiency versus flexibility

Many considerations go into formulating a supply chain strategy, but one concern dominates the rest—the tradeoff between flexibility and efficiency. Most managers, if asked whether they wanted their chain to be flexible or efficient, would answer "both" without a second thought. Unfortunately, the deep tradeoff between the two makes having both an unrealistic goal. Increasing flexibility generally requires a company to increase safety stock and maintain reserve capacity to meet unexpected demand, and increasing efficiency requires driving both of these reserves as low as possible. You can strike any balance you want between the two, but you can't eliminate the tradeoff.

The efficient frontier defines what's possible

However, the tradeoff between efficiency and flexibility isn't absolute. The situation is comparable to the tradeoffs between trading partners discussed in Chapter 3, and applying a tradeoff diagram produces a similar curve. As Figure 14.1 illustrates, there are intermediate "win-win" positions that allow the two qualities to be combined to some degree. But there is also an upper bound, called the **efficient frontier**, that constraints the total of the two. As new practices improve the capabilities of supply chains, this frontier is pushed outward, reducing the need to compromise between flexibility and efficiency. However, you are always constrained by the current frontier, and you have to choose the most advantageous point along that frontier.

The most important consideration in deciding where to place your company along this tradeoff curve is your corporate **positioning strategy**. In the manufacturing sector, positioning is based primarily on three qualities: product, price, and service. The goal of your company should be to stake out a defensible position in the market based on some combination of these qualities. If a dominant company in your industry were firmly entrenched as the low-cost provider, for example, you would probably want to differentiate yourself based on the quality of your products or services.

The tradeoff depends on firm positioning

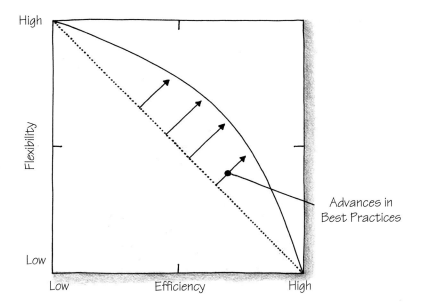

Figure 14.1
The Efficient Frontier

You can't avoid making a choice

Staking out a position for your company involves yet another tradeoff among competing qualities. There has been a tendency in recent years to imagine that it's possible to be the best on all three qualities, as expressed in the mantra "faster, better, cheaper," but the business reality is that these qualities inevitably trade off against each other. The best product costs more to build, and the best service costs more to deliver; realistically, you just can't provide either of these in combination with the lowest prices and still hope to make a profit. Adopting a strategy that calls for being the best in all three qualities is the same as having no strategy at all.

Firm positioning shapes supply chain strategy

Your choice of a positioning strategy places strong constraints on the way you make the tradeoff between efficiency and flexibility in your supply chain (Figure 14.2). If you want to be the low-price leader, your only viable option is to build the most efficient, economical chain possible; if you don't, you will inevitably lose your position to a company that can squeeze more cost out of its chain. If you stake your reputation on the quality of your service, you need a highly flexible chain that can deliver your products quickly and reliably even under the most uncertain conditions. If you take the middle position and

Figure 14.2
The Influence of Corporate Positioning

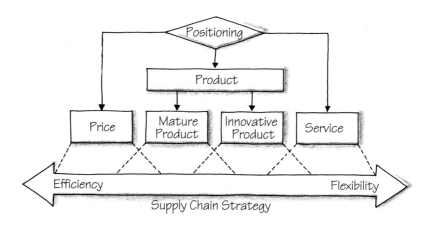

emphasize the quality of your products, your choice depends on the nature of those products; if they are innovative, you need a more flexible chain to cope with uncertain demand than if they were mature products with stable sales.

It's difficult to set and maintain a single, clear strategy for your supply chain, and you shouldn't complicate the strategy if you can possibly avoid it. However, you may not have a choice: If you have a mix of customers and products that just won't fit a single strategy and you aren't in a position to divest yourself of the misfits, you may have to implement two or more strategies within your supply chain. An example in Chapter 13 (see Figure 13.3) showed how you could serve three groups of customers with incompatible requirements by defining three different paths through the same supply chain, each of which reflects a different strategy for delivering the goods. A similar system of overlapping supply chains might be used in the case of incompatible product families.

It's possible to have overlapping strategies

Some very successful companies use multiple supply chain strategies. Wal-Mart moves its goods using a mixture of distribution centers, cross-docks, and direct deliveries, depending on the product, and it sells those goods using a combination of conventional, VMI (vendor managed inventory), and consignment supplier relationships. But the fact that Wal-Mart can handle all these combinations doesn't mean that you can, and trying to combine multiple strategies right away may prevent you from truly excelling at any one of them. Wal-Mart developed its overlapping strategies only after it achieved dominance with a single strategy founded on the relentless pursuit of efficiency. You will likely have more success if you, too, start out with a single, clear strategy and master it before you complicate it with supplementary techniques.

Start simple and build on success

Exploring Your Options

The next step is to scope the design

Once you have decided on a core strategy, you need to set the scope of the design effort. If your company is vertically integrated, so that much of the supply chain is under your direct control, the scope may naturally run from your immediate suppliers to your immediate customers. If not, you will probably need to include your customers' customers and your suppliers' suppliers to achieve major improvements. The more of the chain you can integrate under the new design, the greater the opportunity to build a competitive supply chain. But be careful not to overextend yourself; there are diminishing returns as you add more companies to the design effort, and the overhead of trying to manage too many relationships can easily swamp the benefits of expanded integration.

Focus on the core of the chain

One test of reasonableness for the design scope is the degree of branching. Recall from Chapter 2 that suppliers are often organized into tiers (see Figure 2.10). If you only deal with a handful of Tier 1 suppliers, they need to be included in the design. If their collective supplier base also happens to be small, it may make sense to bring in the Tier 2 suppliers as well. But at some point, the fan-out of suppliers will become too extreme, so that extending the design to include an additional tier would seriously inflate the number of parties involved (Figure 14.3). This link in the chain is often the same point at which supplies become generic commodities that are purchased primarily on price, so there isn't much to be gained by including these suppliers in any case. Similar logic applies on the customer side.

Select partners from within the scope

Once you have set a rough scope for the design, you need to decide which companies within that scope you'd like to have as partners in your efforts to improve the chain. If the design only spans a handful of companies, it may make sense to get them all involved. But that's rarely feasible, and in most cases the collaboration will be

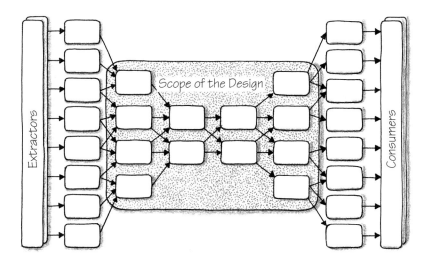

Figure 14.3
Scoping the Design

limited to the companies that exert the most influence over the performance of the chain. Supply chain managers generally know who the key players are, but there may still be some difficult choices. Here are a few things you might want to look for:

1. **Volume of business**—The most obvious candidates are your largest customers and suppliers, since they account for the majority of your business and therefore represent the largest opportunities for improvement.
2. **Value added**—The more a supplier or customer contributes to the quality of your products or the ease with which they flow through the chain to the end consumer, the more important it is to engage them in the design process.
3. **Interdependence**—A small customer that depends on you for custom supplies will be much more likely to contribute to a successful design than a large one that buys interchangeable parts from you. Similar logic applies to the supply side.
4. **Common strategy**—If your strategy is based on efficiency, bring in companies with a proven ability to operate a lean chain. If your strategy is based on flexibility, focus on the companies that thrive on innovation.

5. **Willingness to partner**—There's not much point in working up an integrated design if your trading partners aren't predisposed to making the necessary investment to improve the chain.

Factor in your own core competence

Working through the decisions about who would make the best partners in designing a better supply chain offers a good opportunity to rethink your own role within the chain. It may be the legacy of vertical integration, or it could be the result of mergers and acquisitions, but many companies continue to perform supply chain functions that others could do much more cost-effectively. As these functions become increasingly specialized, it becomes more and more important for each company to focus on its core competence, reserving for itself only those functions at which it truly excels.

The design can clarify your capabilities

The hardest part of identifying your core competence is admitting that you aren't the best at everything you do. Rather than struggling to define your core competence in the abstract, as many companies do, let the design process provide some solid data on your strengths and weaknesses. The technique is simple: Just include outsourcing options for all but the most central functions, and let those options "compete" against your in-house abilities to see which ones produce the best chain. If the best designs all outsource a particular function, then that function probably isn't part of your core competence.

Start by modeling the current supply chain

The starting point for a new design is a working model of the supply chain as it exists today. You can delegate this task to professional modelers, but in my experience you'll get much better results if you assemble a team of operational managers to sketch out a conceptual model first, preferably with the aid of an experienced facilitator. Although software tools may be useful during these modeling sessions, the most powerful tool is a very large whiteboard. The goal of this effort is to develop a shared under-standing of how the chain actually works in its present form, and that usually happens the fastest when all the managers involved are able to look at and work on the same diagrams.

Why should managers build the first model? For starters, most of the knowledge about how the chain works is in their heads, and having them build a model together is a fast, efficient way to cap-ture that knowledge. It's also a good way to discover discrepancies in their viewpoints; if you ask 10 managers how their supply chains work, you will usually get at least 10 different answers, and the sooner those differences are resolved the better. The technique also gets managers from different organizations working together as a team, allowing them to influence the future design right from the outset while also building the relationships that will make organiza-tional change possible. Finally, having operational managers build the model almost always reveals business opportunities that would never occur to technical modelers.

Managers create the best initial models

A proven approach to building the conceptual model is to use a combination of simple diagrams and narratives. Figure 14.4 offers a highly simplified example of the kind of diagram that emerges from these sessions. The example is for a hypothetical lock maker, Amlock, that operates four plants and two distribution centers (DCs). The arrows indicate the basic flow of materials, but they don't tell the whole story; that's where the narratives come in. The basic components for a keyed lock are fabricated in Huntsville, after which the parts for the locking mechanism are sent to Dayton and the remainder are shipped to one of the two Mexican plants for pri-mary assembly. The assembled units and the keyed cylinders are returned to Huntsville, where they undergo final assembly and are shipped out to the DCs. Keyless locks use a subset of the chain; they bypass Dayton altogether, and some of them are fully assembled in the Mexican plants and shipped directly to the DCs.

Use simple diagrams and narratives

Figure 14.4
A Simple
Conceptual Model

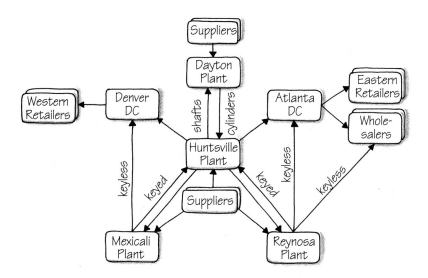

**Look for
opportunities
to improve
performance**

Once the managers in the modeling session agree on how the current chain works, it's time for them to look for opportunities to improve the chain. If the chain needs additional capacity, how should that be achieved? Can existing plants be expanded, or would it be better to close some of them and build new ones? Would it make sense to move some of the operations from one plant to another? Are there ways of reducing the distance materials have to travel as they move through the chain? The Amlock example offers opportunities to explore all these options and more. If the company needs more capacity, it might consider expanding the Mexican plants, adding a third plant, or shutting them both down in favor of a larger, more efficient facility. As for moving operations, it might be possible to move the keying process into Huntsville and close the Dayton plant. Another option would be to transfer final assembly to Mexico, eliminating the need for keyed locks to make the long trip back to Huntsville before going to the DCs.

**The goal is just
to explore the
options**

The purpose of exploring these alternatives is not to make decisions, but to choose the options that should be evaluated in the formal model. This can be a hard discipline to maintain because managers often become enthusiastic about their ideas for improvement and want to see them become part of the final design. For example, the Amlock managers might become so enamored of the idea of moving final assembly to Mexico that they stop looking for other options. This may be an excellent idea, but there isn't nearly enough information in the conceptual model to make decisions about the actual costs and benefits of any one change, nor is there any way to look at the various combinations of ideas to see which configuration would work the best. That's what the formal models are for.

Once the managers have completed their conceptual model and generated a list of options they'd like to evaluate, technical modelers translate their results into a mathematical or simulation model. The first step in this translation process is to assemble detailed information about all the elements of the conceptual model, including the suppliers, customers, products, operations, facilities, and transportation links. Figure 14.5 illustrates some of the information that

The modelers gather the detailed information

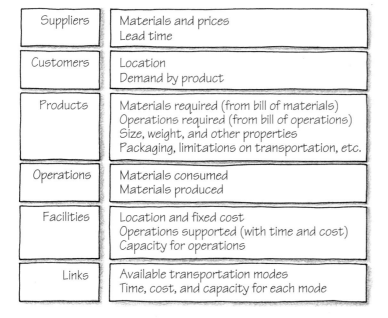

Figure 14.5
Inputs for a Formal Model

would typically be required, but the actual data depends on both the characteristics of the supply chain and the kind of model used. For example, if operations have the same cost and duration at all facilities, these properties can be attached to the operations themselves. Otherwise, the modelers will need separate numbers for each facility, as shown in the table.

Modelers also research each option

In addition to data about existing elements of the supply chain, the modelers need detailed information about the options they are to evaluate: They need to know the costs involved in changing the capacity of each facility, the upper and lower bounds of capacity for each, the cost of closing existing facilities or building new ones, and so on. If you want to explore your options for moving new products through the chain, the modelers will need demand forecasts, bills of materials, planned production sites, and similar information on each new product you are considering.

Designing the Chain

The best designs come from optimizers

The strategy is set, the current chain is diagrammed and described, and the options are on the table: It's time to build a formal model of the chain. If you haven't already done so, you now have to make the choice between a mathematical optimizer and a simulator. A simulator may be a natural next step if your chain is complex and you are still trying to get a handle on how it all works. But if you're ready to move toward decisions, an optimizer will give you more help in choosing the best possible configuration. In the following discussion, I assume that you are using an optimizer, then I add some remarks on the use of simulators at the end of the section. The goal is not to explain how to use either of these systems—your modeling team will take care of that—but to give you enough insight into the process that you can give the modelers the guidance they require and understand the results they bring back to you.

Optimizers come in a variety of forms. They are the core technology underlying advanced planning and scheduling (APS) systems, they are common in stand-alone supply-chain design tools, and they can be purchased—or even downloaded for free on the Web—as plug-in modules for other modeling systems. If you have Microsoft Excel, you already have one on your desktop; just choose Tools and then Solver from the main menu and you'll be presented with a small but powerful optimizer. If you are curious about how optimizers work, experimenting with Excel's solver is an excellent way to become familiar with the technology.

Optimizers come in many forms

Basically, an optimizer is a system with a large number of inputs and a single output—the best design for your supply chain given the inputs (Figure 14.6). All but one of the inputs take the form of **constraints**, which is optimizer jargon for mathematical expressions that describe the current chain and your options for modifying it. The other input is the **objective function**, a formula the modelers construct to reflect your objectives for the design. The optimizer takes the constraints as inputs and uses a variant of linear programming to find the design that best satisfies the objectives, producing the winning design as its output. Your role in all this is to give the modelers the information they need to prepare

An optimizer designs from constraints

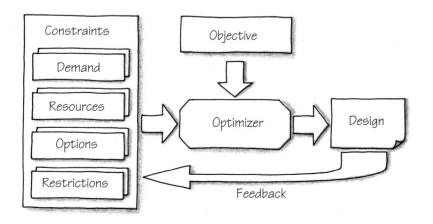

Figure 14.6
Using an Optimizer

the constraints and the objective function, then review the resulting design with them.

**There are
several kinds of
constraints**

Although the constraints are all expressed in the same mathematical form, it's helpful to think of them as falling into four
categories, as shown in Figure 14.6. The demand constraints are
forecasts of how much product has to be delivered in each geographical region, as described in Chapter 13. The resource constraints provide detailed information about the products, facilities,
and other elements of your current supply chain, as listed in Figure
14.5. The options represent the alternatives you'd like the optimizer
to explore, such as changing the capacities of some plants or open-
ing new plants. The restrictions express whatever limitations you
want to place on the design, including the required customer service level, the level of reserve capacity you'd like to maintain, and
the amount of money available for capital improvements.

**The objective
function
provides
the goal**

The objective function represents the quantity you want to optimize in the design. If you have the modelers use total cost for the
objective function, the optimizer will analyze all possible configurations to find the design that meets the expected demand at the lowest cost. If you ask to have the model optimize the order fill rate,
the design you get back will have the highest fill rate you can
achieve, regardless of the cost.

**You can't ask
for conflicting
objectives**

These examples raise an important question: What if you want the
design to optimize two or more quantities, such as cost *and* fill rate?
The short answer is that you can't do it because these two quantities trade off against each other—increasing the fill rate raises the
cost, and cutting costs may reduce fill rates. The most you can ask
for is a good balance between the two, given their relative importance to you, and there are optimization techniques to help you
balance two or more objectives against each other. A simpler solution is to express one of the two quantities as a constraint, leaving

the model free to optimize the other quantity. In the current example, the usual procedure is to treat the minimum fill rate as a constraint and let the model optimize against cost. If it turns out that achieving a fill rate of, say, 97% is too expensive under the best of conditions, you simply ask the modelers to find out how much you could save by lowering it a point or two.

Cost is a common choice for the objective function because, as described in Chapter 12, it naturally aligns other business objectives. However, using cost does tend to favor immediate, operational benefits over longer-term improvements, and it completely ignores the impact of the design on revenue. In my view, the ideal objective function is the "common denominator" shown on the right side of Figure 12.4: the projected profit over a specific period of time, including adjustments for the time value of money. However, using profit rather than cost requires the model to deal with additional factors such as pricing, discounting, and non-production costs, so using profit as the objective function is not yet a common practice.

Cost and profit make good objectives

Designing a supply chain isn't a one-shot deal; it usually takes several passes just to get all the constraints sorted out. The natural procedure is for modelers to run the optimizer on the initial set of data, review the results with you, then change the inputs based on that review. This refinement process offers a good opportunity to ask all those interesting "what if" questions. What would it cost to bump the customer service level up three points? What would happen if you doubled the budget for new construction? How different would the design be if you gave the optimizer the option of shutting down three of your older plants and outsourcing their production? The optimizer can answer all these questions and more.

Supply chain design is an iterative process

You should also perform "what if" experiments to see how the design holds up under variations in demand and supply. Keep in mind that optimizers treat all constraints as fixed values, and that's

Test the design against variable demand

not a realistic assumption. In order to understand the effects of variability in demand and supply, you have to test the design over a range of values for each and see how it performs. If your demand patterns are fairly stable and your strategy is to build a lean chain, it may only take a few of these "what if" experiments to be confident that your design is robust across reasonable variability. If you are designing a flexible chain specifically to cope with high variability, however, you may want to take the additional step of simulating the design.

Simulations validate a design across variability

The limitations of mathematical optimizers are neatly complemented by the strengths of simulation tools. As described in Chapter 5, simulators can assign distributions of possible values to parameters rather than assuming a single, fixed value for each. The simulations run many times, picking a number at random from the appropriate distribution each time they need a value for a parameter. In this way, simulators provide a detailed analysis of the effects of variability, yielding a clear indication of whether a design is robust across typical variations in demand, supply, capacity, and other parameters. The other important advantage of simulators is that they aren't limited to linear relations. For example, if you are concerned about the fact that price breaks and other effects of quantity are introducing nonlinear relations, a simulation model can tell you whether these nonlinear relations are affecting your results.

Use both kinds of models for the best design

If simulations are so much better in this regard, why not use them in place of optimizers? Precisely because they lack the ability to seek out optimal solutions. That's why simulations are a complement to optimizers rather than a replacement. A good way to combine the two types is to use an optimizer to generate one or more candidate models, then use a simulator to stress-test these models under conditions of variability and nonlinearity (Figure 14.7). This approach also makes the best use of the hill-climbing ability of simulation models (see Chapter 5); once you put a simulation model in

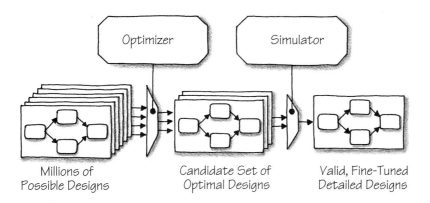

Figure 14.7
Refining the Design

Millions of
Possible Designs

Candidate Set of
Optimal Designs

Valid, Fine-Tuned
Detailed Designs

the region of the desired solution, it can fine-tune the values of one or more key parameters under its more realistic assumptions. In short, using a simulator in conjunction with an optimizer gives you the best of both tools: The optimizer does the heavy lifting of sorting through millions of possible designs, and the simulator does the finesse work of validating and refining the best candidates.

The moment of truth comes when the optimized design is complete and ready for comparison with the current supply chain. Converting an operating supply chain over to a new design is an expensive, disruptive, and risky proposition for all concerned, so the expected ROI from making this conversion has to be substantial to justify the change. The investment side of this calculation includes the initial costs of conversion—the acquisition of new facilities and equipment, the costs of education and training, and other expenses—together with the continuing costs of jointly managing the new chain as an integrated system. The return includes the total savings in operating costs together with whatever increased sales are expected to result.

A new design has to pay its own way

The basis for calculating the expected return on this investment is not the performance of the current supply chain as it operates in today's market, but the projected figures for that chain as it will

ROI should be based on future performance

295

continue into the future, including the effects of all the intrinsic and extrinsic factors reviewed in Chapter 10 (see Figure 10.7). This is an important distinction that may well cast the deciding vote in the decision to make the change. An ROI based on the assumption of a static market with stable competition might indicate that there is little to be gained by changing your current practices. But if the market is demanding increased performance at lower cost, or if your competitors are already integrating their supply chains and upping the ante for the entire market, a realistic forecast could show that your sales will plummet if you don't improve your chain. In that case, what might initially look like a breakeven proposition may actually be a make-or-break decision.

The ability of supply-chain design systems to find optimal solutions gives you a powerful tool for improving your chain, but remember that the most powerful tool of all is still your own experience as a manager. Optimizers can only evaluate the options you give them, so the quality of the design you get is a direct reflection of the quality of your own thinking about your business. That's why it's critical that you and your fellow managers drive the design process, pushing the modelers to try things they would never think of based on your current practices. That's also why you need to be up to speed on the current best practices in the industry, as these are the techniques that allow you to keep pushing the limits of what you can achieve in your design. The next and final chapter explores four of the most exciting developments on the frontier of supply chain management.

15

Maximizing Performance

Chapter 14 described how the strategic tradeoff between efficiency and flexibility is constrained by the efficient frontier, and it offered a way to identify the best operating point on this frontier given a particular supply chain strategy. But the efficient frontier is constantly being pushed forward by new techniques and technologies (Figure 15.1), so opportunities for competitive advantage are constantly increasing. This final chapter looks at four ways in which supply chain leaders are advancing the efficient frontier today: accelerating the movement of inventory across the chain, pooling risk by forming "virtual inventories" across multiple sites, designing products specifically to suit the supply chain, and postponing the differentiation among products as late in the chain as possible.

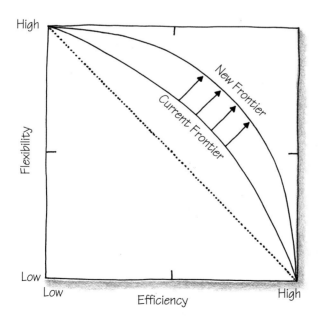

Figure 15.1
Advancing the Frontier

Increasing Velocity

Acceleration helps both flexibility and efficiency

One of the simplest ways to advance the efficient frontier is to accelerate the flow of goods across your chain. Acceleration improves efficiency because inventory doesn't stay in the chain as long, which brings down the costs of holding that inventory. At the same time, increasing the velocity of inventory enhances flexibility because it reduces the time required to change what's in the pipeline in response to changing demand. If it takes six weeks for your inventory to go from production to consumer, then your product mix will always lag behind demand by a couple of months. On the other hand, if it takes six days to go from production to consumer, you can change that mix in a week.

Faster transportation increases velocity

An obvious way to increase velocity is to switch to a faster mode of transportation. If you are sending goods overseas by ship and have the option of using airfreight, you may be able to realize a net benefit from making the switch. But the cost of faster transportation is often substantial, so it's hard to push the frontier very far just by increasing transportation speed. To produce a net advantage, the increased transportation costs have to be more than offset by the financial benefits of decreased holding costs, improved sales, reduced write-downs, or some combination of these factors.

Smarter processing is the better approach

A much more effective way to increase velocity is to improve the way the chain handles goods that *aren't* in motion. Despite all the efforts to improve the efficiency of supply chains over the past few decades, inventory still spends the majority of its time sitting around waiting for something to happen. As noted in Chapter 9, a study of the British auto industry found that steel components spent 97% of their time idle. Your inventory may not be quite that sluggish, but if you gather the data and calculate the results for a few of your own components you may find that you're not much better off.

In short, the better way to increase the velocity of inventory is not to move it faster when it does move, but to get it to spend more of its time in motion. Achieving that goal is much harder than just changing the transportation mode; you have to conduct systematic studies of how inventory moves across the chain, examine each place it stops, and look for ways to get it moving again. To achieve significantly higher velocities, you may need to reengineer your supply chain operations, applying the techniques of JIT, lean production, and related disciplines.

Some process reengineering will be necessary

You can get a quick sense of where slowdowns occur just by looking at the size of the queues of raw materials that build up within facilities, both at the receiving docks and in front of individual workstations. In Figure 15.2, the large queue at Facility F indicates that this facility is a bottleneck, and the empty queue at Facility I indicates that it is being held up by F. When you find a bottleneck, your first choice should be to find a way to increase the throughput for that operation, either by adding capacity or by improving the operation itself. If you can't find a way to fix the bottleneck, then try scaling back the upstream operations that feed into the bottleneck (Facility C in the example). It may seem counterintuitive to

Much of the waste can be found in queues

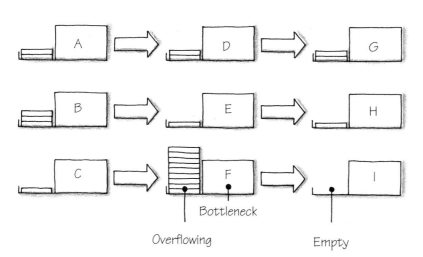

Figure 15.2
Looking for Queues

accelerate the flow of inventory by slowing some operations down, but that's precisely the effect you will achieve. By not pulling inventory into the chain until it has a clear path, you're making sure that inventory moves faster once it does enter the chain.

Eliminate activities that don't add value

For a more revealing view of how inventory spends its time, have someone record the time inventory spends in each location within the chain and plot the results as a time-in-process chart of the sort shown in Figure 9.11. Better still, take this approach one step further by making a distinction between activities that add value and those that don't. The only activities that add value are those that change the product in a way that increases its utility to the customer, usually by changing either its form or its location to bring it closer to the needs of the customer. The study that showed inventory in the British auto industry sitting idle 97% of the time also revealed that when the inventory *was* moving, less than a third of the time was spent adding value. As bad as this may seem, it can get worse because some activities can actually *reduce* value. In the Amlock example of Chapter 14, the time locks spend in transit to the Mexican plants actually reduces their value because it takes them farther away from the consumers who will eventually buy them.

Tracking systems make this much easier

Tracing the movement of tens of thousands of products through your supply chain to identify bottlenecks and unproductive operations can be a daunting task, but this is an area where technology can greatly ease the burden. As described in Chapter 6, tracking systems, supply-chain visibility systems, and event-management software can remove most of the drudgery from this effort and automatically alert you to any slowdowns in the chain. Identification technologies such as barcodes and radio frequency (RF) tags can go even further to make this an effortless activity by automating the entire process.

For example, clothing manufacturers now have the ability to print RF transmitters the size of a grain of salt directly onto the tags sewn into their garments, an innovation that would allow them to track every article of clothing from its offshore manufacturer to its point of sale. In this case, however, the technology may be a bit too advanced for the market; Benetton recently announced that, despite earlier reports, it was *not* going to put these tags in its clothing. The company's customers were disturbed by the idea that the company could track *their* movements when they were wearing the clothes, despite Benetton's promise to disable the tags at the point of sale.

Transmitters are as small as a grain of salt

Although the attempt to increase velocity is primarily directed at the flow of inventory, there are advantages to be gained from accelerating the flow of demand and cash as well. The faster demand moves up the supply chain, the more quickly upstream suppliers can respond to changes in that demand. In addition, accelerating the demand signal is one of the most effective ways of eliminating demand amplification, which is the source of much disruption in supply chains. Finally, accelerating the flow of cash reduces the total cost of debt across the chain, further improving efficiency without impairing flexibility. A case in point is Cisco Systems, which uses instant payment in its supply chain to help suppliers offset the costs of rapid delivery. The moral: When you think about how you can increase the velocity of your supply chain, consider the flow of demand and cash as well as the flow of supply.

Accelerate demand and cash flow along with supply

Pooling Risk

The second technique for advancing the efficient frontier is **risk pooling**. The idea behind risk pooling is to combine the management of inventories that would otherwise be controlled separately so that variability in demand can be handled with less safety stock.

Risk pooling reduces inventory requirements

To see how this works, take a look at Figure 15.3, which compares the inventory levels required to meet a 97% customer service level (CSL) with either three regional inventories or a single, centralized inventory. With regional inventories, each region has to have 150 units of a product on hand in order to meet the target CSL, for a total of 450 units. With a centralized inventory, only 300 units are required.

The advantage stems from offsetting variations

What accounts for the difference? The proper explanation would require an excursion into statistics, but the simple answer is that local variations in demand tend to cancel each other out. In Figure 15.3, random variability might cause demand to be high in the first region, average in the second, and low in the third, or it might lead to some other combination of demand levels, but it's relatively unlikely that it will happen to be high in all three regions at the same time. If the inventories for the three regions are pooled, then the same safety stock can cover the risk of high demand in any of three regions, reducing the total inventory requirements. Depending on conditions, it may be possible to reduce inventories—and, hence, holding costs—by 25% to 35% using risk pooling.

Figure 15.3
Risk Pooling

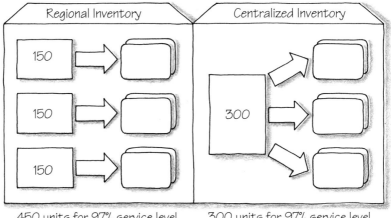

Of course, a decision to centralize inventories involves more than just the requirements for safety stock. It might not be possible to hit your target CSL without holding stock close to your customers, or the costs of using faster transportation might be greater than the savings due to holding less inventory. But risk pooling doesn't require that inventories actually be located in the same place. All it requires is that they be managed as a common pool. This can be done through a variety of techniques, including echelon inventory, multisourcing, transshipment, and direct shipment, as defined in the following paragraphs.

Physical centralization isn't necessary

As described in Chapter 2, many distribution networks have multiple levels or echelons. For example, products might move from a single, central warehouse through several regional distribution centers and then to a large number of widely distributed stores (Figure 15.4). While it is possible for each of these facilities to manage its inventory independently, this is rarely done because it is far more efficient to manage them collectively as an **echelon inventory**. In this approach, the set of facilities leading from the central facility through the retail store is treated as a common risk pool, with the central stock providing backup to the regional stock, which provides backup to the store stock in turn. So long as the delays in getting stock from the next level up the chain are tolerable

Echelon inventory supports risk pooling

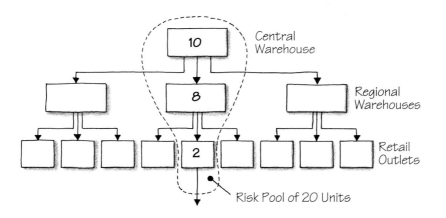

Figure 15.4
An Echelon Inventory System

to the customer, the total inventory in an echelon system can be greatly reduced through risk pooling.

Multisourcing also pools risk

As shown in Figure 15.4, the most common arrangement in an echelon distribution system is for each facility to be served by a single upstream facility. This structure simplifies the administration of the system, but it limits the savings that can be realized through risk pooling. If each facility can receive goods from two or more upstream facilities, then the inventories of those facilities automatically form a risk pool that reduces the need for safety stock. Figure 15.5 illustrates this by showing a variation of the centralization approach illustrated in Figure 15.3. Instead of serving all three regions from a single central warehouse, each region is served by its own warehouse, but the warehouses backstop each other in the event of a stockout. This allows the total inventory to be reduced to 300 units, as with the centralized inventory, but it retains the customer proximity of the regional facilities.

Facilities are grouped into overlapping pools

Shipping from more distant facilities takes longer and is more expensive, so it may not be economically feasible to support all possible links between warehouses and regions. The solution to this

Figure 15.5
Pooling Risk
Across Regions

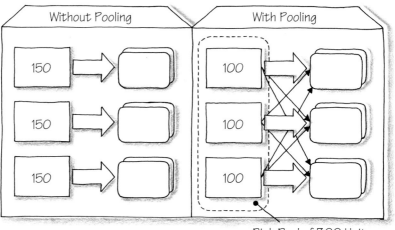

problem is to divide the facilities into separate but overlapping
risk pools, as shown in Figure 15.6. Most of the benefits of risk
pooling are achieved with the first few members in each pool, so
overlapping pools can keep the number of links to a reasonable
level while still achieving significant reductions in inventory. The
strategy works even if shipping products from more distant facilities
results in a net loss on any given sale. Because such events are relatively infrequent, they are more than paid for by the savings in
holding costs.

The benefits of risk pooling can also be achieved through **transshipment**, in which the facilities at a given level of the chain
exchange inventory among themselves. This technique is more
expensive than multi-sourcing because products travel farther on
average, but sometimes it's the only option. This is clearly the case
at the retail level because there are no downstream facilities to
receive merged shipments, and this is where transshipment is most
often practiced. Stores are normally arranged into overlapping risk

**Transshipment
offers similar
benefits**

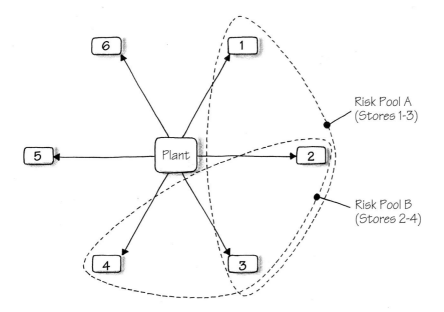

Figure 15.6
Overlapping
Risk Pools

pools based on proximity, as shown in Figure 15.6, and given electronic access to each other's inventory. This allows the stores to deal with stockouts by assuring customers that the product they want is in stock and will be available within a short period, typically the following day.

Direct shipment reduces several costs

Yet another way to achieve risk pooling is through **direct shipment**, in which one or more links of a supply chain are bypassed altogether. In Figure 15.4, for example, a large order might be shipped directly from the central warehouse to a retail outlet, skipping the regional warehouse. As this example suggests, you can think of direct shipment as a variant of echelon inventory in the sense that upstream facilities backstop the inventory of downstream facilities. The advantage of direct shipment is that it avoids all the cost of moving through the intermediate facilities, including the time and expense of unloading, storing, retrieving, and reloading merchandise. Direct shipment is often used to handle large orders that hit transportation breakpoints, such as full truckload (FTL) deliveries, regardless of whether a closer facility has the goods in stock. Not only does this practice eliminate local handling costs, it also reduces total shipping costs by taking advantage of FTL rates. A further advantage of this practice is that because downstream storage facilities don't have to handle large orders, they can reduce both their cycle stock and their safety stock without reducing service levels.

Risk pooling can be applied with any strategy

Risk pooling is an excellent tool for advancing the efficient frontier because pooling can be mapped onto any combination of efficiency and flexibility, depending on your strategy. If you are seeking the most efficient chain, you can trim inventory levels by as much as a third without compromising your service level. If your strategy is based on flexibility, you can respond to greater fluctuations in demand without increasing inventories. If you are looking to strike a balance, you can improve both qualities in whatever mix you prefer.

Powerful as it is, risk pooling is not a panacea, and the leverage you can gain from it depends on the nature of demand. If the demand for a product is highly stable, then you don't need much safety stock to begin with, so there is less to be gained by reducing it. More subtly, if demand in the various regions tends to rise and fall together, then risk pooling won't be very effective because shortages in one region will most likely be accompanied by shortages in other regions. This is not to say that risk pooling can't be used under these conditions. Rather, the point is that the technique produces the greatest benefits when demand is uncertain and relatively independent across regions.

Effectiveness depends on uncorrelated demand

Another caution regarding this technique is that it can be much harder to manage than a standard echelon distribution system. Instead of always receiving goods from a single upstream facility, a facility can pull goods from multiple facilities in the echelon above it, skip that echelon altogether and source from further upstream, or tap peer facilities within its own echelon. To complicate matters further, each of these alternatives may be limited to risk pools whose membership varies with every facility (see Figure 15.6). Properly managed, these sourcing alternatives can push the efficient frontier well beyond its current bounds. Improperly managed, they can leave a company floundering in the hinterland, far away from the frontier.

Risk pooling can be difficult to administer

Designing for Supply

In the 1980s there was a major effort among manufacturing companies to design products that were easier to build. This effort, known both as *design for manufacturing* and *concurrent engineering*, was a significant departure from past practices, in which engineers designed a product and then handed it over to manufacturing to figure out how to build it. By taking manufacturing requirements into account during the design process, companies that adopted this

Design for manufacturing simplified production

approach were able to simplify production, reduce costs, and enhance quality.

This effort now spans the supply chain

Today, design for manufacturing is being pushed outside the four walls of the factory and applied to entire supply chains. The new movement—called **design for supply**—takes into account the entire sequence of operations and movements necessary to convert raw materials into usable products. Many of the techniques are taken directly from design for manufacturing, the only change being a shift in focus from a single company to a coalition of companies. Other techniques provide solutions that are unique to the problems of supply chains.

Simplification and commonality lie at the core

Two of the most basic techniques are simplification and commonality. The goal of simplification is to reduce the number of alternative assemblies by eliminating unnecessary options, even if that increases the cost of components somewhat. For example, it may cost a bit more to build a power supply that works on either 110 or 220 volts, but that one small change can reduce by half the number of different products that have to be produced, shipped, and stocked. Similarly, the goal of commonality is to reduce the number of similar components by reducing the choices available to designers. Instead of allowing each designer an unlimited choice of nuts and bolts, for example, a chain might standardize on a small set of choices and require designers to work with these. This may cause a few products to have larger fasteners than they need, but it also streamlines production by reducing the variety of materials, and it reduces purchasing costs by combining inventories that would otherwise be handled separately.

Modularization increases options and reduces cost

A more ambitious technique is the use of modularity in product design. Rather than designing each new product from scratch, engineers design products as assemblies of pluggable components, using existing components wherever possible. As with simplification and commonality, this technique may increase the cost of an individual product somewhat because it requires interfaces that wouldn't be needed for a product using dedicated components. But these costs can be more than offset by the savings from reusing the same components across many different products. Modularity can also increase customer options by allowing many configurations to be assembled from a relatively small set of components.

Another advantage of modularization is that manufacturers can produce the modules of a product simultaneously rather than building the entire product sequentially. This parallel production permits shorter lead times, improving customer service while reducing holding costs. Parallel production also permits greater flexibility in the choice of production sites by giving manufacturers the option of using specialized facilities for the various components.

Modularity supports simultaneous production

If designers take modularization far enough, manufacturers can create a large number of products from a minimum number of components. They can then produce and ship these components in high volumes, bringing their costs down into the commodity range, yet deliver a final product that is highly customized to the needs of its ultimate consumer. This is what happened in the PC industry, and it's the reason that Dell can sell custom-built computers at commodity prices.

Modularization leads to cheap customization

Another important technique is designing products for convenient packaging. As described in Chapter 13, low-density products are inordinately expensive to ship because they cause vehicles to fill up before they reach their maximum carrying weight. Increasingly, these products are being designed in a modular fashion that allows final assembly to be postponed until late in the chain. A particularly striking example of this is ready-to-assemble (RTA) furniture such as desks and shelves, which requires the final assembly to be performed by the consumer. This innovation has reduced the cost of

Design for supply includes packaging

transportation to the point where RTA furniture is routinely shipped around the world.

Display is now a design concern as well

In the case of retail products, another technique used in design for supply is making sure that the product will display well in stores. For example, electronic games are often designed to be operated within their packages so that consumers can try them before they buy them. Another example is the effect that Wal-Mart has had on packaging dimensions: The store has such a strong preference for goods that fit on its 14-inch shelves that many suppliers have redesigned their products to fit in packages measuring 14 inches on a side. Even when there is no primary packaging, display characteristics have a big impact on design. For example, large plastic items such as cans, storage containers, and lawn furniture are now designed so that they nest inside each other when stacked, reducing the precious retail space required to display these low value-to-volume products.

Collaborative design is becoming common

One further technique is to engage suppliers in the design of a product. In years past, suppliers had little or no input in the design of subassemblies they would produce. Their customers simply passed them a design, and they had to build to its specifications, even if it was a poor design. Today there is much more collaboration in design, with suppliers being consulted on features, construction techniques, and costing in an effort to improve the final product. Chrysler's SCORE program, described in Chapter 1, epitomized the spectacular results than can be obtained by turning adversarial supplier relationships into true design partnerships.

Supply chains now drive manufacturing

The design-for-supply initiative is significant in a number of respects, one of which is the implied shift in the relative importance of manufacturing and supply chain management. Historically, transportation and logistics functions have been subordinate to manufacturing. In essence, manufacturing built what it wanted to build when it wanted to build it, and it was up to logistics to supply them with the necessary materials and take the finished goods off their hands. Today the roles are being reversed, and manufacturing is being viewed as one component of a much larger machine, the supply chain. In the new order of things, the needs and desires of the manufacturing group are often subordinated to the requirements of the supply chain as a whole.

This reversal of roles is a natural consequence of the new competition between supply chains, but it's a consequence that few companies have internalized to date. The main obstacle to design for supply isn't the demands of the technique itself, but the difficulty many production managers have in adjusting to the changing priorities. This is one of the reasons that any attempt to redesign the supply chain has to be embraced, supported, and actively managed by the most senior executives within the company.

This creates resistance to design for supply

Postponing Differentiation

The most exciting innovation in the movement toward design for supply is a technique variously called **postponement**, **delayed differentiation**, or, less commonly, freeze-point delay. The basic idea is to build products in generic form at the plant, ship them to distribution centers close to their destinations, then perform the final operations that result in a specific product (Figure 15.7). This technique pushes the efficient frontier because it offers greater economies of scale in both production and transportation, yet also increases a company's flexibility to respond to changing demand.

Final configuration can be done locally

The classic success story for postponement is Hewlett-Packard's DeskJet line of printers. HP was enjoying rising sales of these printers, and production in its Vancouver plant was ramping up precisely on plan to meet the growing demand. The problem was that the printers had to be configured differently for different national

HP provides the classic example

Figure 15.7
The Postponement
Technique

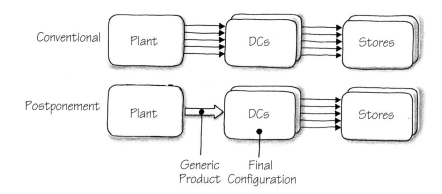

markets, and the company found itself constantly out of stock for some configurations and overstocked on others. A single plant served the entire world and the printers were shipped by boat, so there was no way HP could adjust its mix of configurations fast enough to solve the problem. Instead, the company redesigned the printers to allow the country configuration to be done at its distribution centers. This change allowed HP to produce generic printers in high volumes, ship them in large quantities, and postpone the final configuration until the printers were very close to their target markets.

Postponement increases economies of scale

The HP story illustrates several advantages of the postponement technique. First, it allows products to be specialized to different markets without compromising economies of scale in production and transportation. This advantage is vitally important; in today's consumer-oriented markets, manufacturers must offer products in ever-increasing variety, and that's undercutting the economies of scale associated with large production runs. Postponement offers a way out of this dilemma by allowing the specialization to be done close to the customer. The plant regains economies of scale by producing large batches of generic products, and customers continue to get the variety they want.

Another benefit of postponement is that it takes advantage of risk pooling to reduce inventory requirements. As described earlier in the chapter, risk pooling reduces the need for safety stock by pulling multiple inventories together, allowing local variations in demand to cancel each other out. Postponement achieves the same effect by effectively combining the inventories for an entire family of products into a single pool, significantly reducing the total inventory that must be held in each region.

Postponement offers a form of risk pooling

A closely related benefit is that production can be based on aggregate forecasts, which are always more accurate than detailed forecasts (see Chapter 10). In effect, the postponement technique allows the variations of a generic product to be pulled through the chain by immediate demand rather than being pushed down the chain on the basis of uncertain, item-level forecasts. At the same time, postponement offers an economical way to increase the level of customization by allowing minor variations to be determined all the way out to the point of sale.

The technique relies less heavily on forecasting

Postponement is a form of design for supply, and it can rarely be accomplished without the use of some of the more basic techniques described in the preceding section. Most important, it requires products to be designed and constructed in a modular way, making it easy for downstream facilities to assemble the final configuration. In the case of computer peripherals, for example, it may be necessary to redesign the power supply as a plug-in module rather than building it into the chassis, or to move the logic that differs for PC and Mac peripherals off the motherboard and into an external connector.

Postponement relies on design for supply

Like design for supply in general, the postponement technique can require some difficult organizational changes. One of the obstacles to HP's postponement plan was the resistance of its distribution

The role of distribution centers changes

centers to getting involved in final assembly, a very different activity from the storage and handling operations they were accustomed to performing. If the distribution centers lack the space, equipment, or skills necessary to perform the final assembly, converting to postponement can lead to increases in defects, delays, and other production problems.

Postponement can also apply to factories

If transforming distribution centers into final assembly plants isn't a viable option, postponement can still be applied within the main plant. In this case the technique is based purely on time, and doesn't yield any savings downstream from the plant. However, the increased flexibility that comes from delaying differentiation may still justify the change. In a classic example, Benetton changed the sequence of operations involved in making its sweaters, dying the final sweater rather than dying the wool prior to weaving. Although this change increased the cost of production by 10%, it produced a net benefit because it allowed the company to respond much more quickly to emerging preferences among colors.

You can postpone all the way to consumers

Conversely, if the final configuration process is quite simple, or if retailers have special skills, it's possible to extend postponement out to the point of purchase (Figure 15.8). This is often the case with consumer electronics, which may have to be configured with special cables or adapters, but it can also be seen in the sale of bicycles, which are often specially configured for individual consumers. It is even possible for final configuration to occur in the consumer's own home, as in the case of home entertainment systems. But the modularization needs to be very good for this option to be viable, as anyone who has struggled to sort out the functions of seven different remotes will readily tell you.

Postponement doesn't always reduce costs

Postponement offers many potential benefits, but it's not without its costs. In addition to the quality and organizational problems that can arise when assembly operations are pushed down the supply

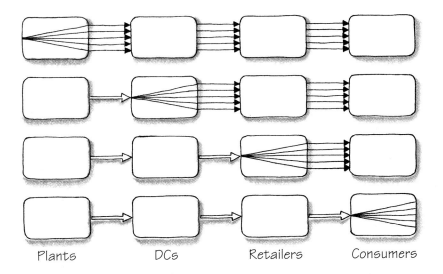

Figure 15.8
Options for
Postponement

Plants   DCs   Retailers   Consumers

chain, the cost of performing these operations downstream is almost always higher than if they were performed at the factory. In addition, the modularization of the product and the resequencing of operations may themselves increase the cost of production, regardless of where final assembly takes place. These costs all have to be offset before the technique can produce any net savings.

Postponement works best when two conditions are met: A large variety of configurations can be derived from a common base product, and the demand across these configurations is hard to predict. This is quite commonly the case with innovative products such as clothing and electronic consumer goods, which usually come in a variety of styles, sizes, and colors, and are subject to fads and fashions. But, as the DeskJet story indicates, even such relatively mundane products as printers can exhibit enough variability in demand to make the technique advantageous.

The technique works best with high variety

The most effective approach is to use postponement selectively across product lines, applying it only where the advantages outweigh the cost. Better still is to apply it selectively *within* a product

Selective postponement is a good strategy

line. In this variation of the technique, you continue to differentiate enough of the product at the factory to satisfy the minimal level of demand you expect for each variation, then use postponement for the uncertain portion of demand, where risk pooling works to your advantage. This approach can offer the best possible outcome: You keep the bulk of your production in your factories where it is cheaper and easier to manage, you reduce safety stocks in your downstream facilities, and you increase your ability to respond to unexpected demand at the point of sale. That combination of benefits provides an excellent example of pushing the efficient frontier into new territory.

Each of the techniques described in this chapter— increasing velocity, pooling risk, designing for supply, and postponing differentiation—can give you a significant advantage over your competitors, but don't think of them as independent initiatives. Rather, think of them as conceptual building blocks for improving your chain, and look for ways to combine two, three, or even all four of them to give yourself as great an advantage as possible. Better still, think about how these four initiatives push out the efficient frontier, then seek out ways to push that frontier even further. Adopting these techniques can put you on the forefront of supply chain management, but inventing new ones is the surest way to turn your company into a true leader.

Notes on Sources

Sources indicated only by author are listed in the Suggested Readings following these notes.

Chapter 1
The New Competition

3   The story of Siemens CT is from *Industry Week*'s profile of its winners of the Best Plants Awards, 2002, which can be found at *www.industryweek.com/iwinprint/bestplants*.

4   Gillette's revamping of its chain is described in "10 Best Supply Chains," *Supply Chain Technology News*, October 2002.

4   The definitive study of Chrysler's SCORE program is the article by Jeffrey H. Dyer, "How Chrysler Created an American Keiretsu," *Harvard Business Review*, July–August 1996.

5   Apple's reconstruction of its supply chain is described by Doug Bartholemew in "What's Really Driving Apple's Recovery?" *Industry Week*, March 15, 1999.

6   The improvements in Amazon.com's chain are described in "How Amazon Cleared That Hurdle," *Business Week*, February 4, 2002.

6   The figure for Dell's 5% margins is from a must-read article by Miles Cook and Rob Tyndall, "Lessons from the Leaders," *Supply Chain Management Review*, November–December 2001.

8   Michael Hammer's characterization of the supply chain comes from his book *The Agenda: What Every Business Must Do to Dominate the Decade*, New York: Crown, 2001.

8   The problems with Kmart's supply chain are described in two articles: "IT Difficulties Help Take Kmart Down," *Computerworld*, January 28, 2002; and "Now in Bankruptcy, Kmart Struggled with Supply Chain," *InformationWeek*, January 28, 2002.

9   Nike's problems with its i2 installation are described in "Supply Chain Debacle," *Internet Week*, March 1, 2001.

10   An analysis of Cisco's inventory write-down can be found in Paul Kaihla, "Inside Cisco's $2 Billion Blunder," *Business 2.0,* March 2002.

11   The Georgia Tech analysis of supply chain problems is reported in Vinod R. Singhal and Kevin B. Hendricks, "How Supply Chain Glitches Torpedo Shareholder Value," *Supply Chain Management Review,* January–February 2002.

13   The analysis of supply chain costs as a function of GDP is from Robert Delaney's Annual State of Logistics Report for 2001, "Understanding Inventory—Stay Curious," presented June 10, 2002, at the National Press Club in Washington, DC. The report can be found at *www.cassinfo.com/bob.html.*

13   The two-to-one advantage in costs between average and best-in-class companies is from Miles Cook and Rob Tyndall, "Lessons from the Leaders," *Supply Chain Management Review,* November–December 2001.

13   One survey indicating that the gap between average and best-in-class companies with regard to supply chain costs is increasing is the KPMG study reported by Derek Slater in "By the Numbers," *CIO Magazine,* February 2000.

14   The example of the major electronics company is from Miles Cook and Rob Tyndall, "Lessons from the Leaders," *Supply Chain Management Review,* November–December 2001.

15   The list of pressures on supply chains is from National Research Council, *Surviving Supply Chain Integration: Strategies for Small Manufacturers,* Washington, DC: National Academy Press, 2000, page 28.

15   The survey of executives is from George Taninecz, "Forging the Chain," *Industry Week,* May 15, 2000.

18   The quote from the National Research Council can be found in their *Surviving Supply Chain Integration: Strategies for Small Manufacturers,* Washington, DC: National Academy Press, 2000, page 24.

Chapter 2
The Rules of the Game

29   The example of Johnson Controls building a seat is described in Robert Handfield and Ernest Nichols, Jr., *Introduction to Supply Chain Management,* Upper Saddle River, NJ: Prentice Hall, 1999, page 8.

39   The audit of the major retailer that needed $200 million in safety stock is described in Miles Cook and Rob Tyndall, "Lessons from the Leaders," *Supply Chain Management Review,* November–December 2001.

Chapter 3
Winning as a Team

46   The shutdown of Toyota's production lines is described in Rushton, Oxley, and Croucher, page 223.

46   The shortages due to flooding are described in National Research Council, *Surviving Supply Chain Integration: Strategies for Small Manufacturers,* Washington, DC: National Academy Press, 2000, page 32.

46   The effects of the terrorist attacks of September 11, 2001, including the costs of shutting down plants and Ford's measures to reduce risks, are described in "Sept. 11 Attacks Reveal Supply-Chain Vulnerabilities," *ZDNet Tech Update,* October 10, 2001.

46   Honda's use of dual suppliers is described in Rushton, Oxley, and Croucher, page 223.

51   The problems in adopting CPFR are described in Carol Sliwa, "CPFR Clamor Persists, but Adoption Remains Slow," *Computerworld,* June 28, 2002.

51   The study of inventory levels conducted at Ohio State is reported in James Gintner and Bernard LaLonde, "An Historical Analysis of Inventory Levels: An Exploratory Study," November 2001. The article is available at *www.manufacturing.net.* The quote is from the same source.

53   The statistics on the scale of Wal-Mart's operations are taken from Owen Thomas, "Lord of the Things," *Business 2.0,* March 2002.

55   The description of how U.S. auto plants have displaced inventory out to dealerships is from Marshall L. Fisher, "What Is the Right Supply Chain for Your Product?" *Harvard Business Review,* March–April 1997.

67   The survey indicating that most supply chain initiatives are internal to a single company is from Miles Cook and Rob Tyndall, "Lessons from the Leaders," *Supply Chain Management Review,* November–December 2001.

Chapter 6
Supply Chain Software

124   The number of transactions per day at Ingram Micro is from Christopher Koch, "Four Strategies," *CIO Magazine,* October 1, 2000.

Chapter 7
Meeting Demand

143   The figures on the number of pallets in a warehouse are from Rushton, Oxley, and Croucher, page 230.

144   The figures on how pickers spend their time are from Rushton, Oxley, and Croucher, page 287.

148   The table on entry error rates is from Rushton, Oxley, and Croucher, page 331.

Chapter 8
Maintaining Supply

170   The Forrester numbers on how many companies are using exchanges comes from Miles Cook and Rob Tyndall, "Lessons from the Leaders," *Supply Chain Management Review,* November–December 2001.

Chapter 9
Measuring Performance

176   The figures for cash-to-cash cycle times come from George Taninecz, "Forging the Chain," *Industry Week,* May 15, 2000.

185   The number of inventory turns for Lear comes from David Ross, *Competing Through Supply Chain Management: Creating Market-Winning Strategies Through Supply Chain Partnerships,* Dordrecht, The Netherlands: Kluwer Academic Publishers, 1998, page 220.

186   The study of the automotive industry in England can be found in David Taylor and David Brunt, *Manufacturing Operations and Supply Chain Management: The LEAN Approach,* Thompson Learning, 2001, page 133. (Not the same David Taylor who wrote this manager's guide.)

191   The source for Caterpillar sending out 90,000 questionnaires per year is Donald V. Fites, "Make Your Dealers Your Partners," *Harvard Business Review,* March–April 1996.

Chapter 10
Forecasting Demand

208   The concept of the tipping point is best explained by Malcolm Gladwell in his compelling book, *The Tipping Point: How Little Things Can Make a Big Difference,* New York: Little, Brown and Company, 2002.

209   The model of consumer choice is described by Paul Ormerod in *Butterfly Economics: A New General Theory of Social and Economic Behavior,* New York: Pantheon Books, 1998.

213   The studies showing the advantages of collaborative forecasting are cited in David Ross, *Competing Through Supply Chain Management: Creating Market-Winning Strategies Through Supply Chain Partnerships,* Dordrecht, The Netherlands: Kluwer Academic Publishers, 1998, page 218.

Chapter 12
Improving Performance

237 The study on how many measures companies use is cited in Miles Cook and Rob Tyndall, "Lessons from the Leaders," *Supply Chain Management Review,* November–December 2001

239 The benchmark figures come from George Taninecz, "Forging the Chain," *Industry Week,* May 15, 2000.

246 The observations on how ineffectively incentives are used are from Miles Cook and Rob Tyndall, "Lessons from the Leaders," *Supply Chain Management Review,* November–December 2001.

247 The observation regarding servicing customers in order of their profit potential comes from David L. Anderson and Allen J. Delattre, "Predictions That Will Make You Rethink Your Supply Chain," *Supply Chain Management Review,* September–October 2002.

Chapter 13
Mastering Demand

264 The cost figures for shipping sugar from Hawaii in bulk rather than bags are from Simchi-Levi, Kaminsky, and Simchi-Levi, page 177.

Chapter 14
Designing the Chain

280 The primary reference for the strategic tradeoff between efficiency and flexibility is Marshall L. Fisher, "What Is the Right Supply Chain for Your Product?" *Harvard Business Review,* March–April 1997. Chopra and Meindl explore the issue on page 33ff.

Chapter 15
Maximizing Performance

301   The announcement of Benetton's use of RF tags appeared in the *San Francisco Chronicle,* March 12, 2003.

302   The average reductions in inventory due to risk pooling are from Simchi-Levi, Kaminsky, and Simchi-Levi, page 59.

Suggested Readings

Intermediate Level

David **Simchi-Levi**, Philip **Kaminsky**, and Edith **Simchi-Levi**, *Designing and Managing the Supply Chain: Concepts, Strategies, and Case Studies*. New York: Irwin McGraw-Hill, 2000.

> A clear, authoritative text written for an executive-level course, this highly regarded book is an excellent next step for managers who want to learn more about supply chain strategy and advanced techniques.

Alan **Rushton**, John **Oxley**, and Phil **Croucher**, *The Handbook of Logistics and Distribution Management (2nd Ed.)*. London: Kogan Page, 2000.

> This book offers a detailed, pragmatic examination of the tactical and operational issues in managing a supply chain, supported by numerous photographs and real-world examples.

Martin **Christopher**, *Logistics and Supply Chain Management: Strategies for Reducing Cost and Improving Service (2nd Ed.)*. Upper Saddle River, NJ: Financial Times Prentice Hall, 1998.

> A systematic, readable treatment that offers valuable insights into the management processes necessary to implement advanced supply chain techniques.

Advanced Level

Sunil **Chopra** and Peter **Meindl**, *Supply Chain Management: Strategy, Planning, and Operation*. Upper Saddle River, NJ: Prentice Hall, 2001.

This comprehensive textbook may be slow going for some managers, but it offers a high payoff in terms of articulate, practical guidance on all aspects of supply chain management, and its excellent organization makes it easy to read selectively.

Jeremy **Shapiro**, *Modeling the Supply Chain.* Pacific Grove, CA: Duxbury/Wadsworth Group, 2001.

For those with the necessary background, this is the best available treatment on the application of linear programming and other mathematical techniques to supply chain management.

Collections of Articles

John A. **Woods** and Edward J. **Marien**, *The Supply Chain Yearbook, 2001 Edition.* New York: McGraw-Hill, 2001.

Combines reprints of many contemporary articles from management periodicals with an excellent compendium of associations, Web sites, journals, and other useful resources.

Harvard Business Review on Managing the Value Chain. Harvard Business Review, 2000.

Eight reprinted articles on supply chain management published in HBR between 1993 and 2000.

Glossary

activity-based costing (ABC)

A technique for allocating indirect costs to production activities, making indirect costs more comparable to direct costs and permitting a better assessment of the true cost of creating each product.

advanced planning and scheduling (APS) system

A type of software that uses mathematical models and related techniques to find optimal solutions to complex production and supply problems. See **optimizer** and **linear programming**.

advance shipping notice (ASN)

A document sent by a supplier to a customer to indicate when an order will be shipped. ASNs are usually transmitted electronically.

aggregate forecast

A forecast based on product or customer data that has been grouped by similarity. See **aggregation**.

aggregation

The practice of grouping similar products or customers to simplify planning and achieve more stable forecasts.

assemble-to-order strategy

The practice of building product components in advance of demand, but postponing final assembly until demand is realized. An intermediate strategy between the **make-to-stock** and **make-to-order strategies**.

available to promise (ATP)

The inventory status of a product that is currently on hand and available for immediate shipment. See **capable to promise**.

back scheduling

The practice of scheduling activities by working backward from the planned completion date, adding activities to the schedule in the reverse order in which they will be executed. See **forward scheduling**.

backhaul   A shipment that moves in the opposite direction along a route just taken by a vehicle in making a delivery, allowing it to make use of its hauling capacity on the return trip.

bill of lading   A document listing all the goods contained within a shipment and stating the terms governing its transportation. Some bills of lading also serve as title to the goods.

bill of materials (BOM)   A listing of the parts and materials that become part of a finished product, organized in a hierarchical structure that reflects their components, subassemblies, or intermediate forms.

bill of operations (BOO)   A list of the procedures necessary to produce a finished product from its constituent materials, organized as a hierarchical structure that reflects the sequence in which these procedures must be carried out.

bullwhip effect   An alternative name for **demand amplification**.

capable to promise (CTP)   The inventory status of a product that is not immediately on hand but that can be produced within the required fulfillment lead time. See **available to promise**.

captive exchange   A private **electronic exchange** that is owned by one or more of the participating organizations and restricted to selected trading partners of the owning organizations. See **private exchange** and **public exchange**.

carrier   A company that specializes in transporting goods.

carrying cost   The incremental cost of placing orders due to increases in product quantities. So named because the majority of this variable cost is the expense of carrying inventory that is not immediately consumed. Also known as **holding cost**. See **order cost**.

cash-to-cash time	A measure of the efficiency with which cash is used in the business. Calculated as the interval between the time a company pays for raw materials and the time it receives payment for the finished goods produced from those materials.
category management	The practice of organizing inventory management, promotions, and related activities around products that consumers view as roughly equivalent in meeting their needs.
collaborative planning, forecasting, and replenishment (CPFR)	A multi-industry program that uses the Internet to achieve cooperation across the members of a supply chain to better forecast, plan, and execute the flow of goods.
conceptual model	A representation of a real-world system, such as a supply chain, that is constructed out of terms and concepts of the sort listed in this glossary. Conceptual models are expressed as diagrams and descriptions. See **mathematical model** and **simulation model**.
confidence interval	A range of numbers within which a predicted value will fall with a specified probability. For example, 9 out of 10 observations will fall within a 90% confidence interval. Confidence intervals are often shown in graphs as small bars above and below the expected value to indicate the range of likely values.
consignment	An inventory control practice in which a supplier maintains ownership of inventory on a customer's site until the inventory is sold, monitoring its level and replenishing it as needed.
constraint	In an **optimization** procedure, a mathematical expression or equation that restricts the range of solutions the method will evaluate. A typical constraint would be an upper bound on

capital spending in the design of a supply chain. See **linear programming**.

consumer

The individual or organization that acquires a product in order to use it for its intended purpose rather than reselling it to someone else. As the terms are used in this book, a consumer is a special type of **customer**.

continuous replenishment (CR) program

An extension of the **quick response** (**QR**) program to cover the full range of retail merchandise and to add the techniques of supplier forecasting and vendor-managed inventory.

continuous review

An inventory replenishment policy in which a continuous count of inventory is maintained at all times, with orders being placed whenever the count falls below a set threshold. See **periodic review**.

cross dock

A specialized facility for transferring in-transit inventory between trucks. Typically a long building consisting primarily of receiving docks on one side, shipping docks on the other, and assembly areas between the two. Although nominally a type of storage facility, cross docks do not usually hold goods for more than 24 hours.

cross docking

The practice of using **cross docks** or **distribution centers** to reallocate shipments across trucks en route from suppliers to customers, allowing each truck to remain full throughout its journey. Products are moved directly from receiving docks to shipping docks, with no intermediate storage.

customer

The individual or organization that purchases a product or service in a supply chain transaction. The term is used inconsistently throughout the business literature, leading to unproductive debates over who the "real" customer is. In this book, the term is used to denote a role within a transaction and can be applied to any link in the chain. In this usage, the final customer is the **consumer** at the end of the supply chain.

customer schedule

A special format for an order spanning multiple shipments in which line items are grouped by delivery date.

customer service level (CSL)

The target level of product availability for a particular region and product. Service level can be specified in wide a variety of ways, ranging from the maximum distance of inventory from a customer's site to the percent of orders that can be filled from inventory within a specified time.

cycle stock

The amount of inventory required to support the operations of a facility, with no reserve to cover unforeseen events. See **safety stock**.

cycle time

This term is used to denote either (a) the interval between successive repetitions of a cyclical process, as in the cycle time of a machine or assembly line, or (b) the duration of a business process. These conflicting definitions lead to confusion and reduce the value of the term.

days on hand

A measure of inventory level, calculated by dividing the quantity on hand by the average daily consumption. Provides the same information as the **inventory turnover ratio** but in a form more suitable to high-turn environments.

delayed differentiation

A technique in which products with characteristics in common are left in their common form until demand is realized, allowing a better match of production to realized demand. Also called **postponement**.

Delphi technique

A procedure in which forecasts generated by multiple analysts are repeatedly combined and reviewed until a consensus forecast is reached.

demand amplification	The tendency for fluctuations in demand to increase as they move up the supply chain. Often referred to as the **bullwhip effect** in recent literature.
demand lumping	A phenomenon in which an otherwise smooth flow of demand up a supply chain is grouped into larger chunks than is necessary to meet operational requirements. Demand lumping is a major contributor to **demand amplification**. It is known to be caused by batching, forward buying, and hoarding.
dependent demand	The demand for a product from customers who are not the end consumers of that product. So named because this demand ultimately depends on consumer demand. See **independent demand**.
design for supply	The practice of engineering a product in a way that facilitates its flow through the supply chain.
direct shipment	A distribution practice in which goods that would normally move by way of a warehouse or distribution center are transported directly from a supplier to a customer.
distribution center (DC)	A **storage facility** in which goods may be staged, sorted, assembled, packaged, and/or stored temporarily as they pass through a particular segment of a supply chain. Distribution centers differ from **warehouses** primarily in the focus on facilitating distribution rather than holding inventory.
distribution network	The set of facilities and lanes that transports finished goods from a production facility to the downstream customers of that facility. A distribution network may be divided into **echelons**.
dynamic forecasting	The practice of revising current forecasts at the end of each period to incorporate the data for that period rather than leaving

these forecasts unchanged over successive periods. See **static forecasting**.

echelon   In a **distribution network**, a set or layer of facilities functionally equidistant from the production facility that serves them. Comparable to a tier in a procurement network.

echelon inventory   When centrally managed, the total inventory distributed across the echelons of a **distribution network**.

economic order quantity (EOQ)   The calculated amount of inventory that should be ordered at one time to minimize the total cost of replenishment, taking into account the opposing effects of **order costs** and **holding costs**.

efficient consumer response (ECR)   A supply-chain program used in the grocery industry that combines rapid retail replenishment with the techniques of category management and activity-based costing.

efficient frontier   A curve describing the most advantageous possible combination of cost and flexibility in a supply chain. This curve is constantly being advanced by best practices in supply chain management.

electronic auction   An auction conducted entirely over the Internet, with sellers submitting products to a Web site and buyers using e-mail or Web browsers to place their bids.

electronic catalog   A directory of products stored in digital form, usually accessible over the Web, that provides access to product by type and supplier.

electronic data interchange (EDI)   A set of protocols for transferring information regarding demand and supply over private electronic networks.

electronic distribution   The practice of shipping products in electronic form across the Internet or other electronic medium. Electronic distribution is used for music, documents, software, photographs, tickets, and other products that can be transmitted in digital form.

electronic exchange

A digital marketplace, accessible over the Web, that brings together buyers and sellers of a particular type of product and provides them with tools for carrying out transactions.

enterprise resource planning (ERP) system

A suite of software that combines tactical-level applications for production and distribution planning with execution systems for order management, inventory control, accounting, and related operations.

external supply chain

The portion of a supply chain that spans facilities outside the ownership boundaries of a particular company. See **internal supply chain**.

extractor

A special kind of **supplier** that takes raw materials from the earth in either living or inert form. Examples include mines, saw mills, farms, and ranches.

extrinsic factor

An influence on demand or some other supply chain characteristic that is beyond a firm's control, such as the state of the economy or the actions of a competitor.

feedback

A physical or information flow from the output of a system into the input side of that system. The appropriate use of feedback is essential for regulating the behavior of a system. See **positive feedback** and **negative feedback**.

finished goods inventory

The store of completed products on the output side of a production facility.

forecast horizon

The date furthest in the future for which events are predicted in a forecast.

formal model   A business model that can be expressed in mathematical or executable form, allowing it to generate numerical predictions from a set of inputs. Of the three types of models discussed in this book, **mathematical** and **simulation models** are formal while conceptual models are not.

forward buying   The practice of buying supplies before they are needed to take advantage of favorable prices or avoid potential shortages.

forward scheduling   The practice of scheduling activities by beginning with the planned start date and adding activities to the schedule in the order in which they will be executed. See **back scheduling**.

fulfillment cycle   The sequence of events in a supplier organization that manage the three key flows in the fulfillment process: order flow, product flow, and cash flow.

fulfillment lead time   The interval between the time an order is placed with a supplier and the time the goods are received by the customer.

full pallet   A pallet of goods that contains only a single kind of product. See **mixed pallet**.

full truckload (FTL) shipment   A shipment of goods that consumes the capacity of a truck, requiring the truck to be dedicated to the shipment. See **less-than-truckload (LTL) shipment**.

hill-climbing   A technique used to search for a superior configuration of a system such as a supply chain by making a series of small, beneficial changes to the system until no further improvements appear to be possible.

holding cost   The incremental cost of placing orders due to increases in product quantities. So named because the majority of this variable cost is the expense of holding inventory that is not immediately con-sumed. Also known as **carrying cost**. See **order cost**.

independent demand	The demand for a product on the part of its end consumers. So named because it is the ultimate source of demand, and doesn't depend on a source of demand further down in the supply chain. See **dependent demand**.
inter-modal transportation	The practice of using more than one medium of transportation, such as rail and ship, within a single shipment.
internal supply chain	The portion of a supply chain that joins the facilities owned by the same company. See **external supply chain**.
in-transit inventory	Inventory that is currently in a transportation lane between two facilities.
intrinsic factor	An influence on demand or some other supply chain characteristic that is within a firm's control, such as the price of a product or the speed of delivery.
inventory turnover ratio	A measure of how quickly inventory is used once it arrives at a facility, calculated as the annual sales of a product divided by its average inventory level.
inventory turns	Shorthand for **inventory turnover ratio**.
inventory velocity	The speed with which inventory moves through the supply chain. Despite the way the term is commonly used, it does not represent a measure of performance, and companies that seek to increase their inventory velocity continue to rely on such tradi-tional measures as the **inventory turnover ratio** and **days on hand**.

item fill rate	The percentage of line items, calculated across all orders, for which the full quantity of the requested product is available for immediate shipment. See **order fill rate**.
judgmental techniques	The collection of forecasting techniques based on cause-and-effect reasoning rather than statistical analysis. Also known as **subjective techniques**.
just-in-time (JIT) manufacturing	The practice of reducing inventory levels by scheduling materials to arrive just as they are needed in the production process. More broadly, a comprehensive program for improving manufacturing operations to yield higher quality products at reduced expense.
keiretsu	The Japanese term for a type of integration in which a manufacturing firm takes partial ownership positions in key suppliers and appoints its own personnel to some management positions.
less-than-truckload (LTL) shipment	A shipment of goods that consumes only a fraction of the capacity of a truck, requiring that the truck be shared with other shipments. See **full truckload (FTL) shipment**.
level component	In **time-series analysis**, the portion of the forecast demand that is constant and unvarying. See **trend, seasonal,** and **random components**.
linear programming (LP)	A technique for finding optimal solutions to mathematical models in which all relations between inputs and outputs are linear in form.
make-to-order strategy	The practice of making products in response to realized demand rather than making them to stock in advance of demand.
make-to-stock strategy	The practice of making products in advance of demand and holding them in finished goods inventory until demand is realized.

mathematical model	A representation of a real-world system, such as a supply chain, that is constructed out of mathematical terms and relations. Mathematical models are expressed as formulas and/or procedures for solving equations to predict the behavior of the system. See **conceptual model** and **simulation model**.
mean absolute percentage error (MAPE)	A measure of the average deviation between forecast values and their corresponding observed values, regardless of the direction (sign) of those deviations. See **tracking signal**.
merge in transit	A technique in which separate shipments are combined en route and delivered as a single unit.
mixed pallet	A pallet of goods that contains two or more kinds of products. See **full pallet**.
mode of transportation	The medium by which a vehicle moves products from one facility to another. The primary modes are truck, rail, boat, barge, airplane, and pipeline.
Monte Carlo method	The technique of running a **simulation model** repeatedly using random variables on each run in order to understand behavior of the model across normal variations of business conditions.
moving average	The mean value obtained by summing the last N values of a measure and dividing by N, where N is set according to need. Used in forecasting and other applications to obtain a typical value for recent observations of some measure. Increasing the value of N produces more stable values that are less sensitive to recent changes.
negative feedback	A form of **feedback** in which movement of an output of a system in a particular direction is decreased, decelerating that movement. Negative feedback usually leads to stable, bounded outputs that facilitate control of a system. See **positive feedback**.

objective function	In **linear programming**, the equation that defines the quantity being optimized, such as total cost or a weighted combination of cost and other performance measures.
on-time delivery	A measure of fulfillment effectiveness, calculated as the percentage of orders that arrive at the customer site within the agreed-upon time.
optimization	Using a mathematical or procedural technique to explore the space of all possible configurations of a system and identify the configuration that maximizes (or minimizes) a designated output measure. Optimization is usually carried out using a specialized program called an **optimizer**. See **linear programming**.
optimizer	A software program capable of automating the process of optimizing a system using a particular mathematical or procedural technique. See **optimization** and **linear programming**.
order cost	The fixed cost of placing an order, regardless of the quantities involved. See **holding cost**.
order fill rate	The percentage of orders for which the full quantities of all products on the order are available for immediate shipment. See **item fill rate**.
packing slip	A document enclosed with a shipment that lists the goods included in that shipment together with information about the origin, destination, and means of transport.
parameter	A quantity whose value is set prior to performing an analysis that depends on that quantity. Example: Order cost and holding cost are parameters used in the calculation of **economic order quantity**.
Pareto Analysis	A technique for analyzing sales data to determine the extent to which a small number of products accounts for the majority of

sales. A common result, often stated as the 80:20 rule, is that 80% of sales come from 20% of the products.

perfect order A measure of fulfillment effectiveness, calculated as the percentage of orders that ship complete, arrive on time, contain the correct goods, are free of damage, and have accurate paperwork.

periodic review An inventory replenishment policy in which inventory is counted at fixed intervals and orders are placed whenever the current count falls below a set threshold. See **continuous review**.

point of sale (POS) system A software application that prices and records the sale of products to customers who are physically on site and take immediate possession of their purchases.

positioning strategy The set of attributes on which a company chooses to differentiate itself from its competition, together with methods for improving those attributes and communicating them to potential customers. In the manufacturing sector, the most common attributes are quality of product, quality of service, and price.

positive feedback A form of **feedback** in which movement of an output of a system in a particular direction is increased, accelerating that movement. If unchecked by other mechanisms, positive feedback usually leads to exponential growth and "out of control" behavior. See **negative feedback**.

postponement An alternate term for **delayed differentiation**.

primary packaging The level of packaging that immediately encloses a product, such as a bottle, box, can, or blister pack. See **secondary packaging** and **transport packaging**.

private exchange	An **electronic exchange** with membership rules that exclude parties that would otherwise be qualified to buy and sell the products handled on the exchange. See **public exchange**.
procurement network	The set of facilities and lanes that transports raw materials to a production facility from the upstream suppliers of that facility. A procurement network may be divided into **tiers**.
production facility	A facility that exists primarily to create products from raw materials, storing materials and products only as necessary to support production operations. See **storage facility**.
public exchange	An **electronic exchange** that is open to all qualified buyers and sellers of the products handled on the exchange. See **private exchange**.
pull chain	A supply chain in which inventory is produced only in response to realized demand at each stage of the chain, with product being "pulled" down the chain by actual orders.
push chain	A supply chain in which inventory is produced in advance of demand and "pushed" down the chain toward the consumer.
push-pull boundary	The point in a supply chain in which the driving force switches from pull to push, with pull operating downstream to the consumer and push acting upstream to the extractor.
quick response (QR)	A supply chain program on the part of the apparel industry that applied **just-in-time** (**JIT**) techniques to retail replenishment.
random component	In **time-series analysis**, the variability in demand that remains after the **systematic components** have been removed. In other words, the aspect of demand that can't be forecast by the model.

raw materials inventory	The inventory of incoming materials maintained at a production facility for use in the production process.
relation	In systems, a mapping of inputs to outputs that yields one or more outputs for any given input. Relations are usually described by one or more lines in a graph, and they range in form from straight lines (linear relations) to complex curves.
reorder point (ROP)	The level or count at which the inventory for a particular product is replenished.
replenishment cycle	The sequence of events within a customer organization that manage the three key flows in the replenishment process: order flow, product flow, and cash flow.
replenishment lead time	The interval between the time a company places an order for raw materials and the time it receives those materials.
replenishment policy	The set of rules by which a firm decides when to replenish its inventory, how large to make its orders, and how much inventory to maintain on site.
reverse auction	An auction in which customers post requests for quotes and suppliers bid against each other to win the business.
risk pooling	An inventory management technique in which the safety stock necessary to handle expected fluctuations in supply and demand is reduced by treating two or more physically separate inventories as a single logical inventory.
safety stock	The amount of inventory that must be maintained in order to handle fluctuations in supply and demand. See **cycle stock**.

seasonal component	In **time-series analysis**, the portion of the forecast demand that varies in a cyclical manner over the course of the year. See **level**, **trend**, and **random components**.
secondary packaging	The level of packaging that groups a standard number of primary packages together for convenience in handling, storage, and sales. The most common form of secondary packaging is the carton.
sell-through	The amount of stock acquired by a customer under a promotion that is passed on to that customer's customers during the promotional period. Suppliers may limit the amount of product a customer can buy under a promotion to the sell-through amount in order to reduce **forward buying**.
ship complete	A constraint placed on an order that requires all items in the order to arrive in a single shipment.
shrinkage	The reduction in inventory that occurs through pilferage, misplacement, and related forms of attrition.
simulation model	A representation of a real-world system, such as a supply chain, that is constructed out of software objects that represent real-world objects. Simulation models are expressed as computer programs that execute the models to observe their expected behavior. See **conceptual model** and **mathematical model**.
static forecasting	The practice of generating a forecast and then leaving it unchanged until a new forecast is created. See **dynamic forecasting**.
stockout	The situation in which there is not enough inventory on hand to fill a received order.
storage facility	A facility that exists primarily to hold goods in anticipation of future demand. Some storage facilities may also perform final assembly

and packaging in order to move these operations closer to the end consumer. See **production facility**.

subjective techniques   The collection of forecasting techniques based on cause-and-effect reasoning rather than statistical analysis. Also known as **judgmental techniques**.

supplier   The organization that provides a product or service in a supply chain transaction. In this book, the term is used as a counterpart to **customer**, denoting a role within a transaction that can be applied to any link in the chain. In some contexts, the term refers specifically to companies that provide raw materials and is not applied to downstream members of the chain.

supply chain   A network of facilities and transportation lanes that transforms raw materials into finished products and delivers those products to consumers.

supply chain management (SCM)   The set of activities involved in designing, planning, and executing the flow of demand, supply, and cash across a **supply chain**.

systematic component   In **time-series analysis**, any component of demand (level, trend, or seasonal) that can be predicted from the model. In other words, everything but the **random component**. See **level**, **trend**, and **seasonal components**.

tier   In a **procurement network**, a set or layer of facilities functionally equidistant from the production facility they serve. Comparable to an echelon in a distribution network.

time-series analysis   A forecasting technique in which future values of a measure are predicted from a mathematical analysis of historical values of that measure.

tipping point	A phenomenon observed in the spread of ideas in which the prevalence of the idea makes a sudden leap from a slow-growth curve to a different, fast-growth curve. Originally discovered in the study of infectious diseases and subsequently found to apply to product sales, crime waves, and other social activities.
tracking signal	A measure of the bias of a forecast to either overestimate or underestimate the observed value. See **mean absolute percentage error** (**MAPE**).
transport packaging	A level of packaging, such as a pallet, that is added to facilitate shipping and storing large quantities of product. See **primary packaging** and **secondary packaging**.
transportation lane	A designated pathway for moving goods from one facility to the next within in a supply chain. Lanes are categorized as highways, railways, waterways, air lanes, and pipelines.
transshipment	A technique in which goods are shipped laterally within the same echelon of a distribution system, such as between warehouses or between retail stores.
trend component	In **time-series analysis,** the portion of the forecast demand that shows a constant, linear increase over time. See **level, seasonal,** and **random components**.
turn-and-earn system	A policy in which suppliers limit customer purchases to the quantity of goods they "turn" by shipping them out as finished goods to their own customers. Used to reduce hoarding during periods of limited availability.
vendor-managed inventory (VMI)	An inventory control practice in which a supplier monitors and replenishes inventory on a customer's site.

vertical integration	The practice of owning facilities across a large segment of a supply chain in order to control as much of the chain as possible. See **virtual integration**.
virtual integration	A practice in which members of a supply chain collaborate closely with each other in order to gain the benefits of centralized supply chain management while retaining independent ownership and control. See **vertical integration**.
warehouse	A **storage facility** that holds controlled quantities of goods in a particular location within a supply chain. See **distribution center**.
Web services	A set of technologies that allows software programs to invoke each other's functions using **XML** and standard Internet protocols.
work-in-process (WIP) inventory	Inventory currently being used in a production process or held for use within the production area. Includes all materials that have been removed from raw materials inventory but not yet deposited in finished goods inventory.
XML	The extensible markup language for communicating data in a structured format over the Internet.
zero-sum game	Any interaction between two parties in which the total gain across the two is fixed, leaving the parties to compete with each other over their relative shares of that gain. Many supply chain relationships that are traditionally viewed as zero-sum interactions are actually much richer than this, including outcomes in which the total gain can be increased or decreased depending on how the parties conduct themselves.

Index

Forging a Winning Chain

You've read the book. You understand the challenges of the new competition. How do you translate that knowledge into action?

Taylor's fast-track to supply chain success

1. Develop your skills

Successful chains require more than knowledge— they demand the ability to make sound decisions under pressure. Gain that ability through hands-on experience with realistic supply chain simulations.

2. Build your team

Competitive chains are run by teams of managers working together to achieve shared objectives. Build that teamwork by practicing the moves in a business laboratory using advanced collaboration techniques.

3. Design your chain

Today's supply chains are too large and complex to fix with point solutions. Forge the strongest chain by aligning every link behind a single strategy, then test that strategy under real-world business conditions.

David Taylor's fast-track educational program uses graphic presentations, interactive simulations, and challenging competitions to turn the insights of *Supply Chains: A Manager's Guide* into practical working knowledge. Get on the fast track. Contact *dtaylor@supplychainguide.com*.

www.SupplyChainGuide.com

0-201-30994-7

OBJECT TECHNOLOGY, SECOND EDITION

A Manager's Guide

Object Technology, Second Edition: A Manager's Guide covers the key terms, important concepts, and useful applications of objects. Managers, salespeople, engineers, software developers—anyone interested in understanding or implementing object technology—will find this book a lucid introduction to the topic.

Highlights include:

• An explanation of how to use objects to create evolutionary software that rapidly adapts to changing business conditions, eliminating the need for most new application development.

• An introduction to the Java programming language, and an explanation of how its use of message interfaces enables a new generation of portable, mix-and-match, Internet-enabled business objects.

• An update on the state of object databases and extended relational databases, with guidelines for combining the two for optimal information storage.

• An introduction to the new generation of object engines and how they combine storage and execution capabilities for maximum software integration.

Addison
Wesley

informIT

YOUR GUIDE TO IT REFERENCE

Articles

Keep your edge with thousands of free articles, in-depth features, interviews, and IT reference recommendations – all written by experts you know and trust.

Online Books

Answers in an instant from **InformIT Online Book's** 600+ fully searchable on line books. For a limited time, you can get your first 14 days **free**.

Catalog

Review online sample chapters, author biographies and customer rankings and choose exactly the right book from a selection of over 5,000 titles.